WATCHING THE WHEELS

Damon Hill is a former Formula One World Champion who raced against some of the legends of the sport, from Ayrton Senna to Michael Schumacher. The son of racing legend Graham Hill, Damon entered Formula One in 1992, racing for Brabham and then Williams, taking over as team leader when Senna died in 1994. Having lost the 1994 World Championship to Schumacher by a single point, Hill was crowned World Champion in 1996.

After retiring in 1999, Hill pursued various business ventures as well as becoming president of the British Racing Drivers' Club in 2006. He now works as a commentator on Sky F1.

WATCHING THE WHEELS

MY AUTOBIOGRAPHY

DAMON HILL

WITH MAURICE HAMILTON

PAN BOOKS

First published 2016 by Macmillan

First published in paperback 2017 by Pan Books
an imprint of Pan Macmillan
20 New Wharf Road, London N1 9RR
Associated companies throughout the world
www.panmacmillan.com

ISBN 978-1-5098-3193-7

1 3 5 7 9 8 6 4 2

A CIP catalogue record for this book is available from the British Library.

Typeset by Ellipsis Digital Limited, Glasgow
Printed and bound by CPI Group (UK) Ltd, Croydon, CR0 4YY

Visit www.panmacmillan.com to read more about all our books
and to buy them. You will also find features, author interviews and
news of any author events, and you can sign up for e-newsletters
so that you're always first to hear about our new releases.

To Georgie
and all Hills,
past, present
and future . . .

Picture Credits

Contents

FOREWORD

I have known Damon Hill since he was a very wee boy. In my first season of Formula Three racing in 1964, I only saw the top Formula One drivers from a distance: most of them were my heroes. Damon's father, Graham Hill, was surely one of them, and Graham and his wife Bette would often have their children at their side in the years that were to follow.

When I got the contract to drive for BRM, Graham was categorically the number-one driver. In those days, Formula One teams did a lot of testing and BRM used to use the Snetterton track in Norfolk. I was still living in Scotland, so I would either fly down or drive down and stay overnight at Graham and Bette's home. At seven o'clock in the morning, three wee Hills would burst into my bedroom, jumping all over the bed, and they were of course Damon, Brigitte and Samantha. They were tiny tots but full of energy and fun. It's wonderful for me to look back on those days and it's only because Damon has asked me to write this foreword for his book that many more memories have come to mind – Samantha and Damon on top of my shoulders as I gave them a 'horse ride' in the paddock is just one of many.

When Graham and I were racing together there was much more of a sense of camaraderie. All the Formula One drivers spent a lot of time with one another in those days as we had to travel together and usually stayed in the same hotels; it was a much deeper relationship than can be seen in today's F1 world. We holidayed together, laughed and cried together, particularly because so many racing drivers were losing their lives in those years.

So I saw Damon growing up, from a toddler to a young lad riding motorbikes, and I saw him entering the world of motor racing the hard way, with no father to help him and little money. When Graham died in an air crash while flying the plane, with his team driver beside him and his mechanics behind him, all of whom lost their lives, it had a huge impact on Damon, Samantha and Brigitte and, of course, Bette. It must have been a terribly depressing and upsetting time for them all. To pursue his dream, Damon therefore had to go out and secure sponsorship himself, just to survive in the sport.

I don't believe that being the son of a World Champion racing driver makes life any easier, what with all the travel, the sponsor events and the many commercial relationships that have to be serviced whilst also trying to be a good parent. Compared to other 'normal' families, there simply aren't enough hours in the day to spend with them alongside the racing, and having a famous father is yet another element that adds to these pressures. It can sometimes make you feel very proud, but at other times very lonely. Yet Damon has survived all that. He became a World Champion racing driver who had the wisdom to retire at the right time and is now a very talented television commentator and authority on the sport. Damon has done something that his father never managed, and that is to win the British Grand Prix, which must have been an extremely proud moment for Damon.

Today, he is a wonderful father and a husband to Georgie. Damon carries himself with great dignity and is a genuinely good man. I am very proud to have had the opportunity to be the understudy and teammate to Damon's father, a man who not only won the World Championship, Indianapolis and Le Mans, but who also had the best wee black book with jokes that set people into tears of laughter, and I feel very privileged that his son has asked me to write this foreword.

I counted Graham as a great friend, and the fact that he won the World Championship, Indianapolis and Le Mans – the only man to do so – was a phenomenal achievement.

Graham Hill would be incredibly proud of his son, and he would be especially pleased to see how he overcame such difficulties, particularly when his family life, which for many years had been so blessed, was put into turmoil when they lost their father and husband. Damon not only survived this, but has made a respectable life for himself, built with great dignity and love for the family unit.

Today, Damon is his own man. He lives his life to the full and protects and cares for his family with such love.

Well done, Damon.

Jackie Stewart
2016

INTRODUCTION

For those of you who supported and followed my career back in the day, and wondered where the hell I went and what I got up to after I stopped racing, this introduction is a brief answer to that and an explanation as to why I haven't written a book until now.

Winning a Formula One World Championship is a big deal. People don't forget it, and it defines you. You are introduced as 'the 1996 Formula One World Champion' twenty years later, and that's very nice, but it doesn't tell the whole story of who you are. We all have our professional lives and our personal lives, but the professional life is very much a necessary front. Behind all those apparently very 'together' facades lie the deeper concerns of life, relationships, fears, moral questions, doubts and needs. We are not the perfect and impervious heroes we like to project, and this is never truer than in the public arenas of sport, politics or the media. Being 'out front' requires a certain degree of chutzpah or good bluffing abilities. Of course, there are a few who are not troubled by an ounce of doubt or insecurity, but they are the rare self-possessed individuals.

A confident person can be very alluring. My character was assessed in all kinds of ways during my career, but I don't believe anyone ever found me to have an overabundance of confidence. I wish I had that strut that some sports people have, but the truth is that I had been shoved into the limelight almost from birth and had developed a deep distrust of situations that I could not control. When Ayrton Senna was killed in 1994, I found myself in a rather unexpected place as team leader against a man called Michael Schumacher, who had yet to win even one Formula One World Championship. I gave it all I had, and more. I never doubted I had driving ability, but just how good was I? I was to find out soon enough, and so was everyone else.

Being at the sharp end is not just about whether you can drive. It also involves an uncomfortable amount of scrutiny, some of it very personal. If there is any weakness, someone will stick a chisel in and crack it wide open. It was a new and totally surreal experience. I had just wanted to drive, win and go home, but more is expected from sports stars. People want something extra, and I was not sure I had whatever that something was. I knew I had something missing. But what was it? Was it charisma? I was not a natural showman like, for instance, Graham Hill, and that spot had already been taken anyway. Or was it simply total confidence: the sense of a right to be there? I think it was more the latter, but it was also to do with the legacy of Graham Hill and the fear of intruding on hallowed ground.

For most of my formative years my father was a very famous person. Then he died in a terrible and unexpected way. This cast a huge cloud over my early years, and it also left what they call 'unresolved issues'. I thought I could solve all these things by getting to the top. I thought, as many people do, that famous, successful people have got it cracked, but it isn't as simple as that. When I gave up my racing life, those issues started to catch up with me again.

Most people have good days and bad days. In sport, you just have to hope that you have a good day when you really need one, but sometimes you have really bad days for no apparent reason, and this is called 'being depressed'. Depression is like being buried alive or having someone sitting on top of you all the time. You feel unbearably heavy. It's like carrying around a dead body; it's exhausting. You just want to curl up and cry, but you can't. You are like a battery that has gone permanently flat, and there is no way, you think, that it will ever come back to life. We've all been disappointed, been kicked out of the World Cup a few too many times, and it feels awful, but we get over it. Hope springs eternal; maybe we'll win in four years' time? But depression is total despair: the thought – the absolute rock-solid, certain conviction – that we will never, *ever* win the World Cup.

A few years after I stopping racing, I accepted that I was depressed and badly needed someone to talk to; someone who was not a friend, my wife, or involved in any way in my life. Someone independent and trustworthy, who could help me unravel the mess of thoughts that was preventing me from being able to cope with life. I was – I thought – just a bit unhappy, but in fact I was pretty badly depressed. For some people – very tragically – depression gets to be just all too much. Thankfully, I never went over that precipice, but there were some bad days, for sure, and I can imagine how it might come to that. What probably saved me from God knows what, was being able to talk to a therapist.

It came as a massive relief to realise that there were people who really did understand the root causes of depression. As it turned out, I had a bagload of those things, notoriously called 'issues', that needed to be dealt with before I could do anything successfully, never mind write a book about my life. Because, simply put, I had no confidence in anything I believed or thought. It would have been a really bad book anyway, full of anger and fury and possibly a bit crazy. I'll try to keep this one in the middle of the road; no pun intended.

Issues are basically acquired and habituated responses to situations that either scare or confuse us. The origins of these issues may be something innocuous that happened long ago, when we did not have the capacity to deal with the situation. Say, for instance, being scared of dogs or spiders in childhood. When we are more mature, we can understand that not all dogs or spiders are deadly (although some really are, so best to check) and we can then approach them without irrational fear, but if there is an unexpected shocking event, then things can get a bit more complicated. The issues present at the time of the event become internally 'petrified' (in both senses), and everything gets stuck together in one messy tangle of emotions. Getting out of these patterns is tricky. Similar situations can resurrect these long-forgotten (or so one thought) traumatic events, so it's easy to keep falling back. This can be inconvenient when you are trying to keep a career in F1 on the tracks.

It could be a relatively minor fear, such as the spider one, or it could be something far more serious or disturbing: something no one could be expected just to brush off as an irrational fear or an overemotional reaction. Something like what happened on the night of 29 November 1975, when our family's world was dramatically and catastrophically altered forever, as my father's plane crashed into Arkley golf course killing all his key F1 team personnel and himself. That sort of event would do the trick.

That was the night the points on the railway track of our lives were instantly switched from one destination to a completely unanticipated one. A sudden tragedy like that is an emotional nuclear bomb. Shock waves reverberate outwards for years and years. And at the epicentre there is a crater; a deep, deep scar that you think will never heal.

Later in this book I go through the events of that night in detail to try and convey the sense of terror I felt. The accident changed my life completely, obviously because I'd lost my father, our family leader and protector, but also because it created longer-term effects that resurfaced during my career and left a great many questions that needed to be answered when I retired. When I look at what drove me to keep trying to get to F1 and what happened when I finally got there, I find it difficult to separate out a 'pure me', carving out my own authentic career, from the wounded boy determined to relive his father's life in order to put right that shocking loss. During my career I was always confused about whether I was authentically a racing driver or someone tasked with a mission to complete before I could become my true self.

Therapy raises these questions all the time: who am I, and who am I not? Erroneous ideas about one's self can range from the slightly annoying to the very damaging. One of the lesser issues I had was the concept that I had been an 'unfairly lucky' child, born with a silver spoon in my mouth. I was always asking myself whether anything I achieved was because I had been especially advantaged in some way. Society can sometimes perpetuate these notions; being privileged is seldom a cause for applause. I could almost interpret my struggles as an attempt to earn acceptance, to show I have earned what I have, to destigmatise myself from the idea of being undeserving.

Very keen not to spoil his children, my father always brought us to book if we started to show signs of cockiness. We were taught to be nice, polite children, which is terrible training for F1, I can tell you. I was told off once by Frank Williams for asking if I could use the telephone in the truck. I guess he was more used to Alan Jones or Nigel Mansell.

My father pretty much drilled out of us any idea that we should expect things, but this made us almost too frightened to ask for anything. We became too self-effacing and reserved. For all his concerns about breeding spoilt brats I think his approach equipped us badly for the big, bad world, in which tons of confidence and a healthy awareness of one's right to exist seem to pay dividends.

Another issue was peer relationships. Of course, it was hardly my fault that my father was successful; I can see that now. But when you are young, all you want to do is fit in, and I always felt as if I stuck out. It is difficult to melt into the background when your father is one of the most famous men of the era. When I was growing up, it was always about avoiding the subject wherever possible, for fear of incurring jealousy or arousing too much curiosity. These might seem like minor matters, but they were part of a larger general compound of issues that conspired to undermine my confidence, both when I was racing and after I stopped. Without the ever-present competition to distract me from addressing these issues, they all came flooding in at once when I retired.

Nature's mechanism for telling us when things are not right or when we are on the wrong path, is to make us depressed. If life doesn't tally with what our instincts are telling us is right, it can bring depression. Depression is a mental indicator of the need to change things; a sign that our life is being appropriated by others or blocked by wrong choices. It may also point up the need to address anxieties that have their origins in very early childhood, or further back still, in the womb.

If a mother is experiencing extreme anxiety or fear at the time of her pregnancy, these emotions affect the embryo, because high levels of cortisol are very damaging to the development of the brain in fetuses. The offspring of such pregnancies have lower cognitive development and a higher than normal incidence of schizophrenia and severe depression in adulthood. So if, for example, a child is conceived and born in a time of war, or a similarly stressful situation for the mother, such as being married to a Formula One racing driver at one of the most dangerous times in the sport, this stress can have unwanted consequences for the infant. In other words, stress and pregnancy are not an ideal combination for bringing a child into the world.

Quite apart from what they put themselves through in motor sport, both my parents experienced high levels of anxiety in childhood. My mother grew up in Catford in south London. During the war she would help her father clear up incendiary bombs. She remembers hiding behind a bus during a dogfight that was taking place overhead. When the shooting stopped she opened her eyes and saw that the bus had left. The next street to where she lived took a direct hit. No more neighbours. She would have been killed at school but for the fact that they had split her class in half due to limited staff, so that the two groups of children went in on alternate days. The unlucky half all perished. To hear her talk about it, you'd be forgiven for thinking that this was all very normal and to be expected.

My father grew up in Hendon, on the other side of London. In his autobiography *Life at the Limit* he talks of the terror of hearing the doodlebugs cut out and the dreadful wait for them to explode. He mentions a vast explosion in 1940 that blew out the doors and windows of his house. It was believed to have been the largest bomb that fell on England during the war and it wiped out rows and rows of houses a mile away. For a boy of only eleven years of age, it must have been incredibly frightening, but it was the same for everyone, so you didn't make a big deal of it: spirit of the Blitz.

For my parents' generation, danger was a trifling thing that you got over and didn't make a big fuss about. After all, if you were being paid to do something you loved, like racing a car, how could you complain about danger when guys and girls only a few years older than you had fought for their lives and the freedoms you now enjoyed? We have an extraordinary capacity to normalise the craziest and most extreme situations. But from what we have learned there must come a counter-response sometime, a debt repayment to our souls. Now we have terms to describe 'abnormal' behaviour caused by these extreme experiences, terms like post-traumatic stress disorder. We are making progress simply in acknowledging that, to paraphrase the neuroanatomist Dr Jill Bolte Taylor, humans are 'feeling things that think', rather than 'thinking things that feel'.

It is inconceivable that my father and mother were not deeply affected both by the war and by the 'peacetime war' of motor racing, with its own unique death toll of brave lads, most of whom were close personal friends. It would be fair to say that they must have normalised high levels of stress and excitement – hence all the wild partying, perhaps. For me, the way they lived seemed normal. Why wouldn't I feel at home in a high-stress environment, too?

The other thing that could have precipitated my depression was withdrawal from high levels of adrenaline. Adrenaline is a very powerful drug. When I was racing, journalists would always call us drivers 'adrenaline junkies'. I thought they had no idea what the hell they were talking about. The thing is that you become acclimatised to high levels and come to know how to deal with it. When you stop, you get a withdrawal effect. No adrenaline, no life. Where's my excitement fix gone? Life can seem very dull when you leave the F1 paddock. The world seems to be in slow motion; simple things like getting the phone fixed take forever. When you're used to having a team of highly trained engineers mending complex machinery in under five minutes, if can be a frustrating new life on Civvy Street.

I didn't wind down from F1 by doing some lesser form of racing until I got too old or bored with it. I just stopped. I went cold turkey, in effect. The reason I did this was because I had a terrible fear that I would die like my dad, post-retirement, and all that I had put myself through to achieve security for myself and my family would have been for naught. So I was dealt a double dose of issues to sort out. This is a real problem for ex-servicemen, too. Going back to a normal life after combat is almost as big a killer as being in combat. I'm not comparing what they go through to having been paid a healthy retainer to swan around in racing overalls, but the principle is the same.

The saying 'never explain, never complain', attributed to everyone from Benjamin Disraeli to Jack Nicholson, is good advice, I'm sure. I would not like this book to be read as an excuse or a complaint. I am certainly not out to make my achievements seem greater or to garner sympathy. If there is an ambition in this book, it is to rub a little salt of reality and truth into my public image and perhaps to encourage discussion about these issues. As I know only too well, there is no getting away from the fact that people know my face, as I was once very much centre stage sport-wise. So this is a chance to explain (not complain) and to show the human being inside the sport hero image.

George Michael once made the point that famous people aren't famous so much because they *have* something others lack, but more because they *lack* the thing that others have, or that they *perceive* others have. They think that fame is the solution. They see society valuing famous individuals and make the not unreasonable leap of logic to assume that worth can be measured in column inches, a good photo, wealth, fans or, as it is nowadays, Twitter followers.

That is not to say that famous people are not really talented, because they deserve the recognition, but often their determination to achieve a goal is connected to an inner sense of incompleteness, as if their life will have no value unless this goal is achieved. This is a huge spur, but it is like living perpetually under the sword of Damocles. Couple that fear to an innate talent and you have a formidable competitor who is literally fighting for his or her life, because failure to achieve the goal will equate to nothingness. Being or nothingness. 'To be, or not to be?' Life reduced to a simple binary equation. But this philosophy is flawed, because we all '*be*', like it or not. And there is nothing wrong with just 'being' . . . unless you are in F1, of course.

The problem with the 'fame philosophy' is that it presumes a normal state of insignificance: I am nothing *unless* I can achieve my goal – an attitude I was rather too familiar with in my career. Compare that view with an assumption of unconditional self-worth: to be content and confident in and of one's self, not to feel a need to justify one's value, to be able to give, because one has something *to* give. Surely this is the best state to be in? Nothing can touch you. We've all met amazing people like this; they are not needy, not ambitious or competitive (unless playing a game); they contribute solutions, not problems. They are those wonderful, perfect people. Don't you just hate them!

That's another symptom of depression: envy. And why would you not be envious of other people's happiness if you have none of your own? So then you hate yourself even more, because you cannot be one of those beautiful people. It's a nasty downward spiral into the abyss, and I don't recommend it. I've learned that to love someone else, you have to love yourself first. It's a cliché, I know, but it's one of the greatest truths of all time.

Another pitfall of fame is that society likes to relive past glories, making it difficult for an individual to move on and be recognised as someone different from their former self. I am now fifty-five years old and I am no longer that chap who won the F1 World Championship twenty years ago; nor do I want to be. So, for me, this book is a necessary thing, a kind of salute to the Damon of the past and an introduction to the more rounded and less driven person I am today.

In this book I describe my parents, who I believe had a difficult relationship with each other. This was exacerbated to an extent by being in the public eye and by my father being an unusually busy person in a very dangerous job. The problems in their relationship, and what we saw and felt as their children growing up, did not always fit with the image they projected. There is nothing wrong or unusual about that. If things had evolved normally, no doubt we would have come to terms with it and moved on, but in our case there was a sudden tragic accident leaving very many unanswered questions and making it more difficult to work out precisely what is myth and what is truth. This is why I have included a section on my parents. I am a product of their lives and I had to understand them to discover who I really am. But also, if we are not to repeat the bad parts of relationships, we have to try to work out what exactly needs to be exorcised and what needs to be cherished. It has taken a long time to unravel the truth about their relationship, partly because grief is a kind of insulation against investigation. We don't like to speak ill of the dead, but I had to know what the truth was about adults if I wanted to be one myself. When you don't want to talk about something, it gets submerged and finds another form of expression. I have learned to talk about fears. It's the best way to put them to rest.

So I have examined myself over the years and found myself wanting in certain respects. Otherwise, I'm perfect, which is exactly the kind of thing my dad would say! Self-knowledge is the only way to become a better person, or at least to become someone one can tolerate and forgive, but it also illuminates the world and the people around us. We become better at recognising devious strategies and insincerity. Perhaps we become less trusting, more circumspect, but also less naive about the world, which can only be a good thing. I'm hoping this extra insightfulness will add something to the telling of my story. You'll have to be the judge of that.

To get to the point of being able to write a book about my career and life, I have had to clear up a lot of 'residue' from my upbringing. This required a certain amount of courage, because the bogeyman looms large in the mind of a child – the child still inside us – and so it took time. But enough time has passed now to get on with things I've been putting off, and I feel ready to take control of this story. I no longer feel driven by some unconscious force to live a certain way or to fulfil some mission or quest to complete the final leg of the journey home, the part fate decreed my father could not make.

For most of my life I needed an answer to the big question: am I just a Graham Hill repeat; Graham Hill, Part II? Or am I Damon Hill, Part I? No doubt, if my father had not died when he did and the way he did, my life would have been completely different. From the moment his plane hit the ground, an unconscious process was set in motion that led me to the World Championship. Of that I have no doubt. We can never know the lives we might have led but for a simple twist of fate. But no one likes to think they are acting out some pre-programmed existence, driven by unresolved issues that aren't even their own.

So, when I stepped out of an F1 cockpit for the very last time in my life, at Suzuka in 1999, after years of chasing cars around tracks as if it was the most important thing in the world (which it certainly was to me at the time), I had at last won a breathing space to reflect on my achievements and to take stock. The idea was to use that time to unravel some of the big questions about my life and life in general, but I had no idea what a can of worms I had opened. I had quite a lot more questions than I had bargained for, which in many ways is in the nature of depression.

When you disappear from the limelight people think all sorts of things. But it was always part of the plan. I'd been fighting to get to this point, where I could detach from the madness and find my true self. John Lennon wrote a song called 'Watching the Wheels'. It was written when he dropped out of the whole fame game while living in New York with Yoko and just baking bread and looking after Sean, their new son. It has the lines, *They give me all kinds of warnings to save me from ruin*, and, *They give me all kinds of advice designed to enlighten me*. And that is exactly what happened to me.

People don't seem to like the idea that you have dropped out; they tend to take it personally if you don't want to come out and play. I went for years not even listening to the news or going to an airport. I just took the children to school, walked and read. It was great. But they write stuff and imagine stuff and make up stuff to fill the blank space you gave them – the blank that they find unsettling, perhaps. But all that time I was trying to free myself from a lot of complicated tangles so I could come back clearer than I've ever been about who I am.

So I've held my tongue and kept my powder dry, enjoying the show and literally watching the wheels go round and round. But now it's my turn to tell it like it really happened, from my point of view. They say if you have ten years to chop down a tree, spend nine sharpening your axe. Well, the nine years are up!

I hope you enjoy the story. I think it's a good one. It even made Murray Walker stop talking because he had a lump in his throat.

1 » THE LEGEND OF GRAHAM HILL

There were several people who were my father. There was the actual person who lived in the house and who went places with us, and there was the legend in the newspapers, on TV and at racetracks. There was the very serious man who did a very dangerous job, and there was the clown who made everything a big joke. I think I have a good handle on who Graham Hill was now, but when I was growing up, he was a demigod: a slightly intimidating but, at the same time, a lovely, generous, gregarious man who made our lives shine with light.

He was not what one might call a romantic man. He might even be called an insensitive person. When I needed to go back, after I had retired, and sort out where I might have been confused about things, it became clear that the blissful life I had enjoyed had a subtext to it: one of which I was luckily not completely conscious at the time. That was because I was in the Garden of Eden; I was a child still maturing. Now I am fifty-five and, having brought up my own family of four children, all of them born just before or during my career, I can see the problems that my parents faced and how difficult it must have been for them to cope.

My story is really about two generations of Hills. My parents laid the foundations for my life and, without question, the path my father carved led me to become a Formula One World Champion like him. But who I might have been if he had not died when I was fifteen is another question. Looking back, it sometimes seems inevitable that I would follow my father's course; at other times it seems incredible that I'd want to. If I was a product of my parents and their life in the glitzy, glamorous but tragedy-blighted world of Formula One, then they were a product of the austere and war-ripped early twentieth century.

It's quite possible that my mother's father, Bertie, fought in the First World War, as his wedding photo shows him in uniform. My mother was born in 1926 and Norman Graham Hill was born the year of the Great Crash, 1929. So they were only very young by the time they were into the chaos and destruction of the Second World War. So the 1950s, which was when they met, must have seemed a blissful release from all that.

It was into the post-war culture of 1960s England, trying to leave the war and stuffy old traditions behind, that my parents brought a family: Brigitte, me and Samantha. But they also brought us into the world of motor racing at its toughest and most intense period. After their experiences in the Blitz, I've often wondered if they were creating their own kind of peacetime, one spiced with a little wartime fear and danger, just for continuity. Overwhelming whatever was happening in the liberal Sixties was the contradictory culture of motor racing, which counterbalanced extreme brutality with an exaggerated lust for life. Through all this, my parents had their own personal life to cope with. Add a bit of fame and a lot of media interest into the mix and you have some powerful influences on a child's development. It created a distorted and unrealistic model of the world, one that had to end sometime, somehow.

But this unusual life my parents had created was my normality when growing up. There was reality, and there were the myths and legends of Graham Hill. Naturally, these myths had a huge influence not only on my view of my father but also on how I saw the world as it responded to the mythology. We love a good story, clearly; sometimes at the expense of the truth. To a large extent, the mythology became a cage for my parents' relationship, one that my mother has never really escaped from since the accident.

Ironically, because my father was so famous, I'm lucky that I have so much information to draw on about my early life and the life of my parents. Both wrote autobiographies and there are copious photographs and press cuttings. But the truth is never clearly on display. I have had to work hard to separate the meaning from the simple words. The magnificent image of Graham Hill, the Legend, often obscures the complications that his life and career created for his family.

Clearly I inherited a lot from my father, but, just as clearly, I am not him. To know who I am, I had to differentiate myself from him. To do that, I had to know all about him. I had to know more than just the cherished image of a media darling with his good looks and a talent for a great quote. But just as importantly, I had to accept his genius, his uniqueness and his popularity. It must have been a tough job being a father and keeping the Graham Hill show on the road. But within the world that he created and the zeitgeist of the Sixties and early Seventies, I formed a view of the world and a set of beliefs about it.

The early legend of Graham Hill describes a young man not content to have a safe passage towards retirement. He jacked in his safe job with Smiths Instruments to risk all on motor racing. He had no idea how it would turn out, but he gambled, and he won. A story my father was very proud to tell was that he and Harry Hyams – who was to become a very successful, not to say notorious, property developer – were identified as the 'two boys least likely to succeed' by their headmaster. Dad had a strong, independent spirit and faith enough in his own instincts to stick two fingers up to those who would try to define or limit him. Being 'press-ganged' through national service into the navy did nothing to change his attitude towards authority, but I have a feeling it did more for him than he ever cared to acknowledge.

In his autobiography, *Life at the Limit*, he gives credit to the navy for teaching him a great deal about life; notably, the officer training where he learnt public speaking – of which he became something of a brilliant exponent in later life. He also learned leadership by being placed in charge of about forty to fifty 'chaps', something he must have found useful when he had his own team.

I have no doubt his navy discipline helped when he had the gruesome task of taking charge of the shell-shocked Lotus team after Jimmy Clark was killed at Hockenheim in 1968. Years later when I was racing, I was sitting in the bar of an hotel when Clark's mechanic, Dave 'Beaky' Sims, sat next to me. He related the story of how my father had told them all what to do: to collect all the bits of the car they could find, to put them in the truck and to drive to the port and not to stop for anyone; just get back to the factory as quickly as possible. He said they would have not known what to do had it not been for Graham's courage and leadership.

Indeed, my father went on to rebuild the confidence of a stricken and broken team by winning the F1 Championship later that year. Impressive stuff, really. The episode was to have a sad parallel in my own career when we lost Ayrton Senna. Without doubt, I took strength from this story, but the situations were otherwise very different. I was not in a position to take control of the team like he had, nor did I go on to win the Championship, but otherwise I was hugely inspired by his example. A very positive legacy.

He also credited the navy with some seamier lessons in life, such as how to get plastered by noon every day. Unbelievably, the navy still issued tots of rum for the officers – a tot being a whole eighth of a pint of neat rum – at twelve o'clock. Another eye-opener was a visit to Tangiers, where he thanks the navy for introducing him to something he called 'an exhibition' and 'extracurricular activities'. We can only imagine what he might have been referring to there. I think it is sufficient to say that he went into the navy an innocent, but came home less innocent. What he also did, though – a variation on the theme of ships passing in the night – was visit Monaco.

His ship, HMS *Swiftsure*, docked in Monaco in 1951 and off went Dad to the casino, where he says he won 'a few bob', not having any idea that one day he would become known as Mr Monaco after winning the race five times and hobnobbing with the Rainiers. He admitted that, at the time, he had no idea there was a Grand Prix there at all, and knew nothing about racing. Still slightly innocent, then. He would win a hell of a lot more 'bobs' at Monaco in the years to come.

My father was not impressed that the navy took two whole years out of his life when he felt he could have learnt it all in one; a very typical attitude from a would-be racing driver. He also took a dim view of having to go back for the next three years to do three weeks on, which is why he grew a ridiculous moustache, which he described as 'RAF fighter pilot'. He knew only clean-shaven or a full set was permitted, but he seemed to have got them flustered and thoroughly revelled in his 'anti-stupid-rules' attitude. He enjoyed seeing them go puce with rage at this early version of a long-haired hippy. But he gave the navy a dilemma. Dad was expressing his freedom in a way they didn't approve of, but could do nothing about. He was hardly Che Guevara, but he was clearly ready for something different; a life in which he was free to live as he pleased. While he was still 'property' of the navy, he met a woman called Bette Shubrook.

Why my father wanted to marry my mother will always remain a mystery. It was a mystery to him; or, at least, he had trouble acknowledging how he truly felt about her. He might have been prompted to propose by a love rival when – at her house one day – he discovered she had all the papers necessary to move to Canada with another man. I think this must have rather hurt his pride. He clearly didn't like the idea of coming second in any situation.

In his autobiography he talks of proposing to her, even though he thought he wasn't the marrying type. He says that he heard himself say the words but felt as if wasn't really him talking. In my mother's book, *The Other Side of the Hill*, she has a slightly more detailed recollection. Her reaction was to say: 'What on earth are you talking about?' 'I don't want you to go – marry me,' he insisted. To which she replied that he must be out of his mind, because he didn't have any money. 'Well, are you going to marry me or not?' was his final offer.

Because he'd already started racing, the only free weekend on which they could get married was 13 August 1955. Their honeymoon was punctuated by – if not carefully arranged around – various sporting events in which my father took part. He based himself at Bognor Regis for easy access to Goodwood, where he had scrounged a few laps in someone's car. And then he 'met a mate' – quite by chance, of course – who was competing in a regatta on the Isle of Wight and asked my father to join him. Rather than explaining that he was on his honeymoon, Dad accepted – and they won the event. This might perhaps have placated his new wife if he hadn't greatly upset her by kissing the famous singer Carole Carr ('this lovely bird' as he refers to her in his book), who was dishing out the prizes. What a great honeymoon!

I'm not sure that the pattern changed much over the duration of their entire marriage. My father did what he wanted and my mother slotted in behind, always slightly short-changed. I fear I could be accused of the same thing but, in my defence, I was indoctrinated by the master himself. It took a good woman to show me the error of my ways, or rather, his ways, but not before I had pulled a similar stunt on our honeymoon, albeit under a bit more pressure than my father . . .

In 1988, Georgie and I were both twenty-eight, and had been living together for a while. We wanted a family, but had jumped the start slightly: Georgie was already pregnant. Naturally, we wanted our child born in wedlock, but we had a limited window for the wedding. The problem was that I'd managed to wangle a drive in a F3000 race in Dijon on the weekend in question. This was obviously vital for my career, which was in a pretty crucial phase at the time (isn't it always?). While Georgie was in a meeting at work, I phoned to tell her the good news about the race. The air became so blue, I was told later, that the people she was negotiating with just caved in to her demands immediately and she got the best deal possible for her company. Nevertheless, she agreed to my plan. But we would have to work quickly if we were to get married, have the reception, drive from Putney on a Friday night to catch a plane from Heathrow to Geneva and then drive to Dijon, consummate the marriage (not that it really needed it by then) and get to the circuit in time for qualifying in the morning.

On the day itself, it all went perfectly. The church in Wandsworth was filled with all our friends, my family and many of my father's closest friends too. The sun blazed as we exited to a recording of the Beatles singing 'All You Need is Love'. We had a wonderful reception at the London Rowing Club just nearby, and then, at the airport, we met Clive who worked for Nicholson-McLaren Engines and was cadging a lift with us, to his acute embarrassment. The three of us drove through the night to get to the bijou economy hotel overlooking the rear end of Dijon train station.

In the morning, I had to leave Georgie to fend for herself and make my way to the track in thick fog. The boys had decaled the rear wing with the words *Just Married*. It was a nice touch and much appreciated by Georgie when she eventually arrived at the track, slightly hungry – being pregnant – and not having been able get anything to eat at the budget hotel because I hadn't left her any money. Like father, like son? A tradition of insensitivity to our brides, or just an overabundance of enthusiasm? Whatever protestations I might make about being different from my father, I have to admit it would appear that neither my dad nor I behaved particularly gallantly in the crucial hours immediately after our marriages.

There must have been something about Bette Shubrook that my dad wanted or needed. Perhaps it was simply money.

She had a reasonably well-paid job at Lillywhites, and he did admit to having bought a pair of climbing boots at Lillywhites in 1953 when he was persuaded to climb Snowdon by some medical student members of the London Rowing Club. They wanted to emulate Hillary and Norgay, who were halfway up Everest, but also to get away from the crowds in London celebrating the Coronation.

There is some confusion as to whether my dad rowed in the navy, met Mum and introduced her to rowing; or whether they met through rowing. Whatever the case, my mum must have been pretty good because she ended up being victorious in the European Games in 1953. My father coached the eight she was in and took some of the credit, but the fact remains that my mother would probably have won an Olympic medal if they had admitted women in those days.

Years later, in a 1958 American car magazine article about a new Lotus Formula One driver called Graham Hill – at that time a total unknown – he was referred to as being married to 'the famous oarswoman, Bette Shubrook'. This part of the Hill family legend has become somewhat obscured over the years, but it shows I have double competitive genes and that Mum was not one to blow her own trumpet at the expense of her husband.

Rowing provided multiple benefits for my father. He became very fit and understood how to dig deep, learning also that you have to keep pushing to the finish because you can't always see your opponent. It obviously honed and satisfied his competitive urge, but there was also a strong social aspect that enabled him to transcend social boundaries. He became good friends with Lord Snowdon through rowing. This friendship nearly had tragic consequences, though, as Snowdon was due to fly with Dad to take photographs that fateful weekend in November 1975.

Dad wryly pointed out that, in the only two sports at which he ever excelled, he was sitting down, and in one he was facing backwards. Finding a wife was a bonus he probably hadn't expected from rowing; nor was finding a perfect crash helmet design. From the very start, he carried the distinctive rowing cap design on his helmet. He was to make the London Rowing Club cap – navy-blue with eight white stripes, representing oars, around the crown – the most famous rowing design in the world. It always stood out on a grid and seemed perfectly to symbolise his conservative attitude. I was extremely proud to carry on the heraldic tradition, as was my son Josh, despite neither of us having been proper members of the club – but maybe we both felt that we were honouring GH as well the club that gave him such great pleasure. I bet the founders never thought their club design would ever be used for motor sport, let alone be carried to three Formula One titles and thirty-seven Grand Prix victories.

We are lucky that we still have so many photos of my parents at that time. My mother was a glamorous-looking woman, whose attractiveness was not in doubt. But, in addition, I wonder if my father had not been drawn to her sportiness and competitiveness? At their first meeting at a Boxing Day regatta at Auriol Rowing Club in 1950, he failed to make much of an impression on her. So, the next time, he turned up in true officer and gentleman style wearing his navy uniform. That seems to have done the trick. She was outgunned.

A photo of them laughing and clearly very happy at some party or other shows Dad with one hand on a pewter jug of beer and the other arm around Mum, who is daintily holding what looks like a small sherry. The extraordinary thing about my dad in this photo is his ridiculous handlebar moustache. No wonder he upset the navy so much, with that thing on his top lip. One wonders how the hell my mum could be attracted to a man who looked like that. In another photo of Dad in a preposterous banger of a car (possibly a Morris Eight) he is wearing a sheepskin coat and a flower-pot hat, looking for all the world like Terry-Thomas in *School for Scoundrels,* except that the film wasn't made until 1960, so maybe Dad was the inspiration? But he always looked as if he was having a lot of fun, even if he was broke.

The best pound he ever spent was at Brands Hatch in 1953 to pay for four laps in a Cooper Formula Three car. My father insisted that the moment he went on the track in a racing car, a light bulb went on in his head and he knew this was what he wanted to do with his life. Quite where this instinct originated would appear to be a mystery, as his father never drove a car in his life and Dad had only just learned to drive himself. So much for being in F1 by the age of seventeen, like Max Verstappen.

Those early years are vital to laying down the instinctive reactions. All current F1 drivers have been karting since early childhood. This early learning makes it easier on the brain later on, and they have spare capacity for other things – like talking on the radio and thinking tactically – because the tough bit is being handled automatically in their unconscious. Undoubtedly, both my father and I were handicapped by our late starts. In today's sport, we would have had a tough job to compete against drivers who have been in karting from as young as four years old.

Modern science has also shown that the young have difficulty making the connection between their actions and the consequences until they are in their late teens, or even early twenties. Their prefrontal cortex is not yet completely wired up, making rational decision-making less easy. If you want to train racing drivers, it's best to get them young, before they can think about all the things that could go wrong.

At the age when Michael Schumacher was developing his karting skills, I was riding my minibike and charging up and down the driveway to our house in my father's Mini Cooper S. Not ideal groundwork for what was to come later, but still way ahead of my father. But at least he made it to F1 by twenty-nine, three years ahead of me.

If we are looking for a possible cause for my father's speed epiphany, Graham's mother, the irrepressible Connie (Con-

stance) would be an obvious starting point. She rode a
motorcycle, just before Graham was born. If there is a link
going back through the generations, then it must be through
the motorcycle rather than the car. My father's first motor
sport competition was in motocross events, or 'scrambling', as
it was called at the time. Just like me, his early mode of transport was a motorbike. An accident on his Velocette in 1958
put him in hospital for three months and left him with a limp
and a characteristic stride that seemed to betray his determination. But the experience may also have left him with enough
evidence of a link between his actions and their consequences
to protect him through his later career. He would go on to
break both legs good and properly in 1969 when thrown out
of his Lotus F1 car in Watkins Glen during the USA GP, so
that evened things up a bit on the hobbling. But I can be proud
to say that we probably both owe our love of speed to his
mother, my grandma.

By the late 1950s, my father had worked his way into
F1 through pure determination and perseverance, a quality I
either learned from his legend or have inherited as an intrinsic
Hill characteristic. Now his life and my mother's were entirely
dominated by the demands of the competitive world he had
chosen. The culture suited his personality completely, and it
also influenced much of my early life. If something needed to
be done to win, it was done. No obstacle was insurmountable.

Modern F1 was founded upon get-up-and-go freethinking
types like my father. Both Bernie Ecclestone and Colin Chapman, founder of Lotus, were his contemporaries as well as key
and influential people in my father's life. They would all contribute massively to defining the sport we have today. It's hard
to imagine either Bernie or Colin fitting into a strict regime.
My father worked as a mechanic for Colin in return for getting a drive. When he turned out to be quicker than Colin, he
was taken on as a driver and suddenly became a driver in
demand, being offered money to race all kinds of other cars
by various entrants. On pure performance, he had become a

professional racing driver. It seemed so simple and organic back then. They all travelled together, socialised together and lived in each other's pockets. Sadly, they also went to many of their friends' funerals.

But motor sport was a place where they could make their own rules, get on and escape the austerity and depression of post-war Britain. And the world needed people like them in order to be free to rebuild. When you hear of what they all got up to and the freedoms they enjoyed, it must have been a wonderful time. They were a law unto themselves and, in the background, you can detect the Sixties culture brewing up in these stories of their beginnings. The Sixties, a wonderful period to be born into, would be the very best of times for my father: a time when his star was at the highest, winning two world titles and the Indy 500 in 1966. Throw in England winning the World Cup, the Beatles, the Stones and the moon landing, and the vibe was distinctly optimistic, despite the Vietnam War. My father was right there in the centre of it all – which meant that we were, too.

In the course of his career he earned many accolades and admirers. He was a living legend. Sadly, he died at the age of forty-six. But his reputation would live forever as the racing driver who overcame all odds and who remains the only man to have won Indianapolis, Le Mans and the Formula One World Championship.

It is the stuff of legend how my father knew no one, had no money, but would sit in the Steering Wheel Club in Mayfair and make half a pint last all night in order to be in the right place to meet the right people. There are countless stories describing a person who would not give up until he had given things his best shot. For the son of such a man, that is both inspiring and a lot to live up to. My father gave the name 'Hill' a certain meaning. It carried all the qualities of the legend with it. If I was going to be a true Hill, I would have to earn it.

2 » FAME AND ATTENTION

When you look at early photographs of me, it is easy to understand why I ended up having a go at what my dad did. It looks as if I'm being literally shoehorned into the cockpit at every opportunity. The pictures also show how early I was introduced to the limelight, albeit reflected from my gregarious and publicity-loving father. Maybe it was all a bit much too soon. I have never felt entirely comfortable with being in front of the camera, although I was never really given a choice.

There were, however, some unforeseen benefits to this publicity. When I was about twelve, together with 'young Geoff Hurst' and 'young Barry John', 'young Graham Hill' was used in a Weetabix advert. We were dressed in the appropriate kit for our sport and we each received £200, which was an enormous amount of pocket money in those days for kids so young. I thought: 'This is it, boys! The big time!' But my ego was rudely brought into check when my father threw in a tenner and said I had to share it three ways with my sisters. Seventy quid each, which left me feeling confused about whether I'd been swindled or overpaid. It took me a while to see that he was being as wise as Solomon. He hated greed and we always had to share. He was fundamentally a stickler for correct values.

On the downside, I was also bamboozled into appearing on *Jim'll Fix It*. I was supposed to have always wanted to start a race that my dad was in. I had never, ever, expressed such a wish, but it was a ruse to help promote a charity saloon-car race at Brands Hatch. On I went and did the whole sordid charade, and felt entirely fraudulent as Savile gave me my 'Jim

Fixed It For Me' medal. I thought the whole atmosphere in the studio was very weird. I hated every minute of it, being singled out as a 'special child' – and I didn't even get paid!

Because of my own experiences, I am very circumspect about exposing young people to fame and have made a point of not exploiting my own children. Fame is an intoxicating, mind-altering drug and can ruin any chance of normal peer relationships. I think it was Gore Vidal who said that the tragedy of the rich and famous is that they have only them- selves to mix with. Thankfully, not all rich and famous people are like him, but I did find when I was at gatherings of famous people with my parents that no one seemed relaxed, everyone trying too hard to have a good time while looking like hunted animals.

Everyone, that is, except my father, who took to attention like a dog at Crufts. He loved it, and it loved him. He swung away in the Swinging Sixties and played up to the part beau- tifully. With his David Niven fighter-pilot moustache and his Terry-Thomas image, he provided the public with a hero who represented the ideal Churchillian. Graham Hill would fight them on the beaches, and in the streets, and would, never, ever, surrender without a damn good fight. He became synonymous – perhaps to his detriment, because he had incredible talent, too – with the concept of gritty determination, which is one small step removed from 'a good trier'.

Perhaps I adopted this same attitude and made the mistake of thinking that you needed to show you were working hard just to impress. But he always remembered that he was in a show and people wanted more than just your driving ability, so a bit of over-dramatisation was also a good thing. It's fair to say, however, that both of us were defined similarly, as having achieved success through force of will, rather than abundance of talent. I guess it's all relative, though.

I thought there was virtue in my dad's stoic approach to his sport and his life, and you have to be in total awe of his courage and complete lack of self-pity. He personified the 'can do' attitude, whereby nothing was impossible and you never gave up. He used to joke, 'If at first you don't succeed – give up!' To him, this joke was hilarious, because to quit would be unthinkable. The only snag with his Mr Determined image was that people tend to want superheroes capable of doing magic and making things look easy. They don't necessarily want to think they could do it too. Crowds are fickle and hard to please, but they always love a showman. As expert motor sport historian Doug Nye remarked, 'Graham Hill strode the stage like a Colossus.' That'll do for me. My daddy was a Colossus.

His parties at our home in Parkside, Mill Hill, were notorious Swinging Sixties happenings, often visited by the local police, who would attempt to get Mr Hill to turn down the music, only to be persuaded to join the party. They would return the next day to collect the missing bits of their uniform.

Although my father loved fun, he knew where the line was. But perhaps there was a slight hint of desperation in his attention-seeking. When he appeared in the newspapers – on what seemed like a regular basis – photographed standing on tables with his trousers round his ankles, you had to feel a twinge of embarrassment. Perhaps I'm being prudish? Perhaps I'm being too politically correct? At the time it was OK to have fun, because tomorrow you could be dead. No one begrudged Grand Prix drivers their parties. Indeed, they were encouraged, and the journalists and photographers knew what to publish and what to keep from the eyes of the public.

This collective secrecy was to become a bit of a barrier for me in years to come when I was finding out more about the person my father was. I needed to discover who he really was so that I could grow myself. People don't like to divulge too much truth about themselves or their friends, and I can understand that. But how can children become adults unless they can lift the veil of perfection? We all eventually work out that Father Christmas is actually 'only' Dad. Normal development allows for the process of meeting one's parents on the level to occur naturally. Cut that process short, and one is left with the image of perfection: a mute god, unable to say, 'It's OK. Lighten up. We're only human.'

My father had a reputation as an uncompromising task-master. He could be very tough: hard on himself and hard on those around him. He said it 'got results'. He had enormous self-discipline and a strong work ethic; he worked hard, but he played hard. I don't think there were many people who worked as hard as my father, but maybe the trick is to work better, not harder, and to be a little kinder to those around you. Jackie Stewart, a great friend and admirer of Dad's, described him thus in the foreword to Dad's autobiography (republished after his death): 'When I first met him he was a very intense man – almost frightening people away at times. He deplored dishonesty, he did not suffer fools gladly and was not afraid to show it. He did not change over the years, but he mellowed.'

My mother did comment that she thought Dad was too hard on me, but Sir Frank Williams called me a 'tough bas-tard', which – coming from him – I took as a compliment. I loved my dad for all his toughness. I even liked his tickings off when I needed ticking off, because life is tough and you need to knuckle down sometimes. I can remember little moments that made me jump, like one time when I was standing around daydreaming while he was unloading the luggage from the plane: 'Oi! Damon. Don't just stand there. Pull your finger out!' He had a point. I was swinging the lead.

How talented was he as a driver? The idea of being a 'born racing driver' is a contentious one. Mario Andretti, when asked if he thought he was one, pithily but perceptively replied, 'I don't know. I've never seen a baby born with a steering wheel in his hand.' Motor sport journalism is riddled with phrases like 'he's a natural' or 'he's a true racer'. I have no doubt that some people have innate natural ability, but sports journalists are invariably romantics who worship the sport they have loved from childhood. Their sport is an arena for superheroes only: the 'gods' who cannot be related to in human terms.

My father was all too human. He loathed pomposity, but to be a superhero you had to have a bit of a superior air about you. This was total anathema to him. We all put our trousers on one leg at a time. No one is invincible; some are just a lot more difficult to beat than the rest, as we both found out when we came up against the most naturally gifted and fastest drivers of our respective eras: him with Jimmy Clark and Jackie Stewart, and me with the likes of Nigel Mansell, Alain Prost, Ayrton Senna and Michael Schumacher. They were pretty special, all right, I can vouch for that. So it's all the more satisfying to beat them. It can be done, under the right circumstances.

Stirling Moss had my father as a co-driver for some events and called him 'very mature and intelligent' and 'a man of considerable ability'. But he also added the caveat, 'he wasn't a racer'. I've never understood this distinction. How does one become 'a racer'? If my father wasn't one, was I? But there was a mutual respect there. My father always regarded Stirling as the best there ever was. Stirling remarked that my father was without ego, which is a nice compliment coming from the great man himself.

But I've always felt that my father was never really given enough credit for showing us what could be possible if we only tried. He had tenacity in bucketloads, and I think I am the same. If we want to get somewhere, we just don't give up till it's done. The problem comes when you don't know where you want to go. He drummed into me the adage, 'If a thing's worth doing, it's worth doing properly' – the *Monte Carlo or Bust!* motto – and, 'If you start something, finish it.' I suspect I would never have become World Champion without my head ringing with these words, in his slightly nasal, clipped tone of voice.

I have also inherited from him an admiration for those who have a go and give it their all, since I know a little about how much harder things can be in reality than they look. We tend to get very awestruck by those who win all the time and it is terrific to see someone being brilliant. But in sport, someone who is so far ahead of the competition is somehow not playing right. They are just accumulating results. Schumacher's dominant years cemented his statistics, but I think what he missed was competition. We all need a foil: someone to test us to our limits.

The greatest sporting events happen when two almost equally matched competitors go against each other for the top spot: drivers like Clark and Hill, Prost and Senna, Mansell and Piquet. For me, Michael lifted my game up to his level, if only for a while. But when the difference is small, then is it the most tenacious competitor, the most spirited, the one prepared to dig deepest into their abundant reserves of talent, who will prevail. Surely the man or woman who gives everything they have to beat those for whom things are a little easier deserves more credit, rather than disdain for not having as much natural ability? Tony Brooks, Britain's top driver of the late 1950s along with Moss, did not regard Dad as a 'natural' but thought his accomplishments were 'more meritorious' for the reason that he doggedly persisted and used his head to work it out.

If neither of us regarded as 'naturals', hot favourites, we both revelled in the role of underdog. Perhaps that's a very British concept: Shakespeare's 'we happy few', a description applied to the Battle of Britain pilots. Sir Frank Williams said one of his favourite films was *Zulu*, the story of a few brave men fighting against impossible odds. I think the Williams F1 team relish the idea of being the ones who win with less firepower but with more ingenuity: a Drake against the Spanish Armada. The British like to think that we are amazing for our small size. But who doesn't? It's our favourite story – the long shot overturns the establishment: David and Goliath, Tom and Jerry, *Charlie and the Chocolate Factory*, *Gladiator* and *Spartacus*. Look at Leicester City winning the Premier League with odds of 5000–1 at the start of the 2015/16 season. It's an ancient idea, one that gives us all hope that if we have a go, something good might happen. My father's philosophy was: if you try, you might fail, but if you never try, you will never know whether you could have succeeded.

At Indianapolis in 1966, the crusty old campaigner A. J. Foyt gave the rookies a briefing: 'No one,' he proudly exclaimed, 'wins Indy first time out!' So what did my father do? He loved that story. In 1984, I was told by John Webb, who owned Brands Hatch and was sponsoring me at the time, that I was too old for F1. Right. I can still get the blood to rise just thinking about it. I guess that's what a competitor is?

My father would never accept that there is a natural order, with only the entitled people at the top. He was always respectful of society's conventions and hierarchies, but never believed that one person had a monopoly on being treated with human dignity. He was a humane man, hated injustice and had a true common touch. He could walk with kings and paupers and make each feel just as valued. He supped with the highest in the land, shooting with the Queen and golfing with Sean Connery. He did an inordinate amount for charities, particularly the Springfield Club for Young People in Hackney, where he would regularly pop in for a game of table tennis (at which he was particularly good). He bought his suits from Savile Row, but was never above whatever duty required. On one occasion he promised to take me to a game at Arsenal but had clearly left it a bit late. We stood outside Highbury stadium while he haggled with the touts. All we could get were tickets in the Clock End. For the entire match we stood among the visitors, Dad in an immaculate suit and an enormous colourful cravat. That's what I call style.

Yes, he was not as naturally gifted as, say, Clark or Stewart, but he ground every last drop of talent out of himself, giving no quarter and expecting none in return. That said, I think he had more natural talent than he believed. You don't win Monaco five times by luck. So there was something there.

People talk about 'driving by the seat of your pants', which is being able to trust entirely to your survival instincts to get you out of all situations. Moss could do it, and Clark and Senna too, but the key is concentration. Ayrton Senna famously lost a Monaco victory when he had a massive lead over Prost in 1988. The problem was that he had slowed under the instructions of team boss Ron Dennis, who ironically had wanted to ensure he finished with Prost in a McLaren one–two. This must have broken Ayrton's state of concentration, which, during a race, is a tranquil state of heightened being, believe it or not. Senna hit the barriers and suffered one of his most humiliating defeats. The concentration required – and willingly given – to drive a racing car to the limits is extreme. It does something to you that can't be found in many other places or experiences. The last thing you need is someone coming on the radio to have a chat. In my father's day, this wasn't a problem. You left the grid and never talked to a soul except yourself for the next two hours, because there was no radio.

Ayrton famously talked about an 'out-of-body experience' in qualifying for this same race, whereby he felt he was no longer driving consciously and was, in his words, 'in a different dimension'. He was ridiculed by some but he qualified 1.4 seconds faster than his teammate, so I'd say that was pretty out of this world. I was to experience something of an out-of-body experience myself, in the race of my life in 1994 in Suzuka. Although it never happened to me again, I now believe I understand what Ayrton was talking about. Concentration can be a powerful drug.

If my father had an extraordinary talent, it was for concentration. Determination and concentration are closely linked. Both require the ability not to be distracted, but concentration is also a function of fascination. One has to find what one is doing absorbing, not boring. There is a fascination in driving fast, as in almost any difficult physical discipline. Challenges stimulate questions that demand an answer, and the questions keep coming: 'What if I try this? Or that? Now try this.' It's a scientific enquiry into one's own limitations. The difference with motor sport compared to, say, golf, is that the consequences of getting it wrong could be fatal. This rather concentrates the mind, of course.

Science has now found a correlation between dopamine receptor gene D4 (DRD4) and what scientists call novelty-seeking (NS). This is a euphemism for drug-taking, gambling and general addiction to danger. What the studies suggest is that a certain condition of this gene does not necessarily cause thrill-seeking but can make one more susceptible to addiction to it. Whereas some people would have a go in a racing car and walk away suitably thrilled, others would just want more, more, more. Fortunately, the scientists conclude that this tendency declines with age, so there comes a time when we can walk away from dangerous sports – assuming we can still walk.

But as for natural-born racing car drivers? I'm with Mario. I think natural aptitude exists, but then it's down to the desire to win. Besides, the very first motorised car wasn't invented until the 1800s, and most people would never have had any experience of a car until the mid 1900s. Humans are blessed with a range and variety of natural talents, but I'm not sure Nature had motorisation in mind when she evolved us. I'm sure Darwin would agree that the trick is to find what you are best fitted for, or to be lucky enough for it to find you.

Somewhere in this mix of character and genetic tendencies are the things I share with my father. Some of it is simply hand-me-down beliefs and attitudes gleaned from other times and other people. But some of it can't be denied or altered. It is him, and it is me, too.

It is easy to be bedazzled by my father but it would be a mistake to overlook the influence of my mother or, rather, the effect my father's life had on her and therefore on their children. The sport he loved had a dark side that the participants often struggled to rationalise. Competition in itself is enough to create enormous emotional strain. But the steady drip, drip of death was an additional psychological pressure that created more than the usual stress fractures. Motor sport is not for the faint-hearted. One might have said back then that it was only for the cold-hearted.

My mother endured the most ridiculous amount of stress watching her husband dicing with death and seeing their friends and colleagues being picked off, one by one, year after year. Among all that, she had three children to look after. Four, if you include my dad, who seems to have needed her as a kind of security blanket.

She was three years older than Graham. Us men put on a brave front, but more often than not we need the soft bosom of our mothers to make us feel truly safe from an otherwise terrifying world. Motor racing probably seemed like a jolly good wheeze compared to the terrors of the Second World War experienced by both my parents as teenagers. One can make one thing relative to another, and maybe racing was less scary than being bombed, but exposure to excessive and extended periods of danger builds a 'stress debt' that must be addressed sooner or later. If you add my own career to my mother's experiences, heaven knows how she coped with it all. She is now an old lady, aged ninety, but she's a survivor.

If my father seemed to be a standard-bearer for risk-taking, my mother dutifully supported his life choice, for all its pitfalls. The courage was not all on one side. But in doing so she inadvertently reaffirmed the myth of their marriage: that they coped perfectly well with it all. That would have taken almost superhuman strength. Do we really think Odysseus resisted all the opportunities he encountered on his voyages, or that he never incurred the wrath of Penelope when he came home late from the Trojan War? My father was heroic, as was my mother; no question about that, but they were also just human beings, and of course there were arguments and tears. It has to be said that my father could be insensitive to how my mother was feeling; you can't apply the rules of engagement in the F1 paddock in the home. But stress does not respect these boundaries.

My first F1 group driver photocall was at my christening in July 1961, when I was just ten months old. In attendance (with me in the obligatory small car) were Bruce McLaren, Stirling Moss, Tony Brooks, my father, Jo Bonnier and Wolfgang 'Taffy' von Trips, who had won the British Grand Prix at Aintree two days before. Sadly, he had less than two months to live, dying at Monza in a massive accident that also killed fourteen spectators. Trips had just founded the kart track in Kerpen, Germany, which was later leased by Rolf Schumacher, father of Michael and Ralf, and became their karting kindergarten.

Of the six drivers in this photo, only two have evaded a violent and untimely death: Brooks and Moss. Both, however, had their share of accidents, Tony eventually deciding that it was not worth the risk and Stirling having a career-ending crash at Goodwood less than a year after this photo was taken. Ironically, the accident involved my father, as it was he whom Stirling was overtaking at the time to unlap himself. Of the others, Bruce died testing his own car at Goodwood in 1970, and Jo Bonnier, my godfather, died in the same Le Mans 24 Hours won by my father in 1972. A bittersweet victory if ever there was one.

Looking at photos of racing drivers in that era is a sobering process. Their faces rarely betrayed the fear they must have felt inside and yet they knew the odds were not good, and many of them would die young. It is hard to believe they ever sat in a car, since it was almost certain death. Jackie Stewart counted fifty-seven of his friends and colleagues killed in motor sport. The sport is undoubtedly inhabited by different characters today. I still struggle to understand how my father and his racing friends lived with the constant thought that there might not be a tomorrow. In my own career I knew there were risks; every time I left for a track, I kissed my wife and children, accepting the possibility that I might not come back, but it was nothing to the risks my father faced.

What is perhaps more alarming and more pertinent to this story is the number of deaths and accidents that happen post-retirement. Mike Hawthorn, for example, lasted only months before being killed in a road accident. To Mike you can add the names of Didier Pironi (powerboat), David Purley (stunt plane), Mike Hailwood (freak car crash) and, of course, my father. You might also add the name of Michael Schumacher as a victim of post-career accidents. Sir Jackie Stewart has had a driver to get him around since retiring, perhaps understanding better than most how lucky he had been.

It's a chilling thought that one is as vulnerable – if not more so – post-F1 career. The safety standards in F1 are now remarkable, making it arguably the safest form of motor sport there is. Nevertheless, as Jules Bianchi's accident in 2015 showed, death always seems to find a loophole in the regulations, no matter how hard we try to make F1 safer. Motor sport is, and will always be, a dangerous game, but outside that heavily protected environment, things are perhaps more risky, not less. It was something that I was mindful of when I stopped racing – especially bearing in mind what had happened to my father.

It is no exaggeration to say that the world into which I was born was clouded with the black pall of violent death. Despite their brave faces everyone was affected. Death was what you didn't dwell on, but it was there always, sharpening its scythe and waiting patiently. The sport always needed eager new recruits, and amazingly there were always plenty available. One team boss once rather darkly compared drivers to light bulbs: when one goes out, you just put another in. It took a certain type of man to be drawn to that level of danger and a certain kind of man to want to work with them. The drivers must have seen it as a price worth paying to do what they loved, but maybe it wouldn't be them who paid the price?

Typically, people in F1 at the time didn't talk openly about death; deaths were deemed an inevitable and necessary cost if one was to enjoy all the other things about the sport. But clearly times have changed. We have gradually sidled away from the idea that a short but heroic life is something to be admired. There are always going to be those who hanker for the days when sex was safe and racing was dangerous, instead of the other way round, but perhaps now we want to move on to something more socially acceptable, more skill-orientated? Maybe in time we will look back on the racing of the past, as we do upon the Roman games, as something sick, maybe even pornographic? Maybe, but there is something unquestionably very stimulating about danger. I wonder if we can (or should) ever lose that aspect of our nature?

3 » BORN IN A COCKPIT

People born into show business talk of being born in a trunk. Well, I suppose I was born in a cockpit. From the very earliest photographs of me I can be seen posing in a small car, or latterly, one of my father's racing cars.

Obviously, to begin with, I was too young to really understand what was going on and just went along with the show. But as I grew I started to hate being asked to pose for this kind of cheesy photo ops. I could sense the premise was wrong. Why did they want a picture of me? Not because of *me*, but because I had a famous father. It was the only conclusion I could come to. You have two ways to go from there: strive harder to define your own separate identity, or do something completely different. I tried both.

At first I look reasonably happy. Who wouldn't want to be a racing driver like their daddy? Well, me, evidently. I think I started to find all this posing a bit odd. It's all very well when your grandma wants you to put the funny hat on and smile for her album, but when someone you have never met before starts to ask you to hold your chin up 'like this', or put your leg up on the front wheel 'like this', you start to think, 'Like hell I will.' It made me very self-conscious; press- and camera-wary.

It was partly that I felt distinctly uncomfortable about being singled out for attention when I had done nothing to warrant it. But, more than that, there was something in me that was strongly against being defined by those around me, even if that included my parents. As time went by, I developed an aversion to the photographers' predictable expectations. I dug my heels in and vowed not to give them what they wanted. I learned to do the 'death scowl' that evolved, I suppose, into the intense Damon Hill 'eyes' – which was such a powerful image that I was able to have it trademarked!

But from the moment I was conscious of what was really going on around me, the most relentless question of all was: 'Are you going to be a famous racing driver like your daddy when you grow up?' No, no, and a thousand times, no! Imagine the media's delight when I finally did – but, in my defence, not before some unforeseeable events that rather changed the context of the question. If the world expected me to follow in Graham Hill's tyre tracks, they'd have to back off until I was ready to do it on my own terms.

Therapy famously likes to examine childhood. In the search for clues as to what created me, parental relationships obviously come high on the list, along with whatever else was happening at the time: good things and bad. Although my father was becoming more successful before I was born, and was to become considerably more so after, at the time it is clear that both my parents were living in a time of heightened anxiety as well as fame.

I was born only fifteen years after the end of the Second World War, nine months and seventeen days into 1960, so I was clearly conceived in the off-season. By pure coincidence, I share a birthday, if not his rare talent, with Sir Stirling Moss. 1960 was the first year in which my father drove for BRM, a team that would bring him his first Formula One World Championship after two more years of graft, sweat and dedication. In February, my father would have been racing in the Argentinian Grand Prix, and after that he raced in all the rounds of the F1 Championship (save for Indianapolis and Monza), not to mention a lot of non-championship events.

In July, he set the fastest lap at the British Grand Prix. It must have been a fantastically exciting race because he had stalled on the grid – having qualified second to Jack Brabham – and had worked his way back up through the field from almost dead last until he was in the lead on lap 55 of 77, much to the joy of the British crowd who were willing him on every inch of the way. It would have been a famous victory: an all-British driver/car combination and my dad's first-ever GP win. Sadly, he was somewhat discombobulated by dodgy brakes and spun out only five laps from the end. As it turned out, by the end of his career, fifteen years and many victories later, including no less than five Monaco Grands Prix, he never won the British Grand Prix. But I put that right in 1994. Teamwork, you see? Sadly, though, I never won Monaco. Ah, well. Can't have everything.

But all these exciting and stressful times were going on as I was making steady progress in the womb. To crown the stress-filled pregnancy period for my mother, the weekend I was born, my father was competing in the Lombank Trophy, a non-championship Formula One race at Snetterton, Nor-folk. I bet that was fun for my mother. Unbelievable. Your husband is in a perilous job a hundred miles away and you are giving birth to your second child (my sister, Brigitte, had been born only eighteen months earlier). The details are sketchy, and my mother is not always a reliable witness. Not surprising, considering all she went through. It's amazing she could function at all, what with people getting killed all the time. But you were British and just got on with it, see?

I must have been born early in the morning because my mother rang my father at 7 a.m. (to make sure he hadn't left for the track) and told him the glad tidings. His reply was: 'Is that all you woke me up to tell me?' No, Dad. You ask how Mum is feeling and congratulate her. I think we've come a long way on that front.

Apparently the matron advised my mother that, now I was born, her place was with her husband, because 'he was there first'. Eh? Excuse me! I didn't ask to be brought here! Just to strengthen the bonding process, I had an eye infection and jaundice. On first sight, my dad said: 'He can't be mine. He looks Chinese.' Imagine how proud my mother must have felt.

He didn't mean to be callous. He was a very kind-hearted and generous person. But I guess he had trouble expressing certain feelings. Or, perhaps, he had absolutely no idea what a woman goes through to get us lot into the ballpark. Suffice it to say that my parents' relationship seemed somewhat functional, with my mother doing most of the sacrificing for her extraordinary husband. This was quite normal then, though it seems like abuse of privilege now. My point is that the backdrop to my mother's pregnancy was fear and tension culminating in a conflict of loyalties, and I think her mothering instincts may have been severely compromised by the situation.

My birth came at a particularly busy time for Mum. Dad was at a crucial point in his career and three months after I was born, they moved out of a cramped flat in Belsize Park into what would be our home for the next ten years of my life, 32 Parkside, Mill Hill, London NW7, which was also to become a notorious Sixties party venue.

Just after Christmas, my dad went to Australia and New Zealand to race in the Tasman Series, leaving Mum in this new house with no heating having to look after me and my sister for seven weeks all on her own. She did not cope well. Dad had done a deal with a few 'likely lad' builders to put in the plumbing while he was gone. All nice and warm for when he got back, he must have thought. But their constant to-ing and fro-ing was driving her to distraction. She wrote a stream of angry letters to him and threatened to 'give it all up and leave'. He phoned from the other side of the world (no easy task back then) and told her to kick them out, so she picked their tools up and dumped them in the street. It must have been very satisfying. I've always wanted to do that. But it's interesting to know that all this was going on in the very first months of my life. She was obviously already under an enormous strain, and it prompted her to draft in a nanny so she could spend more time with Graham at the races, too. But the stress had actually started way before this, if you count being bombed.

The Sixties was not a good time for wives. The world belonged to the male of the species and macho men like my father had the upper hand. No doubt he had many 'opportunities'. That was the point, after all, right? To the victor the spoils. But this sort of thing can be tough on wives, as if the fear of tragedy was not enough. And if it was tough on wives, it was also tough on mothers and their children.

I was to put my own wife and family through similar levels of stress and anxiety by taking on F1. I suppose the difference was that I was very conscious of the need to provide my children with a father in the most normal sense, as far as possible. My father's yardstick seems to have been the British Empire attitude to wives: that they were there to support their husbands, no matter what. I'd never get away with treating Georgie like that. Perhaps I was attracted to Georgie precisely because she knew her mind and how to stand up for herself, unlike my mother who was perpetually confounded by my father.

At some point in the Sixties, my mother sought help to deal with her anxieties. She saw a psychiatrist, who promptly – and outrageously – told my father. He blew his top, accused her of causing him embarrassment, and put a stop to it. An incident like this gives clues as to both the state of my mother's mind when I was growing up, and how concerned Dad was with keeping up appearances. It must have been awful for her. She was, literally, driven to distraction. I always felt as if she wasn't there, even when she was. Her mind was constantly defaulting to how things would affect Graham, or she was worrying whether he was safe, or she was with him at the races. Her loyalties weren't so much split as decided for her. The truth was that we were all in his army: our job was to enhance his status and not to embarrass him.

In a TV documentary about his life made shortly before he died, my dad was asked what his family meant to him, to which he replied that they were everything, because if anything happened to them, he couldn't see how he could carry on racing. Apart from revealing his conviction that the wife and family were there to support the husband, instead of the other way around, the tragic irony of this statement was that it was he who would be lost to us, and we who found it so hard to carry on without him.

I think this overly male-dominated and danger-ridden environment affected all too many families at a time when there was very limited support for the families beyond the social aspect of racing. There were divorces, but my parents obviously stuck together. Of the divorced families we knew, I can think of several suicides among the children. I suppose that is not exclusive to motor sport, but there is something about the culture of denial that is unique in our world, whereby when (rather than if) something bad happens, everyone clams up and just gets on with the show.

But this was all in the 1960s. By the spring of 1994, when we lost Ayrton Senna and Roland Ratzenberger within a couple of days, the world had changed considerably. The reaction to that weekend was one of total shock: the authorities moved very quickly to investigate the incidents and decided that this was not something that could be just an inevitable cost of the sport. But back in the 1960s, they took the view that no one was forcing you to do it. If you didn't like the heat, get out of the kitchen. It was to my father's eternal credit that through the pressure group of the Grand Prix Drivers' Association, of which he was a significant member – as was Sir Jackie Stewart – attitudes started gradually to change for the better.

You might accuse me of labouring the point here. It was not all doom and gloom, by a long chalk; our family had a fantastic life, travel, parties, celebrity, fame. But some things about our life were not so fabulous. I can remember being taken to Lydden Hill in Kent in the late 1960s for an event that my father must have been in. It was an autocross: half rally, half circuit, and I think there was a crossover, of all things. A car had slammed onto another and I could hear the driver screaming. My mum just ushered us away, but I remember the shock in the crowd and awfulness of the driver's howling. You don't forget things like that. I can remember thinking, 'So that's OK, then, is it?' In 1971, my sister Brigitte and I were in the grandstands at an F1 race at Brands Hatch. Black smoke started to climb from behind the trees. The race was stopped and we were ushered away once more. The victim was Jo Siffert: a death that deeply affected my father, perhaps because he could see himself in the moustachioed Jo and couldn't understand how he had been killed, because Jo didn't have a reputation as a reckless driver. Perhaps after a lot of deaths, it must be like flying missions: you start to think your number must be coming up. It must get very unnerving.

It seemed that with every year that went past, the deaths got closer and closer to home. In 1968, when I was eight years old, I was watching television with a friend, sitting too close to the screen, when a newsflash came on. Jim Clark had been killed in Germany. I knew Jimmy. I had pushed him around the garden on my toy tractor with my dad – for the cameras, of course. He seemed funny to me because he was Scottish, and I vividly recall saying to myself that I preferred him to my dad. I knew my dad; he was just my dad. But Jim Clark had a bit of mystique around him. My mum came into the room and asked what was on the newsflash. I told her – innocently – but somehow knowing this was heavy stuff and would affect her. She put her hand over her mouth and just left the room.

It's impossible to fully understand when you are only eight, but somewhere, deep inside, you are getting the message: there are some scary things out there and this sport your daddy does has a sting in the tail. I had no inkling that only a few years later I would have a far more devastating newsflash to report to her.

I can still clearly remember my father coming home and just sitting very quietly after the death of Bruce McLaren in 1970. My mother would create the necessary space around him at times like this and we were told that he was sad at the moment because of what had happened. I never saw him cry, or even come close. Graham Hill kept all those feelings inside, or hidden away from us. We were still very young, so I suppose it was right to do this. Sometimes we would catch our parents' distress, usually with Dad comforting Mum. But they would shoo us away, saying, 'It's nothing, don't worry.'

Paul Stewart – Jackie's first son – tells the story of how, in a particularly brutal time in the 1970s, he was taunted at school with the line, 'Your dad's next.' That does stuff to you that you cannot appreciate at the time. It is confusing that the world is responding to you and your family in such a positive way and yet at the same time you are seen as being on the endangered list, a feted but somehow accursed family. My early life was a gradual awakening to this grim reality. I was conflicted with pride for my father and yet aware that some people thought motor racing shallow and irresponsible and, frankly, frightening. I got the distinct impression that some of my school friends' parents disapproved of their children making friends with me, as if the Hills had a contagious risk-taking disease. In a similar line of thought, some mechanics of the time openly admitted to not wanting to get too emotionally close to drivers because you never knew how long they would be around.

My dad always told my mum that nothing was going to happen to him, but if it did, she would be well taken care of. She'd be all right financially, he meant; which was neither true nor a very comforting answer. What was special about him? How was he going to avoid getting killed like so many others? And the truth was, despite his protestations, he had not taken care of her in the way that he had hoped. He would leave her in a dreadfully messy situation that would take years to sort out.

When I did make the decision to go into F1, I was haunted by the thought of repeating this extra tragedy in my career. Racing was a sport I intended to survive, if at all possible, and if I didn't, I was going to make sure that my family were looked after properly.

What was I to take from this life that I had been born into? That to be a real man meant being someone who could deal with the loss of his friends and colleagues without it affecting his lap time; someone who could carry on regardless of the carnage? Was this what a 'real' man was? Would I be expected to do the same? Were F1 drivers the special breed we were all asked to believe they were, or reckless gamblers, in it for the thrills and the money and the girls? These questions were accumulating as I grew. It was a kind of licensed madness, to be honest. The chance of death was the cost of victory; at times it sounded like a hangover from the war. The spirit that was never beaten down, no matter how bad things got?

It was as if to win an F1 race was the only important thing in life; as if the sport demanded sacrifices. Drivers who showed they were not afraid to die were celebrated and lauded above others; almost encouraged to go just that little step closer to the precipice, for our entertainment. I think my father was one for whom the game was to get to the end in one piece, then see what the result was. Calculating the odds and knowing how hard to push your luck was the skill, but even so, the odds in those days were less than favourable. Was this a wise approach to life? I was beginning to have my doubts, even then – especially if you had a family.

In this environment it was all too easy to regard women as doing the supportive bit while men did the heroic job of risking their lives and doing battle to bring home the bacon. But the wives took things into their own hands when the boys got a little too carried away with themselves, and set up a club called the Doghouse Club, or WMRAC, in 1962. It got the name because Betty Brabham was upset with her husband, Jack, for not paying her enough attention at a party. She told the other wives, 'Jack's in the doghouse!', which they all thought was riotously funny, although it was not meant to be. Over the years, the Club became very famous for doing charity fundraising and created safe havens at circuits for the wives and children of drivers, but in its first incarnation, it was a place for the women to rally against their husbands.

At the races I went to, which included virtually every British Grand Prix from 1961 onwards, the Doghouse Club would be a base for the Hill children, a place my mum could leave us while she went off and did 'timing', at which she was something of an expert. She was able – with the aid of about four stopwatches, a pencil and a rubber – to time virtually the whole F1 field, to the extent that her times were often used as a fallback to the official times if there was a dispute. It helped her, she claimed, to take her mind off what was going on in front of her; a calculating distraction.

At the Doghouse there was always plenty of food and cakes and tea. I could be at close quarters with some of the drivers' glamorous girlfriends: another benefit that became more appreciated as I progressed to my early teens. Nice if also a little awkward at times. But my mother had her own opinions of the 'dolly birds', whom she disliked intensely. It's a tough gig, being married to a Grand Prix racing driver. I don't think my father always made it easy for my mother, either. In her book, *The Other Side of the Hill*, my mother devotes quite a lot of text to experiences that involved my dad not putting her in pole position. One time he pushed his luck too far and was chatting to some girls in a restaurant and ignoring my mother. She decided she'd had enough and went home on her own. It was a while before he realised she had gone. He was pretty upset about that, but I can see my mother's point.

I'm not sure these wounds had properly healed at the time of my father's death. My mother had endured a lifetime of stress and more than her fair share of embarrassment and humiliation. When the accident happened, I think she still had a piece of her mind to impart to her husband, judging by some comments in her book, but the tragedy made criticism inappropriate, and he was forgiven whatever transgressions he might have committed. And the fact remained that he was my father and my hero. This sort of thing is at the root of complex conflicts. Where do one's loyalties lie? How to reconcile both sides?

I can see all this now, with the benefit of hindsight and a great many years of letting the dust settle. It makes me sad to think that my parents never had a chance to work things out. That's the annoying thing about accidents. You keep thinking, 'What if . . . ?'

Starting out on my own career after my dad's accident was a mystery tour into the huge void that he had left. He was a much-loved figure, and people tend to be wary of those who might blight cherished memories. The families of the famous can be either an asset or a curse. I came across a range of reactions to my early attempts to climb the motor sport ladder, from the downright negative to the overemotionally enthusiastic. It was tricky to navigate a path that I could be sure was authentically my own and for myself, rather than following some romantic notion of re-enacting my father's struggles against adversity to see how I compared, or living out some wish fulfilment on behalf of others. And yet despite all that, years later I would find myself tackling virtually the same challenges that he had – and doing it all by myself, just as he had. All I had to go on was my instincts and his example. It was a bit like that Johnny Cash song, 'A Boy Named Sue'. He'd left me with some great tales, but the little asides that tell you what is really happening were missing. I'd have to work that out all by myself.

I know that my father would have been amazed and very proud of my achievements. It is very sad that he couldn't have lived to see the day, and yet, if he had lived, it is by no means certain that I would have followed in his footsteps. In response to the repetitious question: 'Is Damon going to become a racing driver like his dad?' Hill Snr had expressed his reservations on the matter, stating clearly in an interview with Barrie Gill in 1968 that he would prefer me not to follow in his footsteps because of the obvious dangers. 'Besides,' he said, 'Damon is too intelligent to become a racing driver.' Evidently not as intelligent as he thought! But it was nice of him to say so. Despite all the carnage, inevitably and inexorably – so it seems – I was lured to the sound of the sirens, albeit with the earplugs of bitter experience filtering out the most seductive calls. I was always all too aware of the downsides. I'd seen what happened at first hand.

The stories that built the legend of Graham Hill were the Hill family creation myth. I hung on his every word, as did a lot of people. It never occurred to me then that there might be alternative approaches. He was successful; everyone recognised it, so he must have been doing something right. The only snag was that they were half-baked teachings. He died before I could challenge his methods, supposing I ever would have. Freud proposed that in early human development, sons, jealous of their father's relationship with their mother and wanting the position of top banana, wish their father dead. Well, he was wrong as far as I can see. There were plenty of times when I wished my father alive again so he could have helped me. But here's the dichotomy: I am proud of doing it all on my own, even though I think I was digging in the wrong area much of the time. I could have done with someone saying, 'There is an easier way to do that.'

My own career could be viewed as an attempt to earn my place within the Hill myth. I was Telemachus to Dad's Odysseus, except that my dad never came home from the wars. Sons of famous fathers typically have a tough job making a name for themselves, but F1 is now populated by sons (if not so many daughters just yet) of fathers who once raced. In my father's day it was different. Most of the drivers of that era did it against their parents' wishes or without their involvement. My father's dad would come and watch him from the privacy of the British Racing Drivers' Club area at Silverstone and then get a lift back home without even saying hello. Connie never came as far as I know. Jackie Stewart's mum vowed never to speak to him if he became a racing driver. He phoned her when he retired, after winning three world titles. She just said, 'You're best out of it.' Not: 'Well done, Jackie.'

Jenson Button's father attended every race to support his son. They were a very close team. Jonathan Palmer has just got his first son Jolyon into a full-time F1 seat with Renault and the younger Palmer, Will, is just behind. The Lewis Hamilton story is well known, with his father, Anthony, holding down two jobs to give Lewis all the help he needed. Now we have Max Verstappen, whose father, Jos, has also supported and coached him. Maybe there is a sense of unfinished business, with some dads fulfilling their own ambitions through their sons. I hope not, but who wouldn't want the best for their children? Carlos Sainz Jnr has recognised that there is a problem associated with going into the same arena as his father, so he chose single-seater racing rather than rallying.

All of which begs the question: if my father had not died prematurely, would he have been guiding my career, or would I have become a surfer-cum-guitarist hippy dropout? As Lennon also said, 'Life is what happens to you while you're busy making other plans.'

4 » THE GARDEN OF EDEN: MILL HILL

I was a very lucky child: that cannot be denied. We wanted for nothing. From the time of my birth in 1960, my parents were living in the rush and excitement of the time of their lives. There was always a celebration going on. Everything was coming good for them after a long, hard road of sacrifices and risks, and I was right there in the middle of it, soaking it all up.

When I was two, my father won the World Championship. When I was five, he won Indy. When I was seven, he became World Champion for the second time. During that decade of the 1960s, he won 50 per cent of the Monaco Grands Prix. He was *the man*, Mr Monaco. It seemed there was always a buzz in our lives and everything he did involved some kind of carnival. For the first ten years of my life, I grew up in a blissful Graham-Hill-themed world.

I clearly had the 'thirst for first' from the get-go, winning the 1961 Le Touquet Beautiful Baby competition, wearing a fetching pair of cougar-patterned swimming trunks. In the photo I do appear very pleased with myself, as well I might: my first victory.

I was born at Hampstead Hospital and for three months lived in Belsize Park, until we moved to 32 Parkside, a very ordinary tree-lined suburban street in the north London post-war overspill, about half a mile from the start of Britain's first motorway, the M1. The house now has a blue plaque celebrating it as a place once lived in by Graham Hill, OBE. We had a reasonably sized back garden that backed onto Mill Hill Park, where I used to ride my bike (illegally) and play football with my friends. The park separated us from a busy road called the Watford Way. Along with the continual drone of truck tyres, you could hear the occasional blast of 'La Cucaracha' from someone's five-tone car horn dopplering into the distance even from the house.

For as long as I can remember, we had a trampoline, a slide and a climbing frame in the back garden. Once, when I was about five or six, I fell off the climbing frame and closed my eyes expecting to hit the ground very hard. To my amazement, when I opened my eyes I found myself dangling by one hand. From that moment on I knew there was some mysterious 'other' in me who would look after me in dangerous situations. Call it the unconscious instinct to survive, if you like. Sometimes we'd all get on the trampoline together: the whole Hill family, bouncing in harmony.

The lawn in Mill Hill was a place of adventure and freedom. This was where I first took the stabilisers off my bike and discovered the miracle of balance. In the summer, we had a rudimentary water park with the hose running down the slide, which dropped into the paddling pool. You'd splash into the pool at high speed and shoot across the flooded lawn. Besides a bicycle, I had a pedal kart which I used to do laps round the small driveway, but it wasn't as much fun as the bike. That enabled me to go on long rides with my friends to new territories such as Burnt Oak. My mum was to call the police on more than one occasion when I went missing. Once I fell off and damaged my arm going up a kerb at too shallow an angle. My 'friends' didn't stop. I'm not sure which hurt more, that or my arm, but my mother rubbed it better and put it in a sling.

Often, while Mum and Dad were away racing or socialising, my father's parents would come to stay and look after me and my sisters, Brigitte and Samantha. They were rather Victorian types who ate offal and kippers. Grandma would make me sit on the toilet if I'd been naughty. She was obsessed with bowel movements. If I argued, she'd say: 'Don't contradict.' I'd say: 'But I'm not contradicting!'

Norman, my grandfather, was a stockbroker – except I think he'd gone more broke than stock. He'd sit around most of the day reading the paper and smoking his pipe, and then listen out for the FT index before going to the pub. When my father and my grandfather were in the house together, I was struck by how my father appeared more dominant than his dad. It was my father's house, I suppose, but I think Norman had been on the wrong end of a deal at some point. Connie was the boss now. Norman had also been captain of Mill Hill Golf Club. He had a lovely swing, judging by a photo I have of him taken in about 1930. Apparently, he was a famous character in the City: bowler hat, umbrella, very British old boy. Never drove a car in his life. Amazing. He liked a whisky.

I gave my grandparents a shock once when I set fire to the garage. I'd been playing with petrol and it got a bit out of control. Because the thing that got burnt was an old pram belonging to one of my sisters, they wondered if I had some underlying psychological problem with her. They phoned my parents, who must have been a bit alarmed, but it was only because I was a curious child and liked to experiment. No real harm done.

Christmases were 'present fests' when we were given too many toys and made ourselves feel sick from too much chocolate. Dad would deliberately have a lie-in and make us wait for him before we could open presents. He was the master of the house. Christmas lunches were full-on Dickensian family things. My mother made the most amazing brandy butter. She used to put sixpences and shillings in the Christmas pudding which, dripping in brandy, would be set alight and brought into the dining room with much ceremony. After lunch, we'd make a long-distance call to Vancouver to say Merry Christmas to Dad's brother, Bruce. I don't think they were very close; friendly to one another, I mean. Then we'd watch a film, like

The Great Escape, or *The Morecambe and Wise Christmas Show,* along with 20 million other Brits.

If I'd been given an Airfix model, which was more often than not, I'd disappear for hours into my bedroom and build it in one go. You were supposed to paint it first and then assemble it, letting the glue dry at each step. But I could never wait. I'd spend hours unintentionally getting high on plastic glue, then complain of a headache.

Because Dad was famous, he would get my mother to send out hundreds of Christmas cards. These weren't any old cards; they were especially commissioned elaborate cartoons depicting his exploits during the season. Must have cost a bomb. I used to help my poor mum put them in envelopes. They were big, measuring about ten inches by six. Boxes and boxes of them, sent to famous people he knew all over the world.

My dad's small office by the front door was adorned rather impressively with wall-to-wall framed photographs of every person he'd had the pleasure of meeting – *Penny Lane* barber style – and pictures of himself up to all kinds of fantastic things. It was a fame gallery. I don't remember there being too many photos of my mother and him in among them. It was most certainly a man's world back in the 1960s. In the downstairs lavatory in Mill Hill, there was a framed cartoon of a shapely, pencil-skirted woman in high heels – supposedly my mum – pushing a BRM, with the caption: 'To "The Lady" Behind That Man Behind The Wheel.' It was a present from a motor club but it was an odd place to display it, on reflection. Clearly Mum's contribution to her husband's success knew its place.

Other walls in the house had beautiful Michael Turner oil paintings of my father in all the cars he raced. Michael Turner is probably the best motor sport artist of all, but there was almost nowhere to look if you didn't want to know we lived in the house of a racing driver. We used trophies as doorstops and flowerpots.

When he won the Indianapolis 500 in 1966, we put up

chequered bunting and *Welcome Home* signs outside the house. That was a big event in his life and it's the only time I can remember us doing this. I think this was the occasion when we had the party in the back garden and I pushed Jim Clark around on my toy pedal tractor for the cameras. The Indy 500 was known as the richest race in the world, and with the prize money Dad bought his first small plane: a Cessna with the wing over the top. Pretty soon after that, he upgraded to the twin-engined Piper Aztec he had his accident in.

When Dad won his second World Championship in Mexico, 1968, we met him at Heathrow Airport with all the British press in attendance. In honour of his win, he had been given some massive sombrero from the Mexican Revolution, so the photos were of the whole Hill family taking turns to wear this impressive hat.

Because my father loved to socialise, and because racing drivers typically seem to have hyperactivity disorder, there were a lot of parties in our house when I was growing up. But because I was too young, I wasn't officially invited. My sister Brigitte and I would be in bed upstairs, unable to sleep for the Chubby Checker and Beatles records blasting out from the valve amp music centre downstairs. In fact the noise of the people was louder than the music. My father had a very distinctive raucous laugh that threatened to take over complete control of his lungs and abdomen if he wasn't careful. My mother similarly could be heard laughing and talking as if everything was either the wildest, funniest or most outrageous thing she'd ever heard. Occasionally she would come up to check on us and we'd pretend to be asleep. She'd lean over and kiss us, clearly a little boozy and smelling of cigarettes and perfume. You could hear her coming because she usually wore those dresses that appeared to be made of metal or glass. She always looked amazing, like Elizabeth Taylor with big hair and lots of make-up. Quite startling, really, to see your mother seem so different.

It's true that my father was away much of the time, as was

my mother. But when he was back, he was back, and you knew it. Once he returned from America and brought me and my sisters some curious bags to put our pyjamas in. They had faces of felt and long tassels of nylon for hair; he said they were 'Beatles bags'. We'd never heard of the Beatles, so we couldn't work out where the beetle bit came in. We'd find out soon enough.

My father could be a bit of a tease. He once had me in tears of frustration because I was telling him all about tanks – the military type – over supper. He said we had a tank in the loft. I said we couldn't have because it would crush the house. But he kept telling me I was wrong, so I kept telling him he must be wrong. He thought it was very funny that I failed to get it, but I didn't quite feel the same way. I could be quite sensitive as a child sometimes.

We had a playroom with a mini piano, on which I used to tinker for hours. I still can't play anything, despite having piano lessons for a couple of years at my big school, Haberdashers' Aske's, where I would be from the age of seven to eighteen. I didn't like the idea that you had to read music. I was very impressed by jazz musicians who never read music: they just played. I switched to trumpet later on because I wanted to be able to play like Louis Armstrong, but I gave up because you had to carry this horrible hard case to school – along with all your other bags – and it would bang into your ankles when you walked. Trumpet was too much hassle. And it hurt your lips. And I was awful.

We did all the normal things in our street, like have huge water fights with the 'other enders' and go conker-hunting. There was a roundabout at the end of the road with fabulous horse chestnut trees. We'd throw sticks up to make the conkers fall off. Often the sticks would land on cars and in people's front gardens, but we weren't really vandals. That was where I met Tom O'Gorman, who lived with his mum in Burnt Oak. I think his dad had left home. Tom was a lot of fun and, unlike me, good at football. He could dribble round me too easily, taking the mickey out of me in a lovely Irish accent and making me laugh. I realised very early on that I was not going to be a footballer, although when we eventually moved to our next house, Lyndhurst, I did play in goal for a Shenley youth team. Proudly wearing my Arsenal kit, I let in about five goals and never went back.

Tom was probably the first friend I had who didn't go to my school or else have parents in motor sport. He was not from a wealthy family by any means. It's difficult to pinpoint the moment when you know you are more fortunate than others, but at some point it dawns on you that the world is not very fair. I can't remember exactly when I saw the film *Kes*, but it made me realise just how lucky I was and how brutal some other people's lives were. Most of my friends had train sets in their loft and Scalextric sets in their bedrooms. I never even went into Tom's house.

I don't think I was a particularly brave child. I can remember we climbed into an oak tree in the park. Getting up was the easy part; when everyone jumped down, I couldn't do it. Eventually they wanted to go home, so I plucked up enough courage to jump. I was right to be cautious: it hurt when I landed.

Not only was I no good as a footballer, I also never showed any signs of talent the first time I sat in a kart. When I was about six or seven, my dad must have been invited to the north-east London kart track at Rye House. He was there for something else, but they let me have a go on the kiddy karts. I kept spinning and stalling. Mind you, I seem to remember the track was flooded. Years later, in the south of France when I was about fourteen, I had a go on a kart at an amusement place and overtook everyone. I looked to see if my father was impressed, but it seemed not. I don't think he wanted to encourage me.

What I did like, and showed aptitude for, was skiing. Around 1966, we had a winter holiday in Kitzbühel and I took to this skiing thing like a natural. In those days, the boots were leather and the skis were wooden; people kept breaking legs because the bindings were not safe. But I loved it and begged to be sent on the school ski trips when I was old enough. That is when I finally found out that I was good at something at school; skiing and swimming. The rest of it just made me feel as if I was getting left behind.

I never really clicked with education, possibly because my parents never did either. My father seemed content just to send me to school and he expected them to do the rest. He was paying, after all. My mother never had an education, thanks to Hitler. At the end of terms, my father would get us all into his bedroom where we'd gather round the bed while he read our dismal results. He didn't even get out of bed to read them! We'd all end up in tears and my mother would scold him for making us cry. This whole school report thing seemed to bemuse him; once he couldn't stop laughing because the report said that I lacked spatial awareness in PE. I think he imagined me stumbling around bumping into things.

Because he wasn't around much, it was easy for me to slip through the education net. I don't think my parents ever realised that you cannot simply send your kids to school and leave them there until it's time to come home again. I have no recollection of ever being told why I had to go to primary school; I was delivered and left to work it out for myself. For years I floundered around not realising that there was a point to it. Judging by my father's attitude towards school, it seemed to me that it was something one just had to tolerate.

I dutifully went through the motions, turning up on time (mostly), drawing pictures, filling in exercise books, and never really understanding why the other kids seemed so uptight about it all. Obviously, their parents were struggling to give them the best education and making sure they did their homework. The school found my biggest flaw, though. I had to have extra tuition for maths at home. Rather than improving my maths, this just gave me the impression that there must be something wrong with me. I couldn't even understand it when the teacher came to my house! I have cried in maths lessons.

I was sent to St Martin's in Mill Hill – 'sent' being the operative word. When my mother was in hospital giving birth to my little sister, Samantha, in 1965 (I would have been almost five years old), she rang home to see how everyone was. When my dad answered, she could hear screaming in the background. I was having a tantrum because I didn't like her not being there and they were trying to drag me out of the house to go to school. I think this freaked my father out a bit. He explained he had a flight to catch and left me with the au pair.

We had a string of au pairs while I was growing up. One was called Patty. She had lovely long hair and looked the epitome of a Sixties girl: what they called 'groovy' in those days. Our longest-serving and most important nanny, for want of a better word, was a woman called Andrea Wesley, from Bicker in Lincolnshire. We just called her Andy. There was no messing around with Andy. She had good solid principles and she knew her rights. This came in handy when dealing with officials, if she had the job of taking us to races. But my mother brought help in mostly to look after my younger sister, Samantha, who was born smack in the middle of the busiest time for my parents. My father loved baby Samantha, and so did my elder sister, Brigitte, and I.

Now I think about it, I cannot remember a single name of any of the other pupils at my primary school. The whole thing could have been dispensed with, frankly, and I wouldn't have noticed. But I do remember having to go with Brigitte to the headmistress's office for her to witness us drinking our orange squash. God knows why. Perhaps Mum had the idea that we needed to be properly topped up with fluid in case we shrivelled up from too much learning.

The embarrassment of being singled out from all the other children just to have this humiliating ritual visited upon us clearly left a big mental scar on me. I can't blame Miss Joss

(I do remember something from school, at least!); she must have been under pressure to ensure that the children of the World Champion should be given extra-special care. This was one of my earliest experiences of being singled out for attention and wondering why, and ever since, I have been hypersensitive to any suggestion that an allowance is being made for me because of my dad. Even now, I fear that some- one will reveal to me that me winning the F1 Championship was all a ploy to boost ratings and make a nice story. Don't tell me it's true!

From time to time, this 'special status' treatment would revisit me. When I was at my preparatory school, Haberdash- ers' Aske's, there was a sports teacher who could hardly contain his curiosity about my father, always asking me ques- tions of a probing nature. I can understand it now, but at the time I found it annoying because I wasn't sure I should be telling him even if I knew the answer – which I didn't, mostly. It also highlighted the fact that my dad was famous. This, I felt, slightly irked the other kids, many of whom didn't know what their fathers did for a living, nor did they seem particu- larly interested ('I don't know. I think he does something in banking, or something'). The teacher's excessive attention just increased my feeling that I was being treated differently, which I really didn't want. At that age you just want to fit in, not stick out.

It reached crisis point in one of his PE lessons on high jump. As you know, you get three goes and then you're out . . . unless you happen to be the son of a national sporting hero and TV personality. Then you get four goes. I kid you not. If looks could kill, I would have died twenty times; I could feel the daggers being drawn by my classmates. I dutifully failed the fourth time. I should have refused to have a go, but you don't argue with the ref. I wanted to win, but not like that.

I started at 'Habs' when I was still living at Mill Hill. I used to go down our street, through the underpass beneath Wat- ford Way, up the other side and get the 113 to Edgware to catch the school coach. I'd do this all on my own, looking like a little businessman with my briefcase. Once, on the bus, I was picked on by a boy from another school who thought he was being very clever. Our school motto was *Serve and Obey*, which was proudly embroidered on the pocket of our blazers. 'Serve an Egg?' he laughed and shoved his face threateningly into mine. All the sycophants in his gang dutifully laughed too. I held my nerve, banking on the likelihood of my daddy being bigger than his daddy, personality-wise.

I think I'm right in saying that we never had a holiday in the UK, apart from weekends at the cottage in Sellindge in Kent, where my dad liked to go shooting with Lord Brabourne. Usually, we'd drive down on a Friday night, through darkest south London and out the other side. The car would be loaded to the roof with milk and eggs, dogs and us. It was a long drive. When we got there, the place would be freezing, but it had a huge inglenook fireplace. My dad, who loved gadgets, had a fan blower to light it. We would chuck a load of logs on and blast it till the wood ignited. Then we would sit there, frying and trying to watch a small black-and-white TV with terrible reception. There was a tiny bar area with pewter jugs hanging up. It would be a special treat for me to crack open a can of Long Life beer and pour it for Dad in the way he had taught me. We'd try some and get foam on our noses.

If the TV was working, we would watch *The Generation Game*, compèred by Dad's friend Bruce Forsyth. Dad was also friends with Jimmy Hill – a trio of big-chinned celebrities. We would all laugh until we cried while watching *The Generation Game*; one of the few occasions my father ever watched television, which to him was a great evil. We were always castigated for watching too much.

Sometimes, we would fly down in the plane: all of us Hills, plus our two Labradors. This was the very same plane in which he would later perish, along with his entire race team: a Piper Aztec, call sign 'November 6645 Yankee'.

The plane was used a lot by my father for his work, as well as for getting us around when we needed it. It's amazing what you can get into a small aeroplane. We have a photo of all of our luggage for our summer holiday lined up next to the plane on the tarmac at Elstree Aerodome. The line goes on for about twenty feet. Dad's mechanic was called Jock because, obviously, he was Scottish. As children, we loved him; he'd make a big fuss over us and the way he spoke was fascinating. He had a heavy Glaswegian accent: a Hagrid prototype. He also had a lovely, shaggy dog called Haggis, naturally. Elstree was also a flying club and sometimes we would have to hang around outside the clubhouse while Dad, being a sociable person, gave someone a game of table tennis. But he placated us by arranging for us to be fed fantastic sausages with Colman's English Mustard. Everything about Elstree Aerodrome seemed friendly and full of good experiences.

Our summer holidays were usually spent abroad. We were probably in the first wave of British tourists to visit southern Spain. The weather was what you'd expect and everyone came home with extreme tans, if not sunburn. I can't recall using much in the way of sun cream and I can remember how much it stung to have a hot bath. It's a bit alarming to think of how much sun we got, but having a tan in the Sixties was a status symbol. This must have made me stand out even more at school; the teachers often commented on it. But there was nothing in Andalucia in the Sixties. It was virtually a desert. Years later, I would use my earnings from F1 to buy a property in Marbella and have very happy and long summer holidays there with my own children.

Around 1970, we stayed in Guadalmina Golf Resort and my father played golf with Eric Sykes, Stanley Baker and Sean Connery. There is a photo of them larking about wearing fezzes because they went on a trip to Morocco to play golf – or so they said. We would fly all the way down there in my father's plane. It was a hell of a long way to Spain in a twin turbo propeller plane, five hours with no internal pressure, and very noisy. You'd also get bounced around by the turbulence, which was bad at the altitude we flew at. But I would spend many happy hours sitting up front, watching my father at work flying the Aztec.

The years in Mill Hill were blissful, but I only had half an idea what my father did for a living. Although we always went to the British Grand Prix and the Italian at Monza (because it slotted in perfectly at the end of the summer holidays), I would hardly ever see him racing as there was not the same TV coverage as there is now. The only time I can remember seeing him win a Grand Prix was in 1969. I was playing with my friend Nick Leston, son of a famous ex-saloon-car racer, Les Leston. We were at their cottage near ours, in Kent. Nick and I were playing in the garden with Major Matt Mason (a small bendy toy astronaut) when my mother came out to say: 'Come and watch Daddy winning Monaco!' I'd rather have stayed with Major Matt Mason, but I dutifully went into the house to see my father rounding Station Hairpin, as it was called then, and witness what was to be his very last F1 Grand Prix win, and his fifth Monaco.

About five months later, my mother came into the bedroom I shared with my sister Brigitte and woke us up to say she had to fly to America to see Daddy because he had 'broken his legs'. This was an extraordinary concept. I had no idea that legs could be broken. In the way that children do at that age, though, I just accepted it all. And I was very tired. Dad had been competing in the US Grand Prix in Watkins Glen, in upstate New York. He had stopped to check a deflating tyre. Getting back in, he could not do up his seat belts on his own but was heading back to the pits. Just then the tyre blew, the car hit a bank, somersaulted and threw him out, badly shattering his knees as they jammed up against the front dashboard bulkhead. His knees were ripped backwards like chicken legs. In reality, he was very lucky to have lived. When asked if he had a message to give to his wife, he said (through firmly gritted teeth, no doubt), 'Just tell her I won't be dancing for a couple of weeks.'

At the age of forty, my father should probably now have called it a day, but he was Graham Hill and these things were sent to try him. Typically, he proved the cognoscenti wrong again and made a miraculous recovery to score an heroic one point on the opening race of the 1970 season in South Africa. It was yet another episode in the legendary life and times of the great racing driver. He even made his recovery a victory, as well he might. It was the stuff of legend; they had told him he might never walk again, but they didn't know who they were dealing with. Whatever he really felt about it, he made it sound like it was just a flesh wound.

During his convalescence, he had appeared on some tele-vised award ceremony via a projection screen, live from his hospital bed, and joked: 'I don't know what you chaps will be doing later, but I will be getting a rub-down from a couple of lovelies. So if you can beat that, good luck to you!' Boom, boom. Mum was in the audience surrounded by the great and the good, and everyone thought it was very funny. And indeed it was, as Dad played to the gallery again. But perhaps my mother didn't find it so funny? I wonder if she ever felt a bit gagged by my father's 'much loved character' status.

Years later, I took her to visit the site of the accident and to pay our respects. We hadn't been there for thirty-five years or so. It was cathartic to realise that we had all continued to survive, albeit always feeling that something was missing from our lives. On the drive up, I had been quizzing her about Dad and his 'naughtiness' – did it upset her? Thinking I would be offering her a chance to offload any anger about it, I was rudely knocked back. 'At least he wasn't boring!' she snapped. But I'm not sure if those were her true feelings.

When he came home, Dad used to get himself around on small wooden boards on castors. It helped that we had par-quet flooring. We children used the boards just for fun, as if they were skateboards. It was great for us even if it wasn't so great for Dad, not being able to walk. He used to get himself upstairs on his backside. He fought his way back to some kind of fitness and returned to racing in true Graham Hill gritty style. He wasn't finished yet. But really, this accident marked the end of his time as a top-line Grand Prix driver. It also marked the end of our lives in the 'Garden of Eden', 32 Parkside, Mill Hill, London NW7.

5 » LYNDHURST

During 1971, we moved into Lyndhurst, a large Georgian house near Shenley in Hertfordshire. It was a beautiful place to live, with fantastic views and a quarter-mile-long drive leading up to an impressive covered entrance that still had the steps in place for alighting from one's carriage.

My dad was very proud of his status symbol, even though it had cost him an arm and a leg at a time when his driving career was on the wane. From this base he would complete the Triple Crown of motor sport in 1972 by winning the Le Mans 24 Hours race to go with the Indy 500 in 1966 and his two F1 world titles, a feat that remains unequalled to this day. He would also start the next big challenge of his life by forming his own Formula One race team, Embassy Racing With Graham Hill.

Lyndhurst was where I grew into my teenage years and became more attuned to the world around me, which included becoming more aware of and interested in Dad's life and his place in the wider world. My bedroom was above his office, which meant I would often wake up to the sound of him on the phone. Muffled laughs and outraged tones with the obligatory expletives vibrated reassuringly through the floor. More than occasionally, I would sit in his office and wait for him to get off the phone, or just hang, which he never minded as I learned what it was like to live in his world. His study was a much larger version of the office at Mill Hill, adorned with many more photos, trophies and souvenirs that he had collected on his travels, including one of President Nixon's presidential golf balls. He liked the joke: that he had one of the disgraced president's balls. Often I would sit there and listen to his business conversations, and over the years I would hear the name 'Bernie' mentioned more and more frequently, without any inkling of who Bernie Ecclestone was and what he meant to my father.

Through our shared experiences as I grew up, my father and I got to know one another and I came to appreciate him as more than just a figure who passed through our lives between his races, bringing a whirlwind of excitement with him. As a family, we had fantastic times at Lyndhurst, and I developed many of my lifelong interests and loves in this house. Our good times here were to be remarkably short-lived, as we had only another four more years of bliss before the world would come tumbling down, but those years seem to occupy a disproportionately large and important part of my life. It was a blissful and magical time, but the contrast with what was to come makes memories of Lyndhurst a painful conflict of extreme opposing emotions. It was, quite literally, the best of times and the worst of times.

Lyndhurst was not only more convenient than Mill Hill for Elstree Aerodrome, but also for my school, Haberdashers'. The house was on a hillside, nestling in thirty acres of fields and woods with an outdoor pool that hardly ever got used, thanks to the English weather. My bedroom enjoyed a magnificent panoramic view of Hertfordshire. Through one window the sprawling houses of Borehamwood were visible, while through the other I could see the planes landing at Elstree. On hot summer nights I could leave the windows open and hear distant motorbikes scratching through the lanes and dream of doing the same one day. If you were into motorbikes, it was a boyhood paradise, but it was a big old spread and it cut me off from the convenience of just popping round to see my friends. Until I was old enough to travel around myself, I became reliant on someone taking me to my friends, or their parents bringing them to me. That meant my schoolmates were really my only friends, because living at Lyndhurst was slightly isolating.

I used to get the coach to school from the end of the drive. The fashion in those days was to wear army surplus great-coats, even in hot weather. My uncle Brian had been in the merchant navy and I had somehow come into possession of his magnificent dark navy coat with impressive brass buttons embossed with anchors. It felt as though it weighed a ton and it almost dragged along the ground. I seemed to spend hours and hours standing waiting for school coaches in that coat, wishing for the day when I was old enough to ride a motor-bike, because then I would be truly free.

When I was about eleven, I went on a school 'educational cruise' on the SS *Nevasa* around the Mediterranean. We started in Venice, where we bought flick knives, and then went to Israel, a cultural trip that was somewhat wasted on children our age. The cruise, though, was memorable for one reason. In the ship's disco, I punched a guy because I thought he was taking my girlfriend, which was all the more ridiculous because I'd never met her before and only danced with her once. He beat the hell out of me and I came home with a black eye. My dad thought that was very funny and I felt I'd gone up a notch in his estimation, even if it did hurt a lot, since I suspect that I broke a bone in my hand.

Haberdashers' Aske's was a public school for boys only, but in 1974 they moved the Haberdashers' girls' school right next door from where it had been in Acton. This meant we could walk up the driveway with members of the opposite sex if we wanted to, but not many had the nerve. If you were in the drama society, you might get to know one and have a conversation, possibly even physical contact.

I did Spanish with my friend Tim Milne. Because there were only two boys out of the whole year who had decided to take Spanish O level, we had shared lessons with the girls' school to make the numbers sensible. I can't remember a thing about Spanish, nor did I get the O level; the whole thing was just too intimidating. Continuing my descent to the bottom of the academic barrel, I paid little attention to what was on offer at one of the top five schools in the country. I was more interested in the company I kept. I would talk endlessly in the cloakrooms and during lunch breaks about motorcycles, music and *Monty Python* with Tim, Rob Sutton and Jim Hobsley, who was in the year above and seemed to know the answer to everything. My enthusiasm for talking about motorcycles would sometimes continue into lessons. On one occasion, I hadn't registered that the volume from our English teacher, Mr Hanbidge, had been going down and down, while my conversation was becoming more noticeable until it was the only sound that could be heard in the classroom. I realised too late. There was a slight silence as the penny dropped, followed by a scream from Frank at absolute maximum volume and fury:

'HILL!!!!'

'Yes, sir?'

'COME HERE!!!!'

I came there and stood meekly next to the desk, shaking.

'GET OUT!!!!'

For all my many academic failings, I did like physics. It made complete sense to me, and seemed more relevant to my interests than any other subject. Understanding this subject complements motor racing perfectly, where everything is basic Newtonian physics – until, that is, you introduce the human element.

Habs was on 'short finals' to Elstree Aerodrome's Runway 27, which means it was within a few yards of the end of the runway – the runway my father didn't quite reach when he needed to most. Small civilian aircraft would constantly pass over just a few feet above our classrooms, many of them with pilots learning to fly. During lessons we would watch them heading towards us on the third floor of the science block while drifting sideways in strong crosswinds. Sometimes I'd see my father's plane landing; it was easy to spot in its red-and-white Embassy Racing With Graham Hill livery. If it was close enough to the end of the day, I'd make a dash for it to see if I could get a lift home with him rather than going on the coach.

Being with my father was as important for me as it is for any son or daughter. The noticeable difference when I was growing up was that I had to contend with him also being a VIP. I was very aware of that and it felt good to have exclusive and privileged access. On the one occasion that my father came to the open day at school I was bursting with pride, but it soon deflated when he very rapidly lost interest in what the school had to show. He was always under pressure of time, and there was always something more important to attend to. He said once that if time is of the essence, he was very short of essence. He had no idea how prescient that was.

Having a famous father also gave me many opportunities to get up close to events and people in the world he moved in; not that I was old enough to really understand what was going on, but I picked up on the vibe, the etiquette, the protocol. No sudden movements seemed to be important, and no raised voices. Being allowed backstage gave me insights into how people behave around famous personalities, and this helped me keep my feet on the ground when I was in F1 myself. My father always used to say that, whoever they might be, they are just people.

Privileged access can also get you into trouble, particularly in F1, where I was able to roam freely into garages and even out onto the track if I wanted. One day in 1973, bored out of my mind while kicking my heels in the back of my dad's team transporter, I found a device used for measuring camber on the wheels: a very important tool when setting up a racing car in those days. Idly, I fiddled with it, taking off the dials just because the whole thing came apart. In a panic, I must have put it back together wrongly. Later that night, after the team had been scratching their heads for hours while trying to set up the car, Dad came up to me and asked directly: 'Have you been fiddling with this camber gauge?' He wasn't angry but I could see he was in a pretty serious working mindset. I was suddenly aware that I'd caused a bit of a situation. Slightly shocked and intimidated by his accusatory tone, I lied and denied knowing anything about it. I think he knew I was fibbing, and although no more was said, I could tell he was pretty peeved off. I always felt guilty about that one because I had lied and lost my bottle. It made me realise that there was only so much I could get away with as a 'son of'. However, it wasn't as bad as being caught stealing the loose change that piled up on the dresser in Dad's dressing room. Every now and then, I would help myself to 50p and blow it on sweets at the tuck shop. On one occasion he caught me red-handed. Busted, I was branded a thief, to go with my fibbing and cowardice – and I wasn't yet thirteen. The look of shock on his face and the seriousness and disappointment in his tone of voice would stay with me forever.

Even when he was at home my father always seemed to be working on some project or other. When he wasn't, I could get his attention by larking about or by doing something we both loved. After the crash that broke both his legs he took up golf as exercise and I quickly learnt the basics, so that on some evenings we'd play nine holes at Porters Park in Radlett. Wandering around the golf course at twilight was one of the few occasions when I could be alone with Dad without the phone ringing or someone asking for his autograph.

The key thing that that brought us together, however, was motorbikes. We had acres of fields and woodland which allowed me to bomb around as much as I liked. When he met the Bultó family in Spain, Dad bought some Bultacos and we would use these to go trials riding through the woods together. Trials is not a speed event; it simply involves balance and a feeling for the throttle. No doubt all of this went into the part of my brain that was to be used for racing later on. There was a lot of maintenance and fixing, which my dad liked to get involved in. Once he got stuck into fixing something, he was all-consumed. When we couldn't get the bikes to run, he would fiddle with the carburation for ages. Although I sometimes wished I'd never asked him to help fix it because he became so absorbed in the problem, I loved these shared experiences and learned much about mechanics and spanners. While I never knew what it was like to be in the car with him, when explaining anything mechanical Dad was in his element, and he knew his stuff, having studied engineering. Most of what I know about engineering I learnt from him, and when my turn came in F1 all that he taught me would be a huge help with setting up the car to my liking and working with F1 designers and engineers. Even before I got into F1 I had a keen understanding what the car needed, and all through my career I loved fine-tuning and getting an 'unfair advantage' by having the car do most of the hard work.

I was given my first motorbike, a 50cc Honda Mini Trail, for passing the eleven-plus; not exactly a tall order, it has to be said, even for me. I'd pestered my father for months because at Silverstone a few years before I'd ridden a Honda 'monkey bike' that belonged to the Shevloff brothers, Nick and Michael. Michael went on to produce the film *1: Life on the Limit*, about the terrible carnage of motor racing in the Seventies, but at the time we were just ten-year-olds mucking about in the paddock on this bike. One of them asked me if I wanted to have a go. There was nothing I wanted more, and just climbing onto the bike made my heart race and my legs shake. When I turned the twist-grip throttle, that was it; I was hooked forever.

Although I had pestered my parents for months, I had no idea my father had bought the bike. We were staying at the cottage in Sellindge and he had tried to persuade me to go to Brands Hatch with him because he was racing, but I declined because I didn't want to be bored at a racetrack. I didn't like all the noise and people constantly asking, 'Do you want to be like your father when you grow up?' I resisted and stayed at home – but my father was trying to present the bike as a surprise. When my mother told me, I leapt into the air in wild excitement. Unfortunately, because the cottage was Elizabethan and at that moment I was standing in one of the low doorways, I hit my head so hard that I nearly knocked myself out and broke my neck at the same time. I still have trouble with my neck because of it. This slightly dampened my delight, but I very soon got over it.

Excited, but still slightly stunned, I went to Brands Hatch to be presented with the amazing machine in front of all the press and the public. Being sensitive about drawing attention to my privileged situation in life, this put me in a rather awkward predicament. A part of me felt annoyed that my dad had turned this into yet another photo opportunity – why couldn't he have done it privately? – but another part of me was so chuffed that I didn't care too much about the fuss. This bike would totally change my life. I rode it every available second I could, and every waking moment was dedicated to it. My bedroom became covered with wall-to-wall posters of all the star motorcycle riders. There were one or two F1 cars or dragsters, but mostly it was bikes. There was also a poster of a semi-naked woman modestly wrapped in a fur coat and draped over a vintage car – which was as far as I dared push the other emerging interests, among them listening to music in my bedroom and learning the guitar. When my parents tried to get me to go to a boarding school, I cited not being able to ride my bike as a good enough reason not to go, and my father said he would never see me if I went to board, so my mum lost that one. But I would never have wanted to miss those experiences on that motorbike. It actually led me to becoming a World Champion.

After British Grands Prix at Brands Hatch, which were held on a Saturday in those days, my father would throw a party in a marquee on the back lawn at the cottage. The next day, the lanes would be littered with expensive sports cars, some completely stuck in hedges; totally outrageous behaviour, of course, but these were different times. The next day, at Mersham Le Hatch on the Brabourne estate, there would be a charity cricket match with many F1 drivers. I rode my father out to the wicket on my small motorbike and ran for him because of his bad legs. Most of the great names of the era were out on the field in relaxed mood after the race and the party – James Hunt, Jackie Stewart, Ronnie Peterson, Niki Lauda, Jody Scheckter, Mike 'The Bike' Hailwood. Dad was totally in his element, on his home turf, with his friends, family and fellow F1 stars and a huge crowd to play to.

Around that time, he acquired a Norton 750 Commando Fastback in light-blue metal flake. He took me for a blast up the lane through Shenley and I'll never forget hanging onto his waist for dear life, the tarmac flying past underneath us with this thing blasting out its unique Brit Bike thunder. All I could see was my dad's long, slightly blond hair whipping about from under the famous London Rowing Club helmet with the reflection of the fast-moving trees wrapping around it. It is a cherished experience, branded into my mind forever.

During what would be the last year of his life, we were on holiday near St Tropez. Some of Dad's friends asked if he wanted to join them on trials bikes in the mountains, and Baron Huschke von Hanstein, the head of Porsche Motorsport, was among the group. A charming man with a massive moustache and huge teeth permanently revealed by his slightly disconcerting smile, he was everything you might expect of a German aristocrat in his seventies. It also turned out that he had been an SS officer. I only had the Yamaha 250 trail bike that belonged to the farm house we were staying at to use. It was not the ideal bike for a fifteen-year-old, but I didn't care and I convinced Dad to let me go along with them. Luckily he agreed, because this was to be a watershed moment: I was allowed into the world of men.

The climb was not easy, made worse by the south of France at the height of a hot summer. I fought that bike up the hill and managed to hang on to my temper and my tongue.

When we got to the top, Dad put his arm round my shoulders and said well done; he was proud of me for getting that thing up the hill. That single moment with him was worth more to me than almost any other I can think of. I also took it as tacit approval of me riding motorbikes, which was pushing it, technically. But how could he have objected? Motorcycles linked all us Hills together. He had ridden them as a young man, his mother had ridden them, and now I could ride them. And I was good, too.

Humour was another touchstone in our relationship. A great treat was to see what made Dad laugh. He loved stupid British humour, of which there was plenty in *Monty Python*. We enjoyed those programmes together; there is even a *Python* sketch that makes reference to my father, when the politically very incorrect Mr D. P. Gumby asks to see John the Baptist's impression of Graham Hill. Needless to say, it is beautifully tasteless. Dad had obviously listened to the Goons when growing up, which meant Spike Milligan was on the list of his favourites, along with Peter Cook and Dudley Moore. Dad had his own brilliant way of telling funny stories. He was much in demand as an after-dinner speaker and, somehow, could make this ultra-dangerous sport of motor racing sound like a *Goon Show* sketch. Sometimes I could make him laugh by acting the fool or saying something that made me sound stupid. Self-deprecation was always the order of the day with the Hills.

Quite often, when he was home and between races, I would go shooting with my father from our cottage in Sellindge, on the Brabourne Estate. I used to load his gun and pick up the animals, some of which were still alive. I would have to wring their necks, which is something I felt queasy about even then. Aside from the actual shooting, my father loved the social side of these outings because it confirmed his acceptance in British high society. The 7th Baron Brabourne, John Brabourne, was a delightful man who loved my father. In addition to having to look after the massive estate bequeathed to him through the family line, he was also the successful producer of films such as *A Passage to India* and *Death on the Nile*.

When I was old enough, my father bought me a .410 shotgun and I would roam around our grounds shooting anything at will: trees, ponds and small animals. A couple of times I used Dad's twelve-bore but it had such a kick, it bruised your cheek and shoulder. I was pretty unregulated at home because no one was ever around to tell me off. I used to help myself to Dad's shotgun cartridges, remove the shot and take them to school. When the groundsman wasn't around, I would chuck the cartridges onto his bonfires. He never understood what was causing the explosions. Because my father was always the joker, I sometimes liked to play a joke on him to make him laugh. Once in a while, when loading for my father, I thought it would be funny to put cotton wool in place of the lead pellets and have random shots go 'pop' instead of blasting some poor bird to bits. This did not go down well when there was a flurry and everyone was competing to get the rare high birds. My dad had a plum one in his sights, only for the gun to 'phutt' at the crucial moment. He let me off that one, but was clearly not very amused.

My father revelled in the old-aristocratic-family factor and the Brabourne family made a big fuss of him. A couple of times after shoots we were invited to have tea at their main house, while the children, including Brigitte and me, were fed in the twins' room at the top of the house. Dad would come up and act the celebrity, be cheeky and make everyone laugh. He could be quite Captain Hook-ish with us children. The tragic postscript to this was that the IRA blew the family's lives to bits in 1979, killing Lady Brabourne's father, Earl Mountbatten of Burma, plus Lord Brabourne's mother and Nicholas (one of the twins), as well as badly injuring Lord and Lady Brabourne.

Because my father was such a busy person, his aeroplane was in constant use and I would take every opportunity to fly with him. I never had flying lessons but he let me bring it in close to landing and do a few turns in the air now and then. He had had it fitted with 'tip tanks' (extra fuel in the wing tips) to increase the range. To get to the south of Spain in one hop at 188 knots maximum velocity meant five hours cooped up in this really very noisy, stinky plane – one that became distinctly stinkier if someone was sick, which was often. Because it was small, the plane would get knocked around in turbulence, and because it was not pressurised, going over the Alps or the Pyrenees would induce altitude sickness, headaches and nausea. It stank of plastic and would be like a greenhouse in the sun. The heater would blow nasty plasticky fumes into the cockpit. Otherwise it was great fun. I loved it and felt totally safe sitting next to him.

We used the plane to go on our summer holidays and to Monza for the Grand Prix. We would fly over the Alps at around 10,000ft, and I used to look at the glaciers and think they must be massive tractor tracks. If we flew back from Kent at night we could see London, just as the wartime bombers must have done, with neat rows of suburbia sprawling over the hills on either side of the Thames Valley; tiny Monopoly houses tidily lined up in avenues and closes with small jaundiced cars crawling along under the sodium street lights. It was very thought-provoking, giving me a sense of our puny scale. All those houses, all those lives, just little ants. It had quite a profound effect on me; I became quite philosophical up there with my bird's-eye view. Flying private is a huge luxury: the freedom to go almost anywhere you like, whenever you want. No wonder my dad loved it. He used to say he liked the solitude; he became a free bird. Nearly always I was given the co-pilot seat, the girls being happy to let the men do the controlling. I would try to understand how it all worked and what Dad was doing. There is a great deal of paperwork involved in flying; it's not just up, up and away. He spent a lot of time playing with maps – the old paper variety – and doing things such as vector calculations with rulers and protractors, while looking as though he quite enjoyed it. He had a pencil and pad strapped to his leg for making notes and some special polarised Ray-Bans that made him look very Top Gun.

I was in awe of him and I'd watch him like a hawk. He was a macho-looking man with strong, hairy arms, his left wrist sporting a chunky Heuer given to him for winning the Le Mans 24 Hours race. He used to chew his tongue. (They now know that this is a good concentration strategy because the tongue takes up so much brainpower.) He'd tweak all the instruments, pull out stops, push levers and controls, much as he must have done in the engine room of the HMS *Swiftsure*, I suppose, only now this was his own ship. His face was a picture of concentration throughout as he checked all the settings repeatedly. It was a rare opportunity for me to be up close, right next to him, seeing how he worked for an extended period without all the normal distractions, and a precious slot for me just to spend some exclusive time with him. I'm sure I acquired some valuable lessons through these experiences. Dad was very responsible. 'Seatbelts?' he would shout out and we'd all answer 'Yes!' Then he'd grab all the throttles and ram them to the stops. We'd start accelerating to the noisy throb of the propellers at what seemed to be a snail's pace at first, but eventually picked up enough speed to bounce one last time on the tyres and up we'd all go into the wide blue yonder: the flying Hill family.

One of the best flying films of all time was *Battle of Britain* (1969), which I saw when it was released. A wonderful bit of British propaganda, but when you are only nine years old, you lap it up. It includes some spectacular flying scenes that I could relate to, having been up there weaving through the cumulus clouds with my dad. Plunging into one is a great buzz. You seem to be travelling slowly, then these massive white candy-flosses loom up in front of you and, instead of swerving around, you just go straight into them. Unlike in a commercial aircraft, you can actually see straight ahead, so you really get an idea of the speed. It's a very similar feeling, approaching the braking spot for the chicane at Hockenheim at 220mph, and years later I would remember these experiences with my father – the sense of being completed immersed in the subjective and sensory experience that made me feel completely and utterly alive.

While school mopped up a lot of my time, home life at Lyndhurst consisted of all the usual things. Evenings were spent having supper and then watching *Star Trek* or *The Waltons*. We had a home help. I don't remember my mother doing much in the way of housework or cooking, but she did do a fantastic Sunday lunch. We had a massive long dining table, which we used if we had special guests. My dad would sit at one end near his office and my mother at the end near the kitchen. I guess that tells you all you need to know. In the middle would be children and guests. We had the occasional visit from wandering fans, but one day I answered the front door to a man who asked if my father was in. Who shall I say it is, please? 'Roy James,' came the startling reply. Having read a book on famous crimes and being au fait with the Great Train Robbery, I knew immediately who he was. I remembered that Roy had communicated with my dad in beautifully handwritten letters from Parkhurst prison, where he had learned silversmithing and calligraphy at Her Majesty's pleasure. What should I have said? 'Mum! There's a Great Train Robber at the door!'? I wasn't sure if this was an off-the-cuff visit or whether Dad had said, 'When you get out, you must pop by for a cuppa.' Seemed unlikely. Evidently he had asked Dad to help him get back into racing. Dad decided to pass him on to Bernie, who gave him the job of making the FIA Constructors' Trophy, still used today. Sadly, Roy couldn't keep on the straight and narrow and died in 1997. Other than that, our life was as normal as it could be, even though many of the guests were from show business, including Eric Morecambe, who always had my father in stitches. He didn't seem to have to do anything to make you laugh.

In his last years of racing my father was having a

documentary made about his life. It was simply called *Graham*, produced and directed by Tony Maylam. They followed him everywhere and filmed twenty hours on celluloid for a one-hour documentary. To give an idea of his typical family life, we were all told to sit around in the kitchen and pretend to be having breakfast as he came in to say good morning. The whole set-up was completely fake; this never, ever happened! We then all had a party in the back garden and played football and jumped on the trampoline. The image of the successful man was complete. I guess there was some truth in there, though it made me aware of how the fame game works. But where Dad's fame really shone was in the birthday parties my parents used to host, when the house became filled with the most dazzling people I had ever seen. I can still vividly recall the year that Emerson Fittipaldi was there – with a very sexy Brazilian woman who patted me on the head while saying, 'Grayham, 'e's *soo* beautiful!' I was lost for words and went scarlet in the face. They were the kind of parties that the whole family were invited to as well, judging by the photograph of my grandmother with Eric and Ernie, with Eric Morecambe putting his cigar on her top lip to make a moustache. Once the party was over, though, it was back to work for my father, back to his relentless ambition to achieve all he could with his life. From 1973, our lives became inextricably entwined with his new venture, but we had no idea this would drag us from the best times into the worst time of our life.

6 » EMBASSY RACING WITH GRAHAM HILL

In the latter part of my father's career sponsors started to arrive in F1, so you tended to remember the message on the car – which is the whole idea, of course. Dad broke his legs in the John Player Gold Leaf Team Lotus. He made his comeback in 1970 at the wheel of a Brooke Bond Oxo Lotus, entered by the charming and debonair Rob Walker, heir to the Johnny Walker fortune. Despite Rob being the most successful privateer, this would be the last season he would enter a car in F1. I suspect, as a close friend of my father, he wanted him to stop racing, but folding his team at the end of the year was going a bit far! After that, Dad drove for Brabham, which was in the process of being sold to a Mr Bernard Charles Ecclestone. This was one of the few teams yet to have a sponsor and instead the car was a distinctively unattractive green-blue with orangey-yellow front wings and split radiators at the front, the combination causing the Brabham to be known as the 'lobster claw'.

I have not forgotten the first time I met Bernie, which was in 1972 when Dad invited him to our house. He came with Carlos Pace, one of his F1 drivers who, sadly, would also die in a plane crash in 1977. My father showed them around the grounds and Bernie looked impassive, rather than impressed, and gave nothing away, which was unusual because most visitors tended to make all the right appreciative noises. I remember thinking, 'Who is this guy?' He seemed to be scrutinising everything; sizing it all up. He was probably thinking what everyone else was thinking: that Graham Hill's best racing years were behind him and that he should enjoy his life in this lovely house with his family. As a driver, Dad's prospects were necessarily limited in the face of a wave of younger, more dynamic heroes, such as Niki Lauda, James Hunt, Emerson Fittipaldi and Ronnie Peterson. By this time my father's old teammate, Jackie Stewart, was only one season away from his third world title and about to get out in one piece at the tender age of thirty-four. But in 1972, plenty of people were not shy of telling my dad that he should be hanging up the crash helmet. One of my favourite photographs is of him giving the V-sign to a commentator who had the temerity to say he was a veteran, with everyone in the background laughing at his response. Old and battered he might have been, but he had lost none of his appeal to the public.

Why didn't he stop? Because he loved it so much. Being a racing driver is a love affair not only with speed and motion but also with the competition and the little kick of fear that you feel you might miss if you don't get off your backside and get stuck in. There is a buzz that comes with just being involved, but not winning is like seeing the woman you love the most go off with another guy: it really hurts. In the film *Graham*, there is a classic interview with his dad, Norman, who says in a wonderfully British-major-general accent, 'People tell me they think he should give up. I say, if you really think that, old boy, why don't you tell 'im y'self!' After which, he gives a massive wonky-toothed smile from ear to ear. The question was, if he were to retire, what would he do with himself? You cannot keep a man like Graham Hill at home to do the garden. I am my father's son in that regard, the only difference being that, having seen what he did when he retired, I have made a point of not starting a Formula One team; it has been the ruin of many a racing driver and businessman. As the joke goes: 'How do you make a small fortune in motor racing?' Answer: 'Start with a big one.' My father's case would confirm this truism, albeit with a new and tragic twist.

By the end of Dad's contract with Brabham in 1972, his relationship with Bernie had rapidly deteriorated. According to Terry Lovell's book, *Bernie's Game*, Dad had been co-opted to take sides in a bitter dispute that had erupted between the F1 Constructors' Association (F1CA), run by Bernie, and the race organisers' counter-organisation, Grand Prix International (GPI), which was run by Henri Treu, the former head of the FIA's Commission Sportive Internationale (CSI). According to Lovell's version, GPI had persuaded my father to start his own team and, in return for help with finding a sponsor in W. D. & H. O. Wills (Embassy), Dad would support GPI and become an FIA F1 ambassador – but also, in effect, a rebel against Bernie and his F1CA. The team was to be called 'Embassy Racing With Graham Hill'. Since he had often been referred to as the Ambassador for Motor Sport, this was a neat way of enshrining the point. Ever quick to find the joke, even in the dark politics of Formula One, Dad liked to quip that he now had an Embassy to work from. My mum was distinctly against the idea as she had been looking forward to enjoying the fruits of their years of hard work and sacrifice, not to mention some compensation for the years of tension and anxiety she had had to endure. She told of the day when Peter Dyke of Imperial Tobacco came to the house to make the plans for the team, and how her heart sank because she knew this would triple the workload that Dad already had. She could see the life she had hoped for, worked for and surely deserved, slipping away again. He had promised her, 'Never mind, darling; when I retire, I will take you all around the world to show you everything.' She would not be enjoying a beautiful retirement with Graham and her family just yet. But this was my father in a nutshell. He just couldn't stop himself – there was always one more mountain to climb, one more ambition to fulfil.

The Embassy team was a big gamble. Dad had to put a lot of his own money at risk and borrowed substantially in US dollars just before the exchange rate swung the wrong way.

This, and the fact that he had loyally stayed in Britain at a time when the top rate of income tax was getting on for 85 per cent, meant he was swimming against a massively strong current. By this time some other drivers had moved to Switzerland and Monaco, but because of his lifestyle – shooting, TV work in the UK on the BBC's *Call My Bluff*, plus his lovely new house, charity work and endless other personal appearances, Dad had decided to stay and hope for the best.

It meant that the team had to succeed: quite literally Monte Carlo or bust, yet again, and joking aside, the mounting stress on my father must have been enormous. I can remember seeing him return home late one night in a cloth cap and a long brown mac, looking for all the world like his own dad. He poured himself a whisky, which was most unlike him. I went back to watching TV. My dad was learning about the hard-knock life of real business, as opposed to the charmed life of a racing driver, and I think he was getting a proper education. It worried my mother sick, especially when he began staying out late at the Clermont Club and Annabel's.

In 1973, the first season with his own team, for which he would also drive, the results were very poor. Dad manfully dragged his Shadow – the name of the chassis – around the GP circuits of the world. I was lucky enough to go as a treat to the debut race in Barcelona. Now twelve, I was starting to get interested in what Dad did for a living, and being around the team was incredibly exciting, especially at that age. I felt part of what was going on, even if I just stood there in team gear. I can remember standing in the pits proudly sporting my Embassy Racing T-shirt and cap when Dad came in for some set-up changes to the car. He was always very pensive at these times, as all drivers were because their lives depended on it: perfect studies of concentration. He would have his gloved hands clasped between the chin-piece of his crash helmet and the steering wheel, staring into the distance. Every once in a while he would look over his shoulder and spot me up on the pit wall and he would just give his famous deliberate, slow, expressionless wink before getting back to work.

And then the race began. I was not used to seeing him right at the back of the grid, as the thunder of cars tumbled past us, and it was then that I started to think: 'Actually, I don't like my daddy doing this.' Mum was there to do the timing dutifully as always, sitting on her deckchair with four stopwatches dangling around her neck and a look of complete focus. She chewed the inside of her cheek a little, but otherwise she was cool and collected. Later that year, I was standing on the pit wall at Silverstone and witnessed the massive Jody Scheckter pile-up which wiped out nine cars; it happened right in front of me. All hell let loose: wheels, wings, bodywork everywhere, and people gasping. It was pretty spectacular. My mother was in her usual place but standing next to her was Lynn Oliver, wife of Jackie Oliver who was driving one of the cars involved. Lynn screamed and my mum hugged her. They both held on to each other until the whole thing had come to a stop. Miraculously, everyone was OK, and once we realised that no one was badly hurt, it was oddly exciting, and a reminder that this proximity to mortality was one of the reasons why people loved to race and loved to watch.

For my father's team the 1974 season as a whole may not have been much to get excited about either, but the following year there was a terrible accident at Montjuïc Park in Barcelona. A rear wing failed on one of Dad's cars and four people standing in a prohibited area were killed. The stress of building a successful F1 team, as well as being one of the drivers, was clearly overstretching my father. It could not go on, and at the 1975 British Grand Prix he announced he would be retiring from competitive racing to concentrate on his team and his family. Everyone breathed a sigh of relief. The announcement was made before a gathering of the press and dignitaries on the lawn of the BRDC, and after he had given his speech, Dad sidled up, put his arm around me and asked, 'Well, what do you think?' I was so taken aback that he'd actually asked me, I bumbled my way to the only answer I could dig up at short notice: 'Er, I don't know . . .' but the fact was, I was very glad: I just didn't have the nerve to tell him. He did an emotional lap of Silverstone in his GH01 car, without his helmet, waving to the appreciative crowd. It was a terrific send-off for an old campaigner who had given it – and them – the very best of himself, and more. But the cruel truth was he had only a little over four months left to live.

Despite retiring from driving, Dad now had to pick his team up by the bootlaces. He was no longer going to be in constant danger, or so we all thought, but the work carried on. Dad upped his workload and the Andy Smallman-designed GH02 by 1976 looked promising. Having found a talented young driver in Tony Brise, Dad was clearly excited at the prospects of becoming a mentor and team owner, rather like Ken Tyrrell had been with a young Jackie Stewart, perhaps. But clearly life had other plans.

7 » THE ACCIDENT

In 1975, aged fifteen, I was on the verge of adulthood. Things my father had taught me had filtered through and I was starting to see him less as a demigod and more like everyone else: a struggling human being, albeit quite an accomplished one. I had successfully ribbed him about small things on occasions, which he took in good spirit: the young pretender probing for weaknesses to gain at least a foothold on power. He knew I was sexually aware, judging by some of the things I joked about. That always opens up possible topics of conversation: not that we ever had any detailed ones, just *Carry On*-type innuendos; very immature, very British. It is a peculiar feeling to watch your own father's character change, but in the time that he had taken on the responsibility of the team I felt that he too was growing up. You can't run an F1 team and be gallivanting all over town every night. While he may not have realised it, I was left feeling that we were closer for the change in his life, and not just because it was good to have him around more. But all the potential outcomes for our relationship were reduced to ashes in one terrible night, 29 November 1975.

The common perception of the events of that night is that Dad was trying to get home in time for a 'party', which is very misleading, and does not help answer the multitude of questions that were asked after that fateful evening. Like, why didn't he divert to Luton, which reported slightly better visibility? Was it because his and his passengers' cars were at Elstree and he didn't want to go through the inconvenience of arranging transport? Had Dad set the altimeter wrongly? Did

Tony Brise fly the plane at some point? Had Dad pushed his luck one too many times? Why didn't he fly back the next day? Did something go wrong with the plane? Putting aside all conjecture, the fact is that the plane crashed. Nothing can undo that. But it is chilling how the fatal decision – whatever that might have been – can sometimes be a banal, seemingly insignificant one, rather than what appears to be the blindingly obvious one.

The 'party' was actually a quiet dinner, arranged by Mum, with our neighbours, Doreen and Herb Jones. Mum had originally expected Dad home on the following day, but the team had finished early with testing the promising new GH02 at the Paul Ricard Le Castellet circuit in the south of France. No doubt he would have liked to join Mum and the Joneses for dinner, and it is true that Mum had put him under some pressure to be more involved in a joint social life, but it seems his decision to come back on Saturday night was more a case of Dad deciding it would be nice to wake up on Sunday morning in his own bed ready for a relaxing time with his family.

Even today, there is still no certainty about what actually happened. We all make mistakes, including pilots, and racing drivers know more than most that we've all escaped death more times by pure chance than we will ever know. But when a big event like this happens, it punches a hole right through the fabric of our illusion of safety, particularly in those vulnerable teenage years when we are just on the cusp of understanding our vulnerability. It startles everyone, and people never forget where they were and what they were doing when they heard the news. For me, the event unfolded bit by bit over the course of a few minutes, but the repercussions lasted a lifetime and have caused enormous pain, confusion, frustration, anger and, finally but most importantly, grief.

The night of the accident was an awful, freezing, foggy evening. It was cold, dark, damp and horrible out there, with nothing but the sound of the trees dripping icy water on the drive. The English countryside in winter has a particular knack of serving up the kind of evening when it appears that the world has come to a standstill. I was watching television with my younger sister, Samantha, in the small TV room by the front door. At around 10 p.m., a newsflash said reports were coming through that a private plane had crashed on Arkley golf course. They then continued with the scheduled broadcast.

Any mention of the word 'Elstree' along with 'light aircraft' would have been sufficient to start the alarm bells ringing in my head. Gradually, I could feel the blood swelling in my cheeks and I started to get a high whistling in the ears as a new reality was pressing up from below. We had been expecting Dad home that night. Like some sick repeat, this matched almost precisely my Jim Clark newsflash experience of 1968, but with one key difference: there was no name. News clearly travels fast, because the accident had happened at 21.30, according to the statement from air traffic control at Elstree. They last heard from N6645Y at 21.29 when a reply was made in response to their clearance to land. The shorthand call sign was '45 Yankee', but Elstree air traffic control reported that all they got was, '45 . . .' followed by a click. This, they presumed, was the precise moment when the plane hit the trees.

From the moment I heard that newsflash, I was on a conveyor belt to a place I didn't want and never asked to go to. Events were taking control of my life and it was a very scary feeling. However grown-up I might have thought myself, I was about to be knocked back to being a helpless child again in the face of an overwhelming new reality that I simply was not yet equipped to deal with.

I was concerned not to alarm Samantha, so I left her in the TV room and slid out in a state of suspended terror. With the whistling noise piercing my ears I stood in the hallway, experiencing a sensation of being in possession of the world's most powerful weapon and knowing that at some point I was going to have to drop this terrible bomb, like it or not, on my mother. At that precise moment in time I was the only person in our whole family to have the knowledge that something truly awful had happened. There was always the chance that I was jumping to conclusions, but I knew. I knew it as well as I knew I was alive, and feeling a fear I had never felt before. I also knew that we had only moments before the life we had would be gone forever, while the future life we had never had – but imagined would always be there – would disappear in a puff of smoke like a dove in a magician's hands. I felt sure I was on the edge of a cataclysm. The nerve endings all over my body tingled in readiness for the first sign of a confirmation that my instincts were correct, no matter how much I hoped they weren't.

My mother was in the kitchen with Herb and Doreen. I knew I had to get close to her because of what I had learned, and, I suppose, it's what frightened children always do in times of anxiety. I crept through the hall and into the cloakroom next to the kitchen. I could hear them chatting, but as I got close the phone rang. I hid round the corner to eavesdrop. My heart was pounding so hard I could hear it through my mouth.

'Who is this? What do you want? I don't understand what you are saying. Please don't call us at home again. This is a private number.' My mum sounded angrily confused and reported to her guests that it might have been a crank call, but it was the first newspaper on the line trying to get that crucial exclusive reaction from the widow. Events were taking over. I had to tell her what I had heard on the TV. I came round the corner and, no doubt white-faced with terror, said, 'Mummy, they had a newsflash . . . there's been a plane crash . . . I think it could be Daddy . . .' At which point the whole world went into meltdown, with Mum screaming and stamping and pulling her hair and shouting hysterically: 'I KNEW IT! I KNEW IT! I KNEW IT WAS ALL TOO GOOD TO BE TRUE! I KNEW IT!'

The rest is a blur of Euripidean proportions. My mother wailed uncontrollably as a lifetime of waiting for this disaster to be realised, and thinking that she had escaped, was unleashed on her. She transformed into Hecuba as our house became overrun with invading armies. There were people everywhere: press, doctors, police, friends; the world, it seemed, invading our house, trying to do something, be useful, or just doing their job. It was pandemonium.

The doctors tranquillised my mum, who had been apprehended running up the drive by a police car coming down, presumably to break the awful news to the family. She had fled out of the door shouting, 'I MUST GO TO HIM!' as she ran. I have no idea what happened to Samantha, whom I had left in the TV room. Heaven knows what she thought was going on. Most of the evening is a blank that I cannot recreate in my head; it's been filled in like a cavity with protective filler. Brigitte was at a party somewhere and the police came to the house where it was being held. The moment she saw the police she says she knew it was about Daddy. I went to bed and slept the stunned sleep of a newly lobotomised patient, suspended between a place that told me that this could not possibly be happening and the disorientating sensation that it actually was. Unconsciously I had been rehearsing this moment for years, but since Dad had retired I had let my guard down – I thought that we had escaped.

I woke up the next day trying to get a grip on the reality of it all. If I had wanted, I could have pretended it had not happened, but I wanted to know this new place, however hard that would be. I looked out of the window and had an epiphany; something I had not realised before occurred to me. Reflecting on the fact that Dad had just retired from doing one of the most dangerous jobs in the world, I realised that there can be no rules. There is nothing written that says, just because you've been good, or just because you are nice, or just because you help others, that you will live to a ripe old age. And just because you have given up doing something really dangerous, there is nothing to say that you will be spared a violent death. There is no benign creator protecting the just. You're on your own, kid. Better look out for yourself, because no one will catch you if you fall. That's the deal, as I understood it to be, right then. It was strangely uplifting: as if a universal truth had been revealed to me; as if I had woken from the dream, the illusion of a secure life that can never be. I came downstairs to have breakfast and the house was still full of people mingling and milling around. Some of them were family friends, but there were also doctors and police, I seem to remember. Foolishly, someone had left newspapers lying around. I perused them bewilderedly. There was the wreckage, on the ground in the broken woods, a charred scattering of what was once our friendly family transport with police and firemen scouring the scene in the fog for clues. Some of the headlines drew their own conclusions before knowing all the facts. What did they care about our feelings? There is something brutal about newsprint. I went back to my bedroom to be alone with my things and my thoughts; no sounds of Graham Hill leaking through the floor any more, just the mumbling of intruders.

Around lunchtime, I was chuffed to be visited by my school chaplain, Mr Morris. He came up to my bedroom, and I was deeply moved that he had taken the trouble to come just to see how I was. I think he was a person I really needed to see at that precise moment: an adult who understood. It was a kind of healing just to know that there were at least some people thinking about me, Damon. Curiously, I was very calm throughout those early days, philosophical, even, and we tried to talk about how I was feeling, but it was too difficult. I hadn't learned to articulate anything yet, only knowing that there was profound sadness that the one man in my life had gone.

As soon as he could, one of my father's closest friends, the ex-England Lion, Larry Webb, came to see us. Both he and my father were learning to fly helicopters and they had got involved in all kinds of capers together, one of which was investing in a dreadful film called *Caravan to Vacarrès* (1974), based on an Alistair MacLean story. They probably did it because Charlotte Rampling was in it, but another reason might have been that there was a part for a helicopter pilot. For some unfathomable reason, they cast my father in this role. He comes in right at the end of the film as the hero and the villain fight together in the helicopter. It's a stinker of a film and the appearance of a recognisable famous person flying the helicopter just distracts us from the main action. My father and Larry were either out of their depth in the film business, or they were having a bit of a laugh at their own expense. Larry was a lovely bear of a figure. He was also a man of few words, but just having him around was hugely reassuring. He had been a successful businessman who liked a cigar, and I had got to know him well as our families had enjoyed holidays together at their place in Portugal. He lived nearby in Hemel Hempstead and on the day after the accident he came over and took me up the drive for a walk and a chat. He smoked a cigar and tried to make conversation. But what was there to say? He'd lost his mate. I'd lost my dad. I made some dumb joke about the irony of dying on a golf course, but mostly we just wandered around numb with grief as we came to appreciate the magnitude of what had happened. The police asked us if we wanted to visit the site and I went with my mum and her friend, Fay Coakley. It was very cold, damp and muddy, and although less than twenty-four hours had passed since the accident, it looked as if the world had already moved on. Dishevelled yellow tape hung roughly around the area and investigators carried out their gruesome tasks. There it was, then. The end. Our life, their lives, in bits all over Arkley golf course. But there was something strangely peaceful about it; the fire had burned out, and there was nothing really to see since the main event had passed hours ago.

*

They say that you shouldn't be friends with your children, but my father had always been my best friend. I loved him and his crazy ways. He was 100 per cent fun, and when he wasn't 100 per cent fun, he was 100 per cent serious and fascinating. For me, being told through my whole life, both before and after he died, that he was an amazing man confirms the truth. My true privilege was not the wealth, the holidays or the fame; it was having had Graham Hill as a father and having learned directly from him about life, about the right approach to it and towards people. Jackie Stewart called him 'one of life's givers'. That was him in a nutshell. Whatever he had, he gave. He gave of himself to everyone he could.

I have no brother and a good deal of my life has been spent surrounded by women: mother, wife, sisters, daughters, and it was exactly at that moment that I really needed my dad. We were beginning to do things together and share 'man' jokes. But he had been asked to 'pay the bill', a phrase he'd recently used in *Graham*, the documentary film about his life. Did he believe in God, they asked. He said he didn't, but added that he knew if he had been left floating in the sea with no hope of rescue, he'd probably start praying. If he was asked to 'pay the bill', though, he would have no complaints. He'd had a fantastic life and didn't feel he had the right to ask for more.

My mother went to five funerals in one week, including that of her husband. The only reason she could not attend the sixth was because there were two on the same day. My father's was almost a state funeral, held at St Albans Cathedral and conducted by the soon-to-be Archbishop of Canterbury, Robert Runcie. Dad's coffin was carried in with his helmet on top. I sat there with my mum and sisters, choking back the sobs. I could not quite understand how it could be him in that box. There was a huge crowd outside the cathedral and there were press photographers as we entered and left. What a carnival. It reminded me of the line in 'A Day in the Life', by the Beatles: *A crowd of people stood and stared / They'd seen his face before*. It seemed mawkish. I had had enough, as I saw it at the time, of people inviting themselves into our lives. All I could think was: 'For heaven's sake, can't we even have Graham Hill to ourselves in death?' I was angry about it, feeling that Dad had given himself to everyone – but not enough to us. Then he died and deprived us of the chance of ever making up that deficit. Who were these people to us, anyway? He belonged to us, not them. I was struggling with this emotion, and if I was angry, imagine what it must have been like for my mother. But people were just paying their last respects to the great man. We all grieved his loss, together. On the way to the crematorium with my mum, sisters and Fay Coakley, I thought I had come to some realisation that helped with these feelings. I concluded that we should be grateful for the time we had had with him, not be angry about the times we'd been deprived of or the future we'd all lost. He had lost the most, after all. As I sat among the gently weeping women, I said: 'We are crying for ourselves. We shouldn't cry.' The sentiment was right, but perhaps I should have cried a lot more than I did. If ever there was a time for grieving, this was it. I meant well, but maybe I was trying not to show weakness, taking on my father's stoicism and trying to buck up the troops. What could I have possibly known about grief by then? It had been less than a week; we were all still in shock. The 'whole' grief would lie buried deeply within me for decades, like a genie trapped in a bottle waiting for the right moment to be released.

There would be an investigation into the accident, of course. I was asked to attend for interview by the Department of Trade Air Accident Investigation team at Shell Mex House in the Strand. Because I had spent a lot of time flying with my dad, they wanted to know if I could give them any clues. I wasn't much help to them, though, and why would I want to implicate my father anyway? Not that I concealed anything; I was already nervous enough, and I wanted to know the truth, just like them. We all did.

The report came out on 29 September 1976. It did not definitively conclude pilot error, but it revealed that the plane was not registered, its US registration having been cancelled in 1974 by the previous owners, much as we have to do when we sell a car in the UK. So it was, in effect, a stateless plane. This had the knock-on effect of negating the certificate of airworthiness, despite the evidence that the plane had been properly maintained. My father had an instrument rating, proving he was qualified to fly at night and in poor visibility. Unfortunately, renewal of this had also been overlooked, meaning he was now no longer in possession of the right licence for flying into UK airspace at that time. It didn't mean he was not capable, and indeed renewal would have been a mere formality, but there is no way to get around it: he was 'driving without a licence'. He had spent weeks away from home in the USA taking his instrument rating exams, too.

But it's no good if you don't fill in the right form, the task of which had been left to his office, and the damage was done. If you were looking for an excuse not to pay out the insurance, there were plenty there. As for what he did wrong as a pilot, they did not specify anything in particular other than that he must have been mistaken as to his true position and descended prematurely. Mechanical failures were all but ruled out, and the air traffic controllers were exonerated. At the time, all we wanted to do was move on from the tragedy, and gradually we stopped puzzling over what might have happened, but my mother was always haunted by the thought that something must have gone wrong. She refused to believe that her Graham would have made a mistake.

Over the intervening years, more information has filtered through to me, giving a clearer picture of the events of that night, starting from the time Dad phoned home to tell my mother that the car testing had been successful, that they were packing up and he would be back home that same night. During that same phone call he asked Mum to remember to phone Peter Wood in the control tower at Elstree and ask him to turn on the landing lights for his arrival. This she did at some point after Dad's call, because she remembered that

Peter complained that since it was a Saturday night he was having a party in the clubhouse (since Elstree was also a flying club), suggesting that he felt slightly put out in some way by this small duty. Years later, my father's closest friend and confidant, John Coombs, told me that Peter Wood was nowhere to be found after the accident. In his words, Peter had 'gone on a bender' and could not be located for days. In 2001 Jan Bartelski published *Disasters in the Air: Mysterious Air Disasters Explained*, in which he wrote about my father's crash in the chapter titled, 'I'll Be Back Saturday Night'.

It was chilling to read, therefore, that Peter Wood was killed when 'a heavy excavating truck ran into the back of his car ten years, exactly to the day' after my dad's accident. When I first read this, my mind did a bit of a somersault because I remembered what Mum had told me about the phone call to him. Could it be that he forgot to turn on the landing lights? Could it be that the 'party' that keeps recurring in reports about my dad's accident was in fact Wood's party, the one at the flying club? Was Dad looking forward to arriving with his team at Elstree Flying Club for a quick celebratory drink with the boys? But how or why does that connect to Peter Wood's accident? It may not at all, but it certainly is another mystery to add to the list. Most importantly to me, Bartelski makes several pertinent points about the accident that justify (to a degree) my father's decision to attempt a landing that night.

He also has some things to say about London air traffic control. He calls the London radar operator's error in vectoring Dad's approach to Elstree 'inexcusable'. The mistake was to tell Dad too early to turn 'left' towards Elstree, on the same line as runway 270. This meant that he was flying parallel to the Elstree runway, but too far south, bringing him over the high ground of Arkley golf course. Bartelski suggests that Dad could have then mistaken a series of red lights from the train stations of Barnet and Borehamwood for the sequence of lights he would have expected to see on a normal approach, all of which sadly misled him. Bartelski's contention is also that the rear lights of a train, temporarily stationary at Borehamwood, might have played a part. Furthermore, he makes the point that the visibility on the ground was only 800ft, but that above 1,000ft it was a beautiful night. Seeing horizontally through fog is much more difficult than looking down from above, plus it can be patchy, revealing some parts, but not all. There is no reason, Bartelski concluded, that a pilot as experienced as my dad could not have managed to land safely that night. His investigation does not shy away from suggesting that, although Graham Hill was a good pilot, he may have overestimated his abilities and taken a risk, but Bartelski also reminds us that this was not unknown in aviation, even among the most experienced pilots. As always in tragic accidents, it is not one factor but a combination that conspires to tip the balance the wrong way. What he did not consider in his book was the possibility that the Elstree landing lights were not on, because he had no reason to suspect that – but of course, if they were not on, that might explain why Dad was 'landing' in the wrong place.

Conjecture aside, however, some uncomfortable truths have to be acknowledged. The paperwork connected with the plane and my father was not in order. This was not good practice, but Jan Bartelski dismisses these oversights as being irrelevant to the actual accident, saying that the instrument rating could easily have been made current simply by applying and it did not mean that Dad was no longer capable of flying to the required standard. I am extremely grateful to him for taking the trouble to choose my father's accident for examination, and his conclusions go some way to reducing the impression of my father as having been stupid or reckless in his attempt to land that night. He was a very professional pilot with 1,600 hours of piloting experience.

In Mum's book, *The Other Side of The Hill*, there is a whole section of contributions from people who had flown with Dad, confirming his flying credentials and their confidence in his abilities. There is no doubt that there are also other stories of near misses and 'exciting adventures' while flying; we cannot deny that, but just because someone is a racing driver, it is often tempting to make the false assumption that they are reckless. People forget that what racing drivers actually do is 'risk manage'; they look at the risks and decide how to avoid being caught out by all the pitfalls. Only by doing this can they hope to be successful. Drivers of Dad's era were just starting to learn to fly because it was a shortcut around the airport hassle. Many had learned while doing the Tasman Series, which was basically a racing holiday in Australia and New Zealand during the winter months. Colin Chapman flew a plane, and famously Niki Lauda is a fully qualified airline pilot with his own airline, or two. Nigel Mansell had to make an emergency landing when all his instruments went down coming into Exeter airport, so can clearly fly if he has to. Nelson Piquet flew, as did Keke Rosberg. They used to race each other back to Ibiza after Grands Prix. The story goes that one of them had bought a faster plane, won a GP and got home before the other one, even though he had left before the end of the race because his car had broken down. Gerhard Berger liked to upset Frank Williams by having the same or a bigger Falcon jet.

Regardless of the perception, my dad loved the freedom of flying. He felt it took his mind off things, and he could live more fully with the ability to get around more easily – plus it added a bit of style to his arrivals. Sadly, though, all the positive benefits had been knocked out in one fell swoop. We, the Hill family, and the families of all those on board, would have to pick up the pieces and go back to living as best we could.

It's a very heavy thought that one's father could have been responsible for the loss of his own life and those of his passengers. I recall their names here out of respect for them and their families and friends: Tony Brise, Ray Brimble, Andy Smallman, Terry Richards and Tony Alcock. I could understand it if there was anger towards my father. He was the

captain: there is no escaping the fact, but I reject any suggestion that he was reckless with his own life or those of his
passengers. You don't race dangerous cars for twenty years
without having an acute instinct for survival. He once declared
that it was his ambition to live to 100, which was not said
flippantly. At the time of the accident, I was too young to
grasp fully how this must have affected the relatives of all
those on board. Naturally, I was lost in my own grief, too, but
over time you start to think about the whole picture. The big
story at the time was that a national hero had been killed. It
was Graham Hill who was known to most people. His loss
was a massive shock to many, many thousands; inevitably, the
mass grief went in his direction. More recently I have wondered how the other families have coped over the years.
Nothing can undo what happened, but remembering them all
is important. Their families suffered the same loss as ours.
Their fathers and husbands all worked together and formed
the nucleus of an exciting new up-and-coming F1 team. They
might have won several of Roy James's trophies by now. More
ifs and buts. But I like to think that 1976 would have seen
something special. Maybe they would have given James Hunt
and McLaren a run for their money?

Soon after the funeral, it was time to get back to some
routine. School was my routine, but my mother was over-
whelmed by decisions she had no way of making without help
from people who knew the machinations of business and the
law. She necessarily became embroiled in the business autopsy.
Dying the way he did, my father had created a massive headache for his estate from a legal and financial point of view. Not
only was the company he owned gutted of all its key personnel, rendering the whole project untenable, the accident had
also left his entire estate exposed to lawsuits because the
paperwork for the plane had not been properly dealt with.
This would have been bad enough on its own, but my father
had also apparently borrowed dollars to fund the team or pay
for our house, I'm not sure which. And just to add salt to the

wound, the pound started to fall through the floor at almost exactly the same time as the accident. My father's friends put together a group of advisers, which included Larry Webb, John Coombs, Henry Taylor and Lord 'Eddie' Portman. They engaged Lord Goodman to help sort out the mess too, but my mother's life was about to get extremely complicated and burdened by things to do with accountancy. It would go on for years and years and years, with the inevitable prospect of being sued for compensation by all the other families. The immediate objective was to protect what was left, and to reduce overheads. It was decided that we could not stay in Lyndhurst and that whatever had a value and was not essential should be auctioned off.

So the house was invaded one more time by the 'vultures' – as I saw them at the time – for an 'Everything Must Go!'-styled auction. All the things my dad had accumulated through hard graft and by putting his life on the line were stripped away: the David Wynne sculptures; his favourite oil paintings that a 'friend' had sold to him at a massively overinflated price; his precious Holland & Holland shotguns, and anything of value that could be sold to pay off the lawsuits that were starting to arrive from the families of the passengers on the plane. One driver even pitched in with a claim because he would be out of a drive now. I felt we were like roadkill; all the crows were having a good peck. My bitterness was offset, though, by the knowledge that these were just material things. Nothing could bring back my father and I resolved not to get cut up about it. They could take everything, as far as I was concerned. Thankfully, they didn't take my things and somehow the motorbikes mysteriously fell into that category, along with my dad's trophies and old crash helmets. It was just the big-ticket items that mattered. The biggest asset, of course, was our home, Lyndhurst.

Perhaps it was easier for me to be philosophical about the change in our circumstances. I was still young; I had my whole lifetime to recover. My mum, alas, would have to get used to a different kind of status, and the material loss affected her deeply. Certainly, it didn't help that she was now having to deal with complicated business issues and depending on lawyers and accountants to tell her how much she could spend. The group of my father's friends tried manfully to unravel his complicated financial affairs and rescue whatever could be saved to keep her and us in at least some comfort. It taught me a lesson about where the buck stops; it was a terrible mess, all round. My mother, having already had a lifetime of grief and anxiety, was now faced with a completely uncertain future with three children to fend for. 'Don't worry, Mum,' I thought to myself. 'I'll sort this out: somehow, some day.' It was a childish, emotional ambition, but I meant it. A bit like dreaming of one day becoming a World Champion.

8 » LIFE GOES ON

As you'd expect, Christmas 1975 was no barrel of laughs. To add more mundane 'first world problems', the house decided to go on strike: things started to break and we had no central heating, as if Mum didn't have enough to cope with. Christmas had traditionally been one of the rare times when we had Dad all to ourselves, and you can probably imagine that Christmas with Graham Hill could be fun. We were encouraged to be naughty and then he'd give us the old: 'Don't do as I do. Do as I say,' chuckling while he said it. All that was over now, and we did our best to put on a brave face.

We only had one more year at Lyndhurst before having to move to a compact but comfortable mock-Georgian house in St Albans. It would have less space than we had been used to, and gave us a sense of being an army in retreat. Mum spent her time deciding what to sell and what to keep, as she let go of the future she had every right to have expected to enjoy with her husband. To add to Mum's woes, she had more sadness to endure. Her sister Dorie, who lived in Australia, had been diagnosed with cancer and was on a tour of Europe with her husband. She visited us en route to Paris. No doubt she tried to console Mum on her loss and talked about her own limited life expectancy. A few days later, they had a car accident in France and her husband was killed. Dorie had been driving. It was as though all the tragedies life had in store for Mum were being visited upon her at the same time. Mum arranged for Dorie to come back and recuperate with us. Two recently widowed sisters; they had even more to talk about now, if they could find the words. Mum says that every time the phone rang, she dreaded what was coming next, especially since Dorie died a few months after returning to Australia. For the rest of her life, Mum has jumped whenever the phone rings.

There are photos of us at events in the years immediately after the accident and they show how grief-stricken we were. Everything we were asked to do involved hushed respect for the 'tragic Hill family'. It was as if we were grief lepers and people gave us a wide berth in case they caught bad luck from us. Every public event was awkward and stilted: the unspoken truth hanging in the atmosphere, the ghost of Graham Hill more noticeable because of his absence. We could not fill that void. I felt I was being shoehorned into the vacancy: 'Sorry, Graham Hill could not be here today, but we have his widow and his fatherless children,' even when we presented Dad's unraced car, the GH02, to the Beaulieu Motor Museum – an event none of us wanted to be involved in. People were clearly trying to show they cared, but some gestures were too over-whelming. I had an invitation from Enzo Ferrari to visit his headquarters at Maranello. What the hell did he want me for? I'm sure it was done as an expression of consolation, and out of respect for my father, too, but if he had only known I had no love for F1, then we could have saved both of us the embarrassment. At the time, I felt that my father had spent more time with F1 than he had with his family. It was my father's thing, and the way I saw it was that it was time to get away from it all. Of course, all the partying and the social invitations stopped. My mother no longer had someone to go with, and it became very clear that it was Graham they really wanted. I understood that, but it must have wounded my mother terribly. The ghost of Graham Hill would always be there, and out of loyalty to him, she would always make sure of that.

It took a while, but slowly my own life found something close to a normal rhythm again, and it was the music and the bikes that helped to lift me out of this quagmire of doom.

While I was still obliged to go to school, it was the music and the bikes that got me out of bed.

The summer of 1976 was the hottest since records began, and I turned sixteen in the September, which meant that I could ride a moped. I wasted no time in passing my test, and Mum had asked Phil Read, the seven-times Motorcycle World Champion, if he could help get me a deal on a bike. It was with great excitement that I plumped for the Puch GP with disc brakes and magnesium wheels. With a maximum speed of 50mph, I was now mobile! I could experience true freedom, and no longer needed to rely on others to get around. My poor mum: she had just lost a husband and now her only son was heading off into the night. The first day I rode the moped to school, it was as foggy as the day my dad died. I cannot imagine how she let me do it, but when you are sixteen you think nothing will happen to you, and the world had just got much bigger, thanks to the miracle of the piston engine and a couple of wheels.

In early 1977, my mother got a call from Peter Gethin, who had raced a few times for my dad and was quite easily the nicest, kindest and – after my father, of course – most humorous man in F1. He wanted to know if I'd like to come and see motorcycle racing at Brands Hatch. I'd never been to a motorcycle race before. I'd seen countless car races and, frankly, they had all left me cold. This was far more appealing than Enzo Ferrari's disconcerting invitation to an audience with the 'pope' of F1, and I was really excited and touched that Peter had thought to ask. I can remember seeing this guy fly past us into Paddock Bend and I was totally blown away, and that is when the bug caught me, just as it had for my father with cars. I started to wonder if I would ever have the courage to ride one of those things. There was something about the bike racing culture that I liked too. It was not made of the same people as F1, who tended to be very professional and serious; these people did it because they loved it, and you could feel it. The crowd, nearly all of whom had turned up with their own bikes, could relate directly to the riders, and it was an altogether different vibe to the cold, even sinister atmosphere that enveloped F1. Bikes also signified the counterculture, which was something that attracted me. I used to read *Bike* magazine religiously, with the great motorcycle writers L. J. K. Setright and Mark Williams prodding the establishment. If you rode a bike, you were making a statement about yourself and about life; you would not be contained in a tin box, and even though I still had years of tedium at school to get through, and owned only a moped at the time, I used to lie on my bed at night dreaming of the life I was going to lead as soon as I was old enough.

Absent fathers are never good for discipline; it's too easy to avoid detection. Permanently absent fathers are even worse. Much as I respected the teachers at my school, they didn't really have the support of my parents; or, in my case, the one recently bereaved parent who had never received an education herself. Who was going to know if I did no homework? All I had to do was turn up and soft-pedal until it was time to leave. But the skiver in me had to deal with the loyal son, and I experienced two conflicting urges. No longer having Dad around to discipline me, there was the tempting prospect of being 'free at last'. But this was tempered with a guilty sense of this independence having been paid for by his loss. I was free to do whatever I liked; no one could tell me what to do now, but I also felt I had a responsibility not to tarnish his reputation, as if the Hill legacy was a Ming vase that could only be ruined by clumsy and irresponsible descendants. He was not there, and yet he was still there. On the other hand, I knew he had a reputation as a man who lived by his own rules. He had left me with a very contradictory reputational legacy, and I would have to work out all on my own how I wanted to play it.

That said, I was not particularly troublesome or rebellious. In fact, if I could have slipped by unnoticed, that would have been ideal for me. So imagine my horror when, in the chemistry lab at school one day, a conical flask of magnesium and hydrochloric acid exploded in my face with a very loud bang. It didn't just happen on its own, of course. I had been experimenting, although not in the way we had been told. Remembering that the test for hydrogen was to see if it burned with a 'pop', I decided to try it out for myself. Someone had lit the gas tap and left it burning, and the next thing I knew I was watching as my hand, holding the rubber tube from the beautifully bubbling bunged-up conical flask, reached across to the flame. I released my grip to allow the hydrogen to escape. KABOOM! Bits of broken glass made it all the way from where I was at the back, to the blackboard at the front of the classroom. Miraculously, all I had, apart from acid all over me, was a small nick on the wrist that had been next to the flask. My ears were ringing a bit, too. Mercifully, no one else was hurt, but I can still remember all the amazed faces looking at me. I had to go and see the Head, of course, but I had finally arrived. Everyone knew I was dangerous!

I used my special status as a semi-orphan to get permission to build a bike bench in metalwork. There was resistance at first, but once the school realised they were up against a motorcycle maniac, they caved in. While all the others were making toasting forks and bookends, I had a full-scale motor-cycle bench in production, and I used it to service my racing bikes in the coming years.

The teachers gave me extra credit for getting my eight O levels, what with my devastating loss and all that, but I didn't feel I'd done anything exceptional. I'd just gone through the motions. The teachers were obviously aware of what I was dealing with, and they must have been keeping a watchful eye on me, although I never made much effort to revise for exams; too busy thinking about bikes. And if no one is going to check up on you, who cares? The night before the exam I would do a bit, but I never had anyone prompting me or giving useful advice such as: if you put in a little more preparation, you could get really good results. I had to learn all this by trial and lots and lots of error and frustration. It was only years later, after I had retired, that I returned to education and took it seriously by studying for a degree with the Open University – so they get you in the end! I'm not sure I can blame my attitude towards education on my father's accident, but in the immediate aftermath my mind was closed to these things. I had too many difficult issues to negotiate: questions and fears about the world I would have to navigate myself through with nothing but the lessons of a dead legend to guide me.

When you experience the sort of thing that happened to me, you go into autopilot mode. You carry around the pain and shock inside. The outside is a mask that deals with the day-to-day. You forget, in fact. You behave normally – unless a little thing happens to remind you, like other kids talking about their dads or someone talking about your dad, and then back it comes again, the awkwardness. I can remember one kid at a party telling me a sick joke about my dad, something about 'What's black and crispy and hangs around in trees?' He had no idea who I was and must have been devastated if ever he was told, but I could stand there and take anything that was lobbed in my direction. I'd learned not to be hurt. 'Fuck it,' I'd think to myself, 'people are stupid.' I'd learned all about the other side of people through my experiences. Have no great expectations and you won't be disappointed: it was a pretty bleak philosophy, but I needed it to get through. You also get good at keeping the lid on feelings, because you don't want to go into them. You just want to bumble along and put more and more distance and time between you and the event, as if it can be left in the dustbin for the refuse men to take away, never to be seen again. In fact, it is more like luggage you've left somewhere with your name and address on it. No matter how far you travel, it will always come back to you and you will have to unpack it, item by item, and put things back into their rightful place. Or, if you choose, you can throw them out, but you have to unpack the bag first. Otherwise it sits there menacingly, like a bomb that could go off at any time.

For some reason, I stayed at school for A levels, even though I clearly had no intention of going to Oxbridge, or any university, which was the school's *raison d'être*. I was a bit of a wandering student, not really engaged with the process. All I thought about was bikes and music. I enjoyed school for the company, friendship and intellectual stimulation; I just didn't want to be in a system and work in an office for the rest of my life, which is how, through my limited vision, I saw all other occupations.

Just as I was coming up to my A levels in 1978, we had one more tragic event to deal with. It was a lovely day in May when Larry Webb, Dad's *Caravan to Vacarrès* friend and trusted adviser to our family in the sorting out of my father's estate, decided to take his wife, Margaret, daughter Emma and the boyfriend of Emma's older sister, Louise, to Le Touquet in the helicopter for lunch. They went missing over the English Channel. Naturally enough, it hit us hard, but imagine what it must have been like for his three surviving daughters. We had lost a father: that was bad enough, but their whole family had been destroyed. As if I needed to learn any more lessons, this taught me yet again that you can make no deals and expect no special dispensations. They teach none of this at school, of course. In the classroom, everything is abstract, intangible. There was I, experiencing these extreme events in my life, and they wanted me to learn about the Corn Laws, or glacial deposits, so that I could regurgitate them in an exam. I think I had every right to take issue with their methods. I was starting to be resolved that neither the continuing catastrophes nor academia would deter me from my ultimate goal of becoming the next Barry Sheene. I suppose when it's raining death and destruction, that becomes the new normal.

As a result, I decided that, as soon as school was done with, I would 'get money, get a bike, go racing'. In anticipation of this great prospect, I took a day off school and went with

my 'bike friend', Dan Brown, to the Brands Hatch bike racing
school to see how I might shape up. They declared me 'Pupil
of the Day', which I accepted with the doubtfulness of a boy
who suspected he was getting sympathy rather than praise.
There had been earlier indications that I had riding talent, my
father having mentioned to friends that he was impressed by
my trials riding skills, but trials riding is not a speed sport, like
circuit racing. Most of the time I was thwarted because I
couldn't get the bike started, which made me angry and frustrated. I could control the bike, but not my emotions. With the
benefit of my perspective as a parent, it is clear to me now that
I really needed more of my father's guidance and time, even
before losing him forever. I had no patience, even if I had skill.
I wanted to show how good I was, or felt I was. But inside
that frustration was my determination to prevail: the will to
win, the need to overcome adversity. And I loved everything
about bikes.

With trials riding, I loved balancing and trying to get traction, the putting on the boots and the helmet and getting
covered in mud. I'm sure this biking helped me later when
racing in the wet, because that is all about throttle sensitivity.
I also became very good at wheelies and I could get the Bul-
taco 350 Sherpa going along nicely in top gear. I once got my
mum to drop me and my bike off at a friend's house and we
found our way onto the M25, which was under construction
at the time. We had about five miles of empty new concrete
motorway to do wheelies on. It was heaven – until I went over
backwards at about 60mph. I stepped off the bike, but my legs
only did about 12mph flat out. My knee collapsed and I fell
face down. I was wearing an open-face helmet, which only just
prevented the beautiful, virgin concrete road surface from
sanding my face off. My right shoulder folded under my chin
and I was sort of pinned down by the drag. Fortunately, I was
wearing a leather bomber jacket that I had found in my
father's wardrobe, and with a sense of pride I could now point

to an authentic scrape mark; my first big accident. I was on crutches for a few weeks, but nothing was broken.

One really good reason for me to fall out with school came about when it prevented me from going to see Mike 'The Bike' Hailwood make his epic comeback on the Isle of Man in 1978. Mike had raced, with limited success, in F1 at the same time as my father. As a former nine-times Motorcycle World Champion, Mike had then decided after eleven years to make a comeback in bike racing at the 1978 TT. It was to become one of the all-time legendary motor sport stories. He won, and I missed it. I had the tickets and we had made our plans, but the friend I was going with felt he had to ask his mum, who wrote to the school to seek permission. The TT is in June – just before exams. The reply in the negative was predictable, but because of the letter, the school would now know why if we bunked off, and I was devastated. I was lucky enough to speak to Mike when he rode the screaming 6 cylinder 250cc Honda around Silverstone for a demonstration in about 1979/1980. He showed me his bleeding toes from leaning the bike over so far; they stuck through the hole in his boots. There was not a flicker of concern. He memorably said of F1: 'I've never seen a more miserable bunch of millionaires in my life!' I was informed that Mike had been killed just before going out to race my bike at Brands Hatch in 1981. It would have been better if they had waited until after the race, but news like that just can't be held back and everyone was in disbelief. He might have recently retired, but by then I understood the deal; there are no rules that say we live to a ripe old age. The way he died was awful. Fog was a factor again: Mike had gone to get fish and chips with his two children, Michelle and David, and his car hit a truck that was doing a U-turn on a dual carriageway. He and the daughter were killed. Another widow.

When I think about my expressions of frustration at this age, it is difficult to know whether they were the function of a natural competitive spirit, or a reaction to grief. If I was an easily frustrated teenager, there were times when I could be very patient. I like to think that the frustration was born of a deep desire not to be defeated by anything – which could be an intellectual challenge just as much as a physical one – but I was inclined to let my feelings show if things became too much. I can still be a little intense sometimes. Oliver, my son with Down's syndrome, sometimes calls me Basil Fawlty. I'm not proud of it and have learned to take out my frustration on golf balls instead. When I was in my twenties, this anger went into my racing as I channelled all my energy into a burning desire to win, but I had to learn the hard way first. Some of it was inherited, because my father had a temper, too. In my mother's book, *The Other Side of the Hill,* written after Dad had died, she tells an occasion when he took out his frustration on her in sharp comments. He could be 'bitingly cruel' to those who riled him, said Nigel Roebuck, one of the all-time great motor sport writers. Leo Sayer enjoys telling a story about seeing Dad at Brands Hatch when he was young. It had been a bad day for Dad; he'd just crashed. He was packing up to go home when Leo plucked up courage to ask his great hero for an autograph. 'I said, "Scuse me, Mr 'ill. Can I have your autograph?" And do you know what he said?"' recalls Leo with a huge grin on his face. 'He said, "F**k off!"' Leo tells it as if he'd had a blessing from the Pope – but you don't get to be a winner without the urgent desire to win. Woe betide anyone who gets between one of these characters and their goal.

If I needed to get a lot of anger and energy out, the Sex Pistols came like manna from Hell. It sounds trite and perhaps a little romantic and clichéd all in one go, but they totally changed my life and that of a whole generation: my generation, Generation X. Having always been hugely affected by music, it was inevitable that I would want to have a go at playing in a band. Bands of that time typically emphasised the proficiency of the musicians: to such an extent, in fact, that they were becoming far too serious about themselves. They created some of the most self-indulgent – if not self-abusive – long-winded, impenetrable nonsense ever committed to vinyl. Contemporary rock music was floundering in a sea of its own egotism. My first ever gig was Deep Purple at the Empire Pool, Wembley. They were dutifully, impossibly loud and everyone wore denim and smoked pot. It didn't do much for me but I felt grown-up, going to a gig. I was also reaching that time at school when the very serious boys would wander down the corridors parading their Emerson, Lake & Palmer albums in plastic carrier bags. Chris Squire from Yes had been to our school, so Yes were a protected species. But we traded albums like Camel and Genesis and Pink Floyd as if they were religious texts or the Dead Sea Scrolls. The Sex Pistols put a stop to that one afternoon in a single five-minute interview that I watched with my best friend and musical collaborator, Robert Sutton, on the very same TV where I'd seen the newsflash about my dad's accident. We could not believe what we were seeing and yelped with delight as Steve Jones lashed Bill Grundy with a torrent of abuse. Grundy had asked for it! Few things can claim to have changed the world forever: Kennedy being shot, perhaps. Or Watson and Crick's double helix. But for a sixteen-year-old, this was a pivotal point in the culture of the world. The next day, the newspapers were seething with the indignation of the nation. A man had thrown his boot through the television. Chelsea Pensioners who had fought in the Battle of the Somme were dragged out of their beds to condemn these horrible little brats. Questions were asked in the House, and poor old Bill got the sack for his trouble. It was all the ammunition the Sex Pistols needed. Stoked by his new-found power to outrage, Johnny Rotten emerged like the genie from the lamp and created a revolution. From the ground arose all the ghastly ghouls of a disenchanted generation who feared they would be the next wave of automata recruits unless they could force their round pegs into a square system. But what did this have to do with me, Damon Hill, from one of the best public schools in England? My street cred was somewhat lacking. I never even got a piercing or dyed my hair. My fashion sense, really an essential part of punk, was very limited, but I did do a good rockabilly look that complemented the biker lifestyle I was gradually acquiring. I'd already got the red leather biker jacket from Lewis Leathers in Great Portland Street, and a bit of Black and White Pluko would keep the barnet at bay when the helmet was off. But the music was easy to mimic, full of anger and fun. What's more, I could play it, and this exorcised energy that had nowhere else to go. I was never going to be a great musician anyway, but I could make a noise legitimately now. If the Ramones could do it, so could we.

A night at the Marquee in Wardour Street was as good as any game of rugby: plenty of jumping up and down, being pushed around and drinking beer. I used to arrange to meet my friends there and ride down from St Albans on my moped. Why I didn't get the train is anyone's guess; I must have been daft. Then, soaked through with sweat after a night of very heavy physical activity, I would mount up and ride home in sub-zero temperatures. I was so cold by South Mimms that I would slipstream trucks to get warmed up by the diesel exhausts. I would have a hot bath at home but my knees would still be frozen afterwards. The next day, my ears would be ringing until lunchtime, but the exhilaration stayed with me much longer.

One of the most exciting nights of my gig-going life was the Pistols at Brunel University. Rotten, despite everything his name proclaimed, was brilliant; sneering in total disgust at the audience and himself. The music was phenomenal, the atmosphere was electric, and I pogoed violently with my school friend, Jeremy Bergman, who was the drummer in our own punk band, the Hormones. That night it seemed we were at the cultural epicentre of everything, but things could never last. The self-destruction got to them; they were consumed by their own nihilism. It was tragic to watch, but it had to end like that. What a glorious catastrophe they were, though.

The Hormones were originally called 'Sex Hitler and the Hormones', which we thought beautifully sent up the spirit of punk nihilism and offensiveness. But we were never meant to be taken seriously. I mentioned it when interviewed about having signed for Williams in 1993, and it became one of those throwaway remarks that stick to the Velcro of history. It is clearly offensive, but at the time we thought it was hysterically funny and a clever nod towards the Pistols. Our band was originally called Roddy and the Hotheads, after Eddie and the Hotrods. We did one gig in the school drama room. The 'fans', who were just our schoolmates, broke the door off its hinges to get in, which made us notorious and got us in trouble. Then we did a small sixth-form common room lunchtime gig as the Hormones. This lasted one song, because we smashed up the equipment after the soundcheck and left the stage in revolt. The band was a short-lived adventure as we only ever did one party gig and never got a booking. It was possibly one of the shortest careers in the history of music.

Poor Mum must have been very worried about her son as she watched all this from a distance. We went to one of the last Parent–Teacher evenings where they talk about life after school. When my mother anxiously asked what would happen to me, my form master, Frank Hanbidge, simply told her: 'Don't worry. Damon will be fine.' How did he know? Because he knew who I was rather than what my results said I was. He was an English teacher, one of the best. He seemed especially interested in his pupils as individuals, and he was always encouraging and looking out for people. He'd given me a quiet talk once because I'd got involved in an incident involving a vandalised phone. I was always on the edge of trouble, but he knew well enough to warn me not to go any further. He was a good man and left a lasting impression on me. The same could be said of my headmaster, but in a less positive way. When the time came to leave school, I was chomping at the bit to get on with some real life and get the racing programme under way. We were summoned to the headmaster's house for a final farewell. I'd been at this school since I was eight. That's ten years of fees paid for by my dad. The Head had a little chat with me and I sat there patiently. 'I hear you like motorcycles?' he enquired, as if he really cared. 'Well, I hope you don't waste your education on motor sport.' I was stunned and fuming and if his intention was to motivate me, that was the kick up the backside that I needed. Now I was absolutely sure I was going to waste my education on motor sport. Worse than that, I would race smelly, noisy, oily motorbikes. The punk rocker in me nearly boiled over. Luckily, I had enough good manners remaining to bottle it up for use when I needed it most.

9 » AN OPEN ROAD

Being determined not to use my education was all well and good, but I now needed to get hold of some money. I had some summer jobs in the holidays and was not afraid of hard work. If didn't have the proper credentials to show brainpower, I could at least use my body power to earn some cash. I worked on a friend's farm in Bedfordshire digging potatoes, which was the hardest work that I had ever done. I also drove a corn kart tractor that collected all the corn pouring out of the combine harvester, and did bailing, which rips the skin off the back of your arms and cuts your hands to bits – but you get a good tan and muscles. Becoming used to these physical jobs would prove to be good mental preparation for when it came to doing a lot of F1 testing, which was extremely demanding in the days before power steering.

If leaving school and going out into the world naked of any decent qualifications might seem frightening or irresponsible, I was either too stupid or too reckless to appreciate how vulnerable I now was. Or perhaps I was buoyed by the confidence I had in my father's legend and the theory that we Hills didn't need or want the support or protection of society's institutions. We could manage on our own and get to where we were going using our own gifts, thank you very much. The decade that followed leaving school was a cocktail of experiences that tested my resolve to make it in the world of motor sport. I started off with the intention of racing bikes and becoming the next Barry Sheene and ended up abandoning that plan in favour of the fallback position of doing the obvious and racing cars, just like my father. When nearly all my

F1 contemporaries were teenage karters and had their dads taking them all over the country to hone their skills, I was doggedly plugging away on my own, crawling up the motor sport ladder at a snail's pace. I started small-time and ended up broke and jobless with a family to take care of and a mortgage to pay. I console myself that I must have learned something useful along the way. Ten years is a lot of wasted time in sport.

Since I was first let loose on the public roads in 1976, I had gradually upgraded from moped to motorcycle with the hard-earned cash from the labouring jobs. Now I had a second-hand Honda CB500 after I had part-exchanged my horrible Honda CB250G for the CB500 the previous June while on the way to the Brands Hatch motorcycle school. I was still at school at the time. Dan Brown had come with me and was amazed when we upgraded to this beautiful black bike en route.

I was now a free man, and with a decent bike, I could now put into action my racing career plan. At some point, though, I would have to pop the question to my mother. The moment came in the cramped kitchen of our house in St Albans.

'Mummy? Mummy?'

'Yes, darling. What is it?'

'Would you mind . . .'

This was it. This was the big moment. I was just about to ask my recently widowed mother, who had spent most of her life tolerating the insane pressures and risks of motor sport, if she really minded that much if her only son went motorcycle racing. I could see it from her point of view and I would have accepted if she had said, 'Over my dead body!' But she didn't. She said, after a large intake of breath: 'I don't mind. But if you are going to do it, do it properly.' I don't think I heard the last bit about doing it properly. Of course I'd do it properly. All I saw was a green light. We were off! Now it was time to race.

Dan and I both entered our bikes with his mate, Eddie Beard, in a club meeting on 23 June 1979 at Lydden Hill. We rode the bikes down to Kent, slept in a tent, put numbers on the bikes, raced them, then rode home. So simple. We never cared about what would have happened if we had fallen off. I raced with a horrible orange jacket that signified my novice status, but since half the riders on the grid were also wearing them, we hardly needed to draw attention to the fact that we had no idea what we were doing.

The thrill of being allowed to go as fast as we liked on our own bikes was completely exhilarating. I was made up: my first-ever motorcycle race, Stage 1 complete. There was no doubt that this was for me. The next goal was to enter as many races as possible and get rid of that horrible jacket. For some reason, probably because we talked incessantly about bikes to anyone in the paddock, I was offered a ride on a classic bike by an old boy who had trouble walking. He was called Brian Coleshill and he owned a beautiful Seeley Matchless G50. He would enter the bike; I would be his rider and get free races. Perfect. He took me for a test day at Hullavington, an airfield track near Chippenham. There were hordes of bikes and we were let out in batches. The 'track' was defined by a few cones on the runways. I let rip on this thing and had a whale of a time: my first time on a proper racing bike, even if it wasn't a contemporary one. Miraculously, I returned it to him in one piece. He took the bike back and said he'd think about it. He must have thought I'd kill myself and didn't want the publicity of having Graham Hill's son wiped out on one of his machines. I never heard from him again, but it was nice of him to offer.

From my perspective there was nothing to worry about, but I understood that without a husband to help with the process of turning a boy into a man, the racing made my mother feel more anxious and out of her depth than normal. I was more concerned about how she was coping than I was about myself, but since there was very little I could do about that, I defaulted to doing what I could about my own life. The way I saw it, the solution to everything would be to become the next Barry Sheene. After all, isn't that more or less what Mum and Dad had done?

In a valiant attempt to jump-start me into full-time employment, Mum organised for me to spend some time with Dan Gurney in California, thinking that I'd learn the motor sport ropes from him. Dan was a F1 driver contemporary with my dad, and a very cool dude. American racers aren't so excitable as us Europeans and Dan was an especially laid-back and intelligent man with his own team, All American Racers, racing in CART (their F1) in the States. In August, I set off on a Boeing 747 jumbo jet, cruising at 32,000 feet, looking down on the little white chips of ice floating off the tip of Greenland, and listening to the Doobie Brothers' 'What a Fool Believes' and the Ramones' 'Needles and Pins' on the airplane loop tape. I was greeted at Los Angeles airport by the Hare Krishnas and I kept an eagle eye out for the Moonies, my knowledge of California having been gleaned from television, the newspapers, Hollywood and my motorcycle magazines. It was eye-opening. The vast freeways clogged with massive cars and guys on Harleys cruising past with bandanas in place of helmets. It was not like little old London.

The one flaw in my mum's plan was that I had no interest in car racing. I went into the workshop a few times, cleaned the engine dyno room with trichloroethylene and generally moped about getting bored. I was much more interested in going to the cafe and talking with a guy called Chuck Palmgrew who raced flat-track oval motorcycles. He was a hero and I hung on his every word. Flat-track oval racing only happens in the US. We do speedway in the UK, but it is a miniature, more specialised version of motorcycle racing compared to the big boy stuff in the States where they race on one-mile oval dirt tracks using Harley-Davidsons: everything in the States is bigger, better and more extreme.

Dan had known my dad very well and we had some clumsy chats about their times together, but I felt like he knew more about Dad than I did. He set me up with his son, who lived with a bunch of other guys and girls in a small house in Newport Beach. I was supposed to be there for four weeks, but I fell in with the other friends and asked Mum if I could stay for an extra two weeks in order to go with them in their VW camper on a surf trip to Baja. Alas, the trip fell apart the moment we got into Mexico. When the camper started to make a farting noise, we had to stop in the middle of nowhere and get some of their mates to come 200 miles and tow us back. My dad always used to play Herb Alpert and the Tijuana Brass at his parties; I presume because he actually liked 'Spanish Flea'. Once we had got the camper moving again, I was able to visit the border town of Tijuana and put a face to the place: border town, keep moving! The problem turned out to only be a spark plug working loose, which could have been easily fixed if we had only known.

I also spent some time with Phil Hill, the other 'Hill' F1 World Champion, and his amazing, fun, psychoanalyst wife, Alma. Phil took me up Pacific Coast Highway to Laguna Seca in his 1929 Le Mans-winning 'Blower' Bentley. It seized up on the way, but he just let it cool down and off we went again. Then he raced it at Laguna! He also took me to the Pebble Beach Concours D'Elegance because 'old cars' were his business. It was a defining experience to be out here on my own, away from the shadow cast by my father which I just didn't seem to be able to shake off at home, and to be treated like a grown-up too. Going to the States as an eighteen-year-old was an initiation into an entirely different world. American kids in LA were pretty unregulated compared with what I was used to back home. I learned a lot, shall we say, and it was great fun. I discovered Kahlúa can be mixed with milk to make more interesting milkshakes, for example. There was a lot of grass-smoking going on. I tried a puff or two but I didn't like the feeling of being incapacitated; I imagine that must be what drowning is like. I figured it would slow down my reactions for racing, too. You'd never leave the grid!

Dan had given me an old Pontiac Grand Ville so I could

get around. While I had no insurance, it had a 5-litre V8 that made a fantastic noise. I freaked them out completely when I parked it facing the wrong way on some street. Evidently you can do all sorts of crazy things in the US, like carry guns, but you can't park facing the wrong way. If my mother had known what the trip to the US was really teaching me, she might have been a bit more worried than before, but this was my life now, tragedy or no tragedy. Besides, I had no love for car racing; the people were just not my type at all. All I wanted to do was ride bikes, listen to good music and have fun. No one in car racing seemed to be happy.

When a journalist later asked Dan about my time there, he said he thought I was a totally lost soul, but I was having a great time in a completely alien environment with people my age who knew nothing about Graham Hill. I was just some British kid who had no idea about anything much except motorcycles and music, and in many ways, this was just what I needed. I had never been anywhere before where virtually no one knew who I and my dad were. But that's what America is supposed to be all about, isn't it? Liberty, and escape from the past.

Once back to normality in the UK, I got into the rhythm of working to pay for my racing. Fay Coakley's daughter, Mandy, was living with Bob Towler, a guy in the building trade. This was at the start of the housing boom. Bob specialised in conversions and my first job with him was in Holland Park. The client's name was Mrs Katzenellenbogen. Bobby Shaw, the decorator who taught me all I know about white emulsion and woodchip, had a natural ability to be cheekily funny. He used to whistle the tune 'Gilly Gilly Ossenfeffer Katzenellen Bogen by the Sea' all the time – I think Max Bygraves did the original. She never twigged. Very childish, but when you are cooped up in someone's flat for days on end with just a paintbrush and a radio, you go a bit mad. Bobby made me laugh a lot. He had an encyclopedic knowledge of contemporary culture and would pipe up with all kinds of urban mythology apropos of nothing.

'He's gay, you know.'

'Who is?'

'John Cassavetes.'

Stuff like that. I don't actually know if John Cassavetes was gay or why it mattered. But it was a constant drip, drip of mythology and opinions formed from years of being cooped up on his own with nothing but a white wall and a radio for company. He couldn't work out why I was working with him when my dad had been a famous racing driver. He came from Hackney and we had very different backgrounds; he took the mickey out of my public school 'nice-boy'ness. I was ribbed mercilessly when Bobby found out that I kept a racing bike in my bedroom since I didn't have a garage at the time. 'You wanna get yourseff a girlfriend, mi'boy,' he'd say. I loved the bluntness of working in the building trade. No pretty bullshit dressing things up to be what they weren't.

This was the kind of education that I had been missing at school. There was the Glaswegian plumber, for example, who had the foulest mouth and mind I've ever had the misfortune to be exposed to. Or the Irish guy who had trench foot and hardly spoke, but was built like a giant. I spent four weeks with him digging out a basement in Holland Park, and when the surveyor came round he had a fit because we had removed too much of the foundations. The whole house could have come down. On another site in Maida Vale we went so deep we could hear, clear as day, the Underground trains.

Ripping out the ceilings of Victorian buildings is nasty work. You get a shovel, hold it above your head and rip the plaster and the lathing down. The whole room fills up with a hundred years of decayed human skin, coal dust and rat faeces. Plus a few old Victorian pennies, if you are lucky. But tough and exhausting as it was, I loved it, and it was just the kind of tonic that I needed to help me stop thinking about my father all the time, and try and make a life for myself.

The job also allowed me to ride my bike every day, and I used to ride down to the King's Road from St Albans each morning on my Honda CB500, reaching Bob's by 8 a.m. He would get out of bed and I'd make coffee for him and Mandy, his girlfriend. He'd sup his coffee, have a Gitanes, scratch his arse, get dressed and then we'd go to Peter's, the taxi drivers' cafe in Pimlico, where Bob would buy me breakfast. When I asked why the hell I had to get here by eight o'clock every day, Bob would simply reply: 'To make my coffee.' When you are nineteen, you have no idea. By the time I got home in the evening I was exhausted, with black crap up my nostrils and in my hair. My clothes were ruined, but the money was good, which was just as well because I was saving up for my next bike.

Travelling up and down the M1 on a bike every day was not without its hazards. On one trip home, just before the Watford exit, a large removal lorry was up ahead with its roof flapping about. A massive strip of semi-opaque fibreglass, the entire length of the lorry, suddenly broke free and flew up into the air, spinning around and around like a huge fibreglass syca-more leaf. It became pretty obvious that it would eventually come to rest either on top of me or just in front. I watched like a rabbit in the headlights as it settled, still spinning, in the middle lane, just in front of me. I had time to wonder what would happen if I rode over it. Would I be rotated and return to the surface of the M1 facing backwards on a motorbike at 70mph? I just managed to avoid it. On another occasion, I was hanging off the bike while having a great time going round Hyde Park Corner. A police motorcyclist pulled me over at the exit of Belgrave Square.

'Do you want to know what I think you are?' he quizzed.

'Er, OK. Tell me.'

'I think you're a c**t!'

I couldn't dispute it, but I had to defend the charge of reckless riding, successfully arguing that I hung off the bike to make it more stable round corners, like Barry Sheene. The judge bought it, but I was done for speeding and Mum was not happy. When I told her the whole story, she was dismayed by the language the officer had used. She complained to the Met. The 'independent enquiry' squad came round for tea and biscuits and concluded that they could think of worse insults. 'Like what?' my mum asked. 'Well, he could have used blasphemy.'

None of these hiccoughs derailed the racing project. I had a goal: get right up to 500cc GP level and race with Barry Sheene – assuming he hadn't retired by then. Barry's talent on and off the bike had made him the most famous racing motor-cyclist in the world. He was the chirpy, cheeky cockney and who wouldn't want to be like him? He'd paid the price, though, famously surviving a tyre blowout at over 170mph at Daytona in 1975 and ending up pinned together like an old rag doll.

Like my father, Barry made a spectacular recovery. He went on to win many more races and the 500cc World Championship in 1976, and it was his crash that really launched him. A documentary was being made about him, covering the accident and its aftermath, falling into place beautifully to create the legend of 'Bazza'. Far from wanting to emulate my father, Barry was the hero I wanted to follow, and that dream was cemented at the epic Sheene/Roberts British Grand Prix at Silverstone in 1979 when 'Our Barry' overtook 'King Kenny' and gave him the 'V' sign behind his back as he did so. One day, I said to myself, one day.

For 1980, I had a new bike but didn't have any way of getting it to the track. I couldn't ride this bike like I did to my first race, because that would be unprofessional. Instead, I per-suaded Mum to put a tow bar on her Ford Fiesta. I bought into the Kawasaki 500 Production series with my lovely brand-new red Z500, which was sponsored by Moores of Watford – but which I paid for. Moores would help by providing a workshop to prepare the bike. The manager, Stewart Fearnside, impressed me because he raced, of all things, a turbocharged Kawasaki Z900 drag bike. He helped me get started. Off I went, sleeping in a tent and travelling all around the country in a 'yuck orange' Ford Fiesta 1300 Sport towing this bike, which was great fun, but left Mum stranded while I was racing, so yet again she would be hanging around a racetrack waiting for another Hill in her family to come into the garage before she could get on with the rest of her day. The trailer was bought for me by Henry Taylor, one of our closest family friends. It was Henry who suggested that Dad should leave BRM and go to Lotus in 1967, which then led to his second world championship. He and his wife Peggy were always there for me after Dad died, and this was just another token of their friendship that I took for granted in the aftermath of the accident.

The racing season in this country for cars and bikes runs from March to October, and I raced on as many weekends as I could get entries for – which meant most weekends. When my friends wanted to party, I was heading off to a windswept racetrack somewhere. In case I broke down and couldn't drive home, I had to try and press-gang reluctant former school friends to come with me. Mostly, they didn't fancy standing around in a field getting cold and wet, then sleeping in a tent and missing the party, but I had to have someone with me, just in case something happened.

When racing bikes, you have to wear a dog tag showing your address, name, phone number and blood type in case you end up beyond being able to explain these details to the ambulance men at the crucial moment. I had started with a cardboard dog tag on a bit of string but, eventually, Mum got my father's St Christopher. It obviously hadn't worked for Dad, but I kept the faith and wore it throughout my whole career.

The Kawasaki Series offered quite good prize money and, by winning the championship, you stood a chance of coming out ahead of where you went in, but I would not call this professional racing. It was more 'hoping to become professional' racing. I had to start somewhere and learn my craft even though, quite honestly, I did not have a real clear plan. I was just racing to see if I could win. If I wanted to get into Grand Prix racing, I would have to progress from production racing to open class 250cc or 350cc national class races. If I could win them, then Grand Prix racing could be on. I had this notion that it was necessary to do everything myself, or it wouldn't count: an extension of the old Hill legend giving me the idea that the only way was the hard way. I was following the family tradition by clawing my way up from the bottom. True to the tradition, too, I was doing it all on a shoestring, though not by choice. I knew if I wanted to get anywhere I would need a sponsor, but I lack the gift of the gab, and while some people I raced with were able to sell themselves easily, I found the very thought of going to family and friends cap in hand a much tougher job than riding the bike.

Eventually, I persuaded an old friend of my father to sponsor me with some proper racing machinery that would allow a go in the open category racing. Ron Shaw was one of those unbelievable characters who had made a fortune by pretending to be less intelligent than he really was. He had white hair and milk-bottle-bottom glasses that made his eyes look like enormous gobstoppers. Most of the time, he had his mouth open and said stuff like: 'I got no idea, me,' or, 'Ow do they do that?' But Ron and his wife, Vee, were sharp as pins, and they were rampant entrepreneurs and fantastic entertainers. They had also been good friends with Bernie Ecclestone and lived right next to Brands Hatch. Ron was from somewhere like Bermondsey and had been evacuated during the war to an old lady's big house in the country. He had never seen anything like it before. He had no idea that some people could have so much money – so he decided to get some for himself. His daughter had just started a company called Thermic Catering, specialising in keeping food warm in the office, and, together with a local bike dealer called David Brown, they put together the deal for 1981 that allowed me to do as many rounds of national racing as I could on a TZ 350. I was hopelessly out of my depth and had bitten off more than I could chew, and I was running purely on enthusiasm, but it was just the sort of education that I needed.

As had happened during my trials riding experiences, I could never get the damn bike to start. In those days, the riders started with a dead engine and when the flag dropped there was the sound of pattering feet until one bike would fire up, then the rest, and we'd be off to the fabulous sound of rasping two-strokes in a massive cloud of white smoke. I say 'we' but I mean 'they' because, more often than not, I'd be still there pushing the bloody bike for about ten seconds or more. But there were some highlights, such as being selected to race in the high-profile new Yamaha Pro/Am series. This was a televised championship that offered really good prize money to established 'Pro' riders and up-and-coming talents: 'Ams', like me. Because there was television and prize money, the racing was fierce and wild. The bikes were provided by Yamaha and they didn't care if you crashed them. So neither did we, but I survived in one piece. I even showed I was competitive on occasions. I was on my way to great things, but I had a lot to learn about how the world really works. The Donington Round is available on YouTube and features a short interview with a very young-looking Damon Hill giving his views on car racing versus bikes. Little over a decade later, I would finish second to Ayrton Senna in an F1 race at this very same track.

10 » SUGAR 27 AND GEORGIE

During 1981, we moved to Vardens Road in Wandsworth, near Clapham Junction. We needed a bit more stimulation than we were getting living down a lane at the back of St Albans, where it felt as if our life had just stopped. Once we had done with schools, the Hill family could move closer to the action.

Brigitte did not go to university, choosing to go directly into work and a job in PR in Hong Kong. Samantha was the most short-changed of us all. Too young to grasp what was going on, since she was eleven when the accident happened and surrounded by a family consumed by dealing with their own loss, she had been sent to boarding school. She was almost forgotten in the chaos of it all. I'm sure Mum did all she could, but many decisions were taken by the trustees of my father's estate. Our lives were in the hands of these remote functionaries, accountants and lawyers, and I had already taken the decision that I wasn't going to wait for people to tell me what I could or couldn't do, but my mother and Samantha remained in their charge. If having no autonomy was utterly frustrating for my mother, being too young to have any self-determination at all was bewildering for Samantha.

Samantha eventually travelled round the world and married a fisherman in Fiji called Jale (pronounced 'Charlie'). She lived in this Pacific paradise for three years before, one Christmas, bringing Jale back to the UK. We all went for a walk on Clapham Common. It was about four in the afternoon, freezing cold and pitch-dark. Thinking this must have been a bit of a strange experience for him, I asked Jale if he had travelled much. He said, 'Oh, yes. A bit. I've been to Tonga.' He was a lovely man, but he couldn't read and the culture shock was too much. Eventually he went back to Fiji, leaving Samantha to look after three young boys on her own; the patterns of family history being repeated, but with subtle twists.

Moving south of the river wasn't quite like turning up from Fiji in the middle of winter, but it was not normally the done thing, although it was much easier for me to get to work. While I was consumed by work and the bike, Mum had this idea that I needed further education. She got me an interview at the South Bank Polytechnic to enrol for, of all things, business studies. I think she thought they'd teach me how to get rich. This was certainly not part of the world domination plan I had figured out, but I dutifully went along with the fiasco, arrived at the interview wearing a sheepskin flying jacket that I had borrowed from Bob 'The Builder' Towler, and acted uninterested. I was trying to get rejected, but they thought I had the right stuff and accepted me, which was a disaster.

That autumn, in theory, I would have to go in to Elephant and Castle every day, and sit in a classroom again. It was never going to work and I had no idea why I was there, who these other people were or what was going on. I absolutely hated it, and in unconscious protest I virtually failed to get out of bed for the whole winter. I never went in for the last term of the first year, which made me a proper dropout. In retrospect, it was clear that I was suffering from depression that winter. I remember listening to a Lennon track in my room when my mate Tim was there, and suddenly crying uncontrollably. There was no warning at all. It was '#9 Dream', and the opening lines are: *So long ago / Was it in a dream? / Was it just a dream?* But what was the dream? Was it the dream of the life we had once had, or was it the dream of the life to come? If I was going to have to give up on the dream of becoming myself, that would certainly have produced a depression. I was not cut out for business studies; I was a bike racer, which meant that I needed to race. But I also needed to grieve,

It's only natural. The top F1 drivers of the day gather round the latest recruit at my christening in July 1961. From left: Bruce McLaren, Sir Stirling Moss, Tony Brooks, Dad, my godfather Jo Bonnier, and Wolfgang von Trips.

My sister Brigitte and I attempt to overtake Dad's new teammate at BRM, Sir Jackie Stewart. Dad looks on with Pam Rudd, whose husband Tony designed the BRMs.

At Lord Hesketh's fun trials day with Dad, Easton Neston, 1974. Motorcycles brought us together.

A familiar sight for me growing up: Dad concentrating at the controls of his Piper Aztec, N6645Y.

An awful day: going to my father's funeral at St Albans Cathedral, with Fay Coakley, my sister Brigitte and Mum.

Wearing second-hand Phil Read overalls on my Kawasaki Z500 at Brands Hatch, doing what I loved most, September 1980.

Doing all the PR and press stuff with Mum before my very first car race,
Brands Hatch, November 1983. All too much, too soon.

Alain Prost seems to be listening to me! Not a bad teammate to have in
your first full season of F1. The active car of 1993 was all new to him.

Senna humiliated everyone at Donington in 1993. A very proud
Tom Wheatcroft celebrates whilst the Williams duo look chastened.

Those are not my real legs! Senna passes me into turn one at
Interlagos, Brazilian GP 1993.

First Prost, now Senna. Sir Frank proudly announces his new driver and my new teammate for 1994. We had no idea what was round the corner.

Georgie and me talking kerbs with Bernie Ecclestone, Imola, 1994, after Rubens Barrichello's frightening crash.

Imola, 1994. After Roland's accident Ayrton had serious talks with Professor Sid Watkins.

The drivers' tribute to Senna prior to the start of the Monaco Grand Prix.

Georgie watching me hard at work.

which I had not yet done properly. I was missing my Dad, no question. We all were.

If only I had stuck at the business studies, I might have gained more of an idea about getting sponsorship. This was to be a really big problem throughout my career. I simply had no idea why anyone would want to sponsor a racing driver, far less a motorcycle racer. It was highly unlikely that they would get any of their money back. I think the potential sponsors sensed my scepticism about the business plan, but I simply couldn't wait to get back to what I loved doing. The other problem with being a student was that I wasn't earning any money. The winter of 1981–2 was a downer and the racing season was about to get under way again, which meant that I had to call time on being a student, swiftly.

The experience, though, was not all wasted. At some point in mid 1981, I gave a young lady a ride on the back of my motorbike. She was visiting friends at a flat opposite our house and, when she challenged me for a lift, I was happy to have the chance to show her I wasn't scared of girls. I'm not sure if it was me or the young lady who was showing off to her friends, but I gave her a lap round Wandsworth Bridge roundabout and brought her safely back to Vardens Road. Her nickname was Georgie. Her real name was Susan George, but she changed it, not because her name was the same as the actress but because she was studying fashion at Kingston Polytechnic and there were too many Susans. Georgie suits her better, somehow.

We didn't get together straight away. On 5 November 1981, a friend of mine was taking her to a fireworks party in Brixton and they picked me up on the way through. I thought she looked very sexy, sophisticated and mysterious: all in black with a bob haircut, not at all like the skinny punkette I'd given a ride to. I sat in the back of my friend's Z28 Camaro – which is a tight fit – and made the usual witty remarks, but there was not a flicker. So I tried all my comedy routines and clever comments. Still she blanked me. Rather than putting me off for life, she intrigued me with her austere and somewhat aloof attitude. But I must have made some impression, because years later Georgie would claim that God spoke to her at the party and told her she was going to marry me, which was eventually exactly what happened, even if it did take a further seven years.

Soon after giving up being a student, I decided to start to earn some real money by doing dispatch riding. The rumours were that you could earn more than £300 per week, and it was the dream job – I could ride my bike all day, get paid for it *and* fund my racing. I converted my Z500 for dispatch work and started with a company called Apollo Dispatch, based in Villiers Street, WC2. When you first joined you had to go into the office and sit around talking 'bike' with all the other misfits. Because the money was so good it attracted all sorts, from students studying nuclear physics to bikers studying the *Sporting Life*. The conversations were pretty diverse. Eventually, you could just jump on the bike at home and call in on the CB radio. My call sign was Sugar 27. It's imprinted in my mind like the bell in one of Pavlov's dog's brains.

We would courier around all sorts of odd packages, including artwork from advertising agencies that was actual physical bits of art, which we strapped to the top box with a rubber bungee. You'd be whizzing along with this huge piece of pith board sticking up and it would either catch someone's wing mirror or fly off at speed. On one occasion, I lost an essential bit of artwork (it was always essential and last-minute; that's why they paid for a bike) in the middle of the tunnel heading towards Piccadilly. I realised as I exited the tunnel that it was gone, and knew I had to get it back. Unfortunately, that entailed going to the end of barrier separating the lanes, doing an illegal U-turn and going all the way back to Knightsbridge for another illegal U-turn, and then heading back down the tunnel again. Which I did, arriving just in time to see the artwork lying intact in the fast lane. Phew! I parked the bike illegally and took one step towards the –

until then – pristine artwork just as a taxi ran over it, punching the hook of the bungee cord right through the middle. Another time, I picked up a small piece of artwork from Lots Road to go to Fleet Street, but when I looked in my saddlebag it was gone. I radioed in and was told to go back and they'd have another one waiting. I dutifully returned to Fleet Street with the parcel and opened my saddlebag again. Gone. Third time, red-faced, I got lucky.

Every December in the run-up to Christmas, dispatch riders would dress up as Santa Claus. By the end of the first week, my beard had an authentic tang of diesel soot. If it was raining, which it was three times out of five, we would stand clutching our deliveries, dripping water all over the carpets in the reception halls of these plush City offices. If it was meant to cheer people up, I never noticed anyone smiling. But Christmas was a good time for dispatch riders. People were in a hurry to wrap up business before the end of the year and I was earning in excess of £300 a week, which made the outfit and the cold bearable.

The summer was a different matter. I would ride everywhere wearing a T-shirt and shorts; and never with gloves. I may have got a good tan, but it was unbelievably reckless. But when you have total confidence in your ability you think nothing can touch you. You trust your survival instincts completely and near-misses seem only to confirm your self-belief. One afternoon, on the way back from a delivery, I got stuck behind a coach while travelling at around 50mph on the Chiswick flyover. When the coach started to move to the left, I thought it was pulling over to the slow lane. Similar to the Hamilton-on-Rosberg move in the 2016 Spanish Grand Prix, I went for the pass, but the coach was actually following the road. I accelerated into what I thought would be an empty lane, but which rapidly became a bike-sized gap between the coach and the barrier. I mounted the kerb between them and did a tightrope-balancing act for about fifty yards before dropping back, a little chastened, but still alive. When I replayed the incident in my head, I had this intimation that it was purely my reflexes that had got me out of that situation and others like it – just like when I had fallen off the climbing frame as a child. I don't think there is a racing driver who hasn't come to trust their instincts, because that's what keeps you alive. The moment you let an external influence into your head, you are at risk. There were many incidents like this on the bike, but these little moments went into the mental bank for later, when I would really need them.

Riding a bike all day around London streets heavy with traffic, in all weathers and often in the dark, is hazardous to one's health; pollution being not so high up on the list, but pretty awful nevertheless. I don't know what my life expectancy was, but if you added in racing motorcycles at the weekends, it was probably not that good. But the dispatch riding provided very good training for the racing. I used to like Belgrave Square because it had almost no grip in the wet. If you pushed the front and rear together, you could learn to two-wheel drift. With the throttle, you could over-speed the rear wheel and keep the bike balanced in a nice power slide.

After many years of riding on the road, you develop a sixth sense for pedestrians and errant traffic. I used to know instinctively if a car would be turning right despite indicating left. Tourists typically look the wrong way and just stroll into the road in front of you. So you stop, so as not to kill them, and they jump out of their skin when they finally look right and catch something out of the corner of their eye. You could predict what they would do before they actually did it. Dispatch riders develop an unconscious picture that tells them which way traffic is going. People in cars get startled by them because they are invariably listening to the radio, staring out of the window and generally being half awake. Half awake on a bike is half dead, so you get good at things like staying alive.

Juan Manuel Fangio, the five-times World Champion, used to tell a good story about the 1950 Monaco Grand Prix. He was leading and yet, for some reason, he knew he had to lift off. The road ahead seemed clear, but he sensed something was wrong. When he got round the blind apex of the corner, he discovered there had been an accident and the track was blocked. His instincts had forewarned him. After the race, he was bewildered as to how he had known, thinking maybe God had intervened, then he realised that something had been different about the picture as he approached the corner. People were not looking at him, as they had always done before and as you might expect when leading; they were distracted by the accident. The background image had changed. His unconscious had registered it and warned him. This is the sixth sense that you need to survive in motor racing, and dispatch riding was teaching me it. Even if I wasn't yet winning races, I was accumulating the skills. The hours and hours I spent on my bike every day prepared me, at least to a degree, for the frenetic action of racing towards the first corner of a Grand Prix – as anyone who has tried to enter Hyde Park Corner in rush hour will appreciate.

Being in a helmet all day can be pretty lonely, but I put my time to good use by thinking of ways to get sponsorship. One thing I learned was the existence and location of many different companies. When I came across Ricoh, a photocopier company based at the back of Euston station, I kept their compliment slip and put it in my pocket to add to the list of possible sponsors.

11 » TWO TO FOUR

In August 1982, I went with Dan Brown on a bike road trip to the San Marino Grand Prix. We got off the ferry at Calais at 6 a.m. and rode to Turin in one hop. The motorway riding was boring and I nearly fell asleep on my bike, something that I would never have thought possible, but it gave me a hell of a fright, which was just the jolt I needed to make me pay attention. We arrived in San Marino and asked where the track was – only to be met with blank looks. Eventually someone worked it out and redirected the hapless Englishmen. The race was being held at Mugello, across the country near Florence. We felt pretty stupid but had a fantastic ride over the spine of Italy with mountain roads, forests and, eventually, the descent into Florence.

It was sweltering at the track, but we were in bike heaven, watching these amazing riders and Grand Prix motorcycles in action and dreaming of one day doing the same. We were on a tight budget, so we didn't eat lunch and just drank water during the day, and to save fuel we would freewheel down the hills. In the evening, we went to the local pizzeria for beer and a massive calzone cooked in an open wood-fired oven. On the way to finally conking out in a budget hotel, we did long wheelies through the pine-perfumed mountain forests. It was an amazing trip; I felt so free on my bike. We routed through Monaco on the way back and went to stay at Henry and Peggy Taylor's home in Golfe Juan, where they ran a boat business. It was good just to hang out with their sons, Tim and Stephen, with whom I had grown up and shared school holidays. While we were there, we met a couple of young English guys, Paul Newman and Lance Lawry, who were from the same corner of London, and we followed them to Saint-Tropez and spent a few days having fun before the long, boring and increasingly cold trip home. It felt good to be completely self-sufficient, and I had all I needed to be happy, but I was to get a rude awakening upon my return.

Ron and Vee must have felt I was not on track to super-stardom and decided to pull the sponsorship. To my dismay, they also pulled the bikes, which I thought were mine under the terms of our agreement. When it came to the detail of deals, I was always woefully naive. I have since learned the hard way, and the painfully slow way. It was then that I got to hear of Mike Agostini, who ran Special Delivery, a dispatch company in the King's Road. More importantly, Mike liked to sponsor motorcycle racing. With a name that combined the two most famous names in motorcycle racing history, how could he not!

One of the best things about Mike was that he let me use the van as well as his bikes. But I had to work for it. On a Friday evening, he had a regular job delivering copy for all the local newspapers to printers in Walsall. This meant that, after a full day on the bike, I had to set off in the van during rush hour, head up the M6, drop the boxes, turn around and come home again. It was a VW Type 2 van; ugly as sin and the rear engine took up most of the space in the back. The only enter-tainment was an eight-track player with a choice of *Peter Frampton Live* or *Band on the Run*. When I started to nod off each time on the way back around Scratchwood Services, I would give it another blast of Paul McCartney and open all the windows.

At the time, Georgie was living in a ground-floor flat in Kew, which meant I could cut round the North Circular and pop in though her window, to avoid waking the rest of the house up, before crashing out. I'm sure she was delighted to welcome in a guy who had spent all day riding his bike and then been in a van for five hours or more, but it was kind of romantic, tapping on the window and being let in.

According to Georgie, she is still amazed she ended up with me. I wasn't what she thought was her type. I hadn't yet learned to appreciate art as much as motorcycles and my reading consisted mostly of *Motorcycle News* and *Bike* magazine. Her listening was more Stevie Wonder; mine was Led Zeppelin. She hung out with 'fashion' and 'arty' types. A grubby dispatch-riding motorcycle racer was not high on her list of people she wanted to associate with, but I wasn't a complete philistine. I had a rather dismissive motor sport way about me: dismissive, that is, of anything that wasn't completely functional. The one thing I did have going for me was that she thought I looked a bit like Donny Osmond. Years later, using my power and influence as a recently crowned World Champion, I managed to arrange for her to meet her childhood crush at a TV studio show: *An Audience With* . . . . It's the type of show in which the camera pans around the audience to catch a famous face. If the camera had caught a glimpse of me it would have shown a very red-faced Damon Hill as Donny launched into 'Puppy Love' just after reading out a letter he'd written to his mother when he had been a lonely little boy on tour, far, far away from home.

Georgie knew nothing about motor racing when I first met her. One afternoon in early 1982, we were sitting on the swings in the park when I broke the news to her. April was nearly upon us and the new race season was about to start. There would be no more free weekends for a while. She had no inkling of the significance of what I was really saying, or that it would hold true for the next eighteen years.

If Georgie was bewildered about her attraction to me, I can only say that I felt much the same. I knew something important beyond the physical was going on between us. There was a bond of something or other: something to do with sadness. Georgie had also lost her father, albeit through parental separation when she was thirteen, leaving her with a slight distrust of men. When we first met, it was only six years after my dad's accident and seven years since her parents had divorced. We were still trying to come to terms with our personal losses. I had done a pretty good job of burying the memory of the accident, or so I thought, but during the process of getting to know each other I had taken Georgie to see where my father was buried. Suddenly, there it was again: buckets of tears.

In Georgie's case, she was very angry towards her father. Of course, this got muddled up with the love she also had for him, and she had a lot to deal with on her own. Later, I was to learn how we act out the issues of our parents in our own relationships. When you don't know this, a relationship can be very confusing as emotions are brought out on both sides for no immediately obvious reason. You cannot understand why things can suddenly change from being OK one second to blowing up the next. But after you learn that there are parental patterns that map themselves onto our own lives, you can start to unpick things, spotting the similarities and consciously realising that you are being toyed with. It comes as a relief to learn that it doesn't have to be a repeat performance of the parents' lives; the tension and frustration is caused by the desire to break out of the patterns, but not being able to. There was an understanding of something deep between me and Georgie that I believe brought us together, but we had some tough negotiations along the way. That's not to say that it wasn't enjoyable arguing with Georgie. I found her a fascinating contrast to my doubts about virtually everything, including myself. She has very strong views: a commitment to what is right, along with a razor-sharp mind and a memory to match. I had to be on top form if I was going to take her to task on anything. Georgie knows her mind, but she nearly always comes round to my point of view. This meant that in the coming years, and against all the expectations she might have had about her own life, Georgie would have to put up with racing if we were going to be together.

It is not just with the benefit of hindsight that I can see the parallels with my parents' early life together. I think that, semi-consciously, I wanted to recreate the conditions to allow me to rebuild the life I had enjoyed as a young boy. All the pointers were there; we were almost broke, just like my parents, and I was a struggling competitor. In Georgie, I had found an ally, someone who made me feel safe, gave me shelter and love and who understood the more serious things in life. I could offer her the same. Just like my parents, we would have to grind our way up to the top through perseverance. Besides, it was the only model I had and it seemed to have worked for them. I don't think Georgie always saw the big picture I had in my mind, probably because I hadn't articulated it. There were a few 'it's the bike or me' conversations, but I somehow won her over and, at the beginning of 1983, I managed to persuade her to move into a dreadful flat with me in Poynders Road, part of the South Circular, on the borders of Clapham and Balham. Romance can get you so far, but the mould and the damp, along with the incessant traffic, would have been a test for any couple moving in together for the first time.

About the same time, I had also been offered a garage in Webbs Road, Clapham, by Barrie 'Whizzo' Williams. Barrie is one of British motor sport's unique characters, having raced almost everything and anything that moves, and he let me use the garage for a peppercorn rent, which meant I could prepare the bikes better. I was one step closer to becoming professional. As soon as I got the keys to the garage, I spent every spare minute I could tinkering with the bikes, teaching myself how to make them go as fast as possible. One night after working late I came home to Georgie, who seemed upset with me. I couldn't work out what I'd done, until eventually it came out: she thought I had another girlfriend. I tried not to laugh, because she was completely serious, but it showed how little she understood about my commitment. I don't think she had ever met a serious sports person before, whereas I had had one for a father. She didn't really understand that the bikes needed a lot of attention and I was being meticulous. Although she had been to see me race a couple of times, she couldn't understand what would make me want to work so late in a cold, damp garage rather than be with her. But this was racing. Winning would be the secret to everything and bring us untold riches. All those hours hunched over the bike in the middle of the night, while our friends were off having a good time, would be worth it in the end – I kept telling myself. As my fourth motorcycle racing season got under way I quickly realised that if I was going to have any chance of making good on my promise to Georgie, I was going to have to prepare better for the races. That meant getting a decent night's sleep before race day.

I had a bit of luck to add to the support I was getting from Mike Agostini. Ray Bellm, a family friend, offered to sponsor me for £2,000, a huge sum. All I had to do was carry the brand name of one of his company's products, Mucron, which claimed to clear up catarrh. I was more than happy with the deal as it meant I could splash out on a caravan to sleep in before races. What luxury: now I would arrive refreshed and ready to go. Christian Devereux, a friend who I had met when he was the controller at Villiers Dispatch, agreed to be part of the team.

One Friday night, we left very late for Oulton Park. I decided to sleep in the caravan with Georgie while Christian drove – which was strictly illegal. About halfway up the M6, we were shaken from our beds with pots and pans flying and the curtains dangling at an unnatural angle. It was obvious what had happened. Christian had fallen asleep and gone up the embankment. When everything had settled down, I peered through the front window to see him sheepishly giving me the thumbs-up sign in his rear-view mirror. He didn't stop, so I had no way of letting him have a piece of my mind until we got there. By then I was too tired, which must have led to increased adrenaline levels the next day that sparked the kind of light-bulb moment that indicated that I was moving to the next level as a rider.

The bike had sprung a puncture only minutes before the start of the race. Having waited all day for one race, I wasn't inclined to miss it. I attacked the bike with all I had: spanners and tyre wrenches flying; swearing, shouting, hitting things with a mallet. I had everything ready just in time and I rushed to the grid. When the flag dropped, I was so pumped up with adrenaline that I took no time to get the bike going and then gave it all I had, slotting into second place behind Graeme McGregor, a top rider of the time. I had never felt like this before. It was almost as if I had ignited a part of my brain that I had never previously engaged and I was more awake and alert than ever. As I swung round Island Bend at the far end of the circuit while hanging on to McGregor's rear wheel, a thought entered my head: 'Hold on, Damon. What the hell do you think you're doing up here with Graeme McGregor?' From that moment on, I dropped back through the field, but it had been enough of a sign that I could be up there under the right conditions. It was as if I had just woken up and realised that I could actually do this. My inner convictions were finally being justified.

Thankfully, we managed to move into a much nicer basement flat on the road where I had met Georgie for the first time and, conveniently, right opposite my mother's house. I had moved all of thirty feet from my former bedroom. Being in a basement had its drawbacks, like the slugs that slid down the hallway from the front door, but otherwise this was a step up from the South Circular Road flat. The new place was on meters. Occasionally, while we were watching television, all the lights would go out, prompting a search for a 50p piece in the dark. Then the gas fire would go out, and you would have to nip out to the corner shop for more change, hoping you didn't slip on a slug on the way. It may have been pretty basic, but it was perfect for us to find out about life together. We were very happy. I was still dispatch riding for the money and really appreciated Georgie's home cooking. After I'd had a soaking wet, cold day alone on the bike, Georgie would have lamb chops and mashed potato ready for me, or sometimes liver and onion; sometimes dumpling stew. That motivated me to press on through the rain and snow to get those jobs done as soon as possible.

I was twenty-three now; many of my friends had left university with degrees. While they were partying every weekend, I had been trying to sleep in a tent or a van and staying off alcohol. I did sacrifice quite a lot of social learning during my hermit life as a dispatch-riding motorcycle racer. But in the middle of 1983, my career and my life were about to take an unexpected diversion. This was something I really had resisted, seemingly since birth, and decided to explore only out of a sense of adventure and curiosity.

Mike Knight ran the Winfield Elf School in France. He had been a racer himself, but had not made it to the lofty heights of F1. His racing school was famous, however, and had been responsible for giving the first big break to Jacques Laffite, René Arnoux, Alain Prost and Patrick Tambay: virtually all of the leading French drivers. But Mike, being English, was frustrated not to have had a British winner of the school scholarship. While putting together a package for non-French hopefuls, he offered my mother a place for me. The offer almost certainly came about through conversation with friends, because she had never intimated that she didn't like me racing bikes, but I had to admit the career prospects in bike racing were not that good – unless you were Barry Sheene. And by then I knew that I was not going to be the next Barry Sheene, though if everyone else knew, they hadn't told me. One day, Mum idly asked me about having a go in cars and mentioned the Winfield offer. I said, 'No thanks. Every penny I have goes on my bikes.' Then she asked, 'What if it was free?' That rather changed the look of things. Pretending not to be interested, I joined an excited contingent of British hopefuls: young racing prospects who had done either karting or Formula Ford at some point, but were of very limited experience. Rather like myself, except that I had at least raced bikes. They were talking about this thing known as *Autosport* (the leading motor sport magazine) and a guy called Dr Jonathan Palmer, who was winning everything in F2 at the time. I had no idea who or what they were talking about. Furthermore, I didn't like the sound of any of it. A doctor? Racing a car? Far too establishment for me. This was exactly the reason I had chosen bikes over cars in the first place. I seemed to get on better with a guy called Peter Chrisp, a journalist who was covering the experience for *Car and Car Conversions* magazine. He seemed to share my sense of being an outsider and my lack of seriousness about the whole project. He was, after all, only there to write a piece, not blitz the competition. I, on the other hand, was only playing at it – or so I thought.

At first the school was a little too safety-conscious for me and gave none of the sense of danger, speed and power I was used to on my bike. The cars were Formula Renaults with Martini chassis; capable of being quite quick, with wings and a 2.0 litre engine. The instructors made us start right at the beginning by driving through cones and practising braking. It was all a bit too easy for me but, having had their fill of crazy people nearly killing themselves and destroying their cars, they were understandably cautious and keen to impose some control. Eventually, we were allowed to have a go at a lap time. Once let loose to attack, I seemed to be getting into it a bit. This was more like it. Without any experience of karting, I seemed to understand instinctively what to do, which was a surprise. But I suppose it's all about conservation of momentum in our sport – that, and a thirst for more speed. It was surprisingly enjoyable. Mike thought I might have some talent, which encouraged me, and without really trying, I qualified for the finals at the end of the year. If my mother was pleased about this, it never really showed, but she must have felt glad it went well. I think her secret agenda was to get me off the bikes.

Georgie thought this was another branch to my eccentricity and made little of it. But down there somewhere, deep in this competitor's brain of mine, a little program was starting to churn through the permutations. What if I won? That could be interesting.

The finals, however, would unearth flaws in my ability. I became too tense and screwed up a couple of gear changes, which cost me lap time. Ironically, given how reluctant I had been to sign up in the first place, I found myself deeply disappointed not to have won. Years later, Mike told me he had been more impressed by my evident disappointment than by my performance, but success meant everything to me, in whatever I did. I was almost manic in my determination to prevail. Perhaps I had my father's fierce will to win after all. All I needed now was the talent behind the wheel, and to do that, I would need to get my bum in a seat and start practising.

The bug had clearly bitten. The more I learned about the long-term prospects for race car drivers versus motorcycle racers, the more I could see the possibility of a 'secure' future earning a living through car racing rather than admitting defeat and getting a job. What would I do, anyway? With no appetite for office work, or any idea what that meant, motor car racing seemed to offer many possible benefits over motorcycle racing, not least of which was the prospect of still being able to walk without a limp for the rest of my life. If car racing had the potential for inflicting serious injury or death, motorcycle racing offered the same possibility, but with the added certainty of broken bones. So maybe the way forward was car racing after all?

It didn't take long for word to get out that Graham Hill's son was trying his hand at racing cars. John Webb, who ran the Brands Hatch circuit in Kent, was a brilliant promoter and could see a good opportunity when it came his way. Hearing that I had shown some potential at the Winfield School, he offered me a drive in an end-of-season mini-championship known as the BBC *Grandstand* Formula Ford 2000 winter series. John figured this would generate a good story and boost interest, but I don't think he realised just how much interest there would be. Nor did I.

Formula Ford 2000 cars were similar to those I'd tried in France, only faster and with a bit more grip. The championship would be contested by the hottest and the best drivers competing in the UK, many of whom had been racing all year in these cars. It was like being thrown to the sharks; I had no idea what I was about to let myself in for. Surprisingly, I wisely decided that it would be good to get a proper feel for what it would entail and went with Georgie to see some racing at Brands Hatch. Virtually the first thing we saw on arrival was Grand Prix driver Eddie Cheever's younger brother, Ross, barrel-rolling his car down Paddock Hill. I looked at Georgie and she looked at me; we must both have thought the same thing, but never said a word. Crashing hugely was evidently part of the game.

In preparation for the race, they gave me some essential testing in an Argo, the car I would be racing. It was not the best car for a beginner, the Argo being of a different design from most of the others and having a reputation for being tricky to drive. Having no prior knowledge of car sport, however, I had no idea about this. I crashed the car comprehensively during testing by going pretty well flat out into a barrier at Snetterton. This was not like bike racing. When the car goes off, you go with it, and it doesn't slow down much, thanks to having far more mass than a bike. I saw stars.

I couldn't understand how these things worked. I kept trying to stick my leg out when cornering, the natural reflex that came with riding a bike. In a car, you are crammed into the cockpit and I found the whole experience very claustrophobic. There also seemed far too much grip for the power available. On my bike, I was used to quite a lot of power with a very small contact patch. I could ride it on the throttle and it wasn't until I was almost in F1 that I would get a car with the right amount of power to suit me, excluding the wet races when there was always enough power to spin the rear wheels on a slippery track. The Argo was not the right car for a novice and the series was too advanced, but in for a penny, as they say.

The first round of the series was my first-ever car race. It was at Brands Hatch and the world's press seemed to have descended on what would otherwise have been a small end-of-season race meeting. John must have been delighted. It was a carnival of press and TV, completely over the top and really the last thing I needed for my first crack at car racing. The pressure was massive. My mother was there, proud as anything and reliving past glories – only this time with her son. I was posing for photographs and doing interviews, not knowing anything about the motivation of the media or how to moderate expectations. To add to my woes, I didn't technically qualify for the race, but given the amount of press interest, the organisers took a vote and let me start. It was the high jump experience at school all over again. I felt humiliated and just wanted to get out. But it wasn't over yet.

Finally I got into the car, where I could experience something close to tranquillity. The race started and I ended up spinning and stalling at the exit of the famous, plunging first corner, Paddock Hill Bend, the scene of Cheever's massive accident a few weeks before. I was trapped at the bottom, right on the exit, as cars appeared to be dropping out of the sky towards me and shaving the front of my car at about 130mph. I was terrified. The marshals got the car started and I trundled sheepishly back to the pits where they told me to get back out and have another go. As much out of shock as anything else, I did as they said. It was probably the least impressive, most useless, and most publicised race debut in recorded motor sport history. I had learned another lesson – if I was going to take this on, I would need to take it seriously.

So that was it. The inevitable had happened. I was back in the cockpit of destiny. This time, however, I was a collaborator instead of an unwilling and powerless pawn. I did it partly out of curiosity, partly out of desire to have a go, partly because I needed a career and partly because the opportunity was there for the taking. But I also did it because there was clearly an urge in me to see how I would get on trying to follow 'the old man'. This is where the question arises as to whether my career was my choice or whether I was inevitably drawn to it, like some long-lost comet always returning to the sun.

Some people believe that life is not about what you want from it, but about what life wants from you. Let's suppose there was some hidden hand nudging me in a certain direction. All I can say is that it did a good job of making me look out of my depth and completely unlikely ever to win a race in any category, let alone become F1 Champion one day. The net result of my racing debut was to show the world that I was hopeless. I did improve over the remaining few races, but the damage was done as far as public perception went. Failure can have two effects: one, you scuttle off, tail between your legs and do something else; or two, you put your foot down and say, 'No. Not having it.' One thing was certain: the baptism of fire had highlighted the need to be sensible and start at the beginning, not halfway up. The car racing crowd is very different from the biking crowd. It is significantly more complex in a social sense. There is more planning, strategising, politics and business when dealing with cars, and the pressure in car racing is considerably higher, as is the negativity. This is partly explained by the sums of money involved, but there is probably something deeper going on; the joy of driving is not felt so much by the people involved. I often think the actual driving art in F1 is forgotten, as though it is incidental to the important business of the sport. If you ride a motorbike on the road, you relate to what the motorcycle racer is actually doing out there on the track. Bikers can empathise with the competitor more readily in motorcycle racing. I sometimes wonder if F1 is not more about lifestyle. Despite these reservations, I resolved that I should see if I could succeed in car racing. Something had annoyed me about not having shown what

I believed was my true potential. It was unfinished business, and I had an itch that needed scratching, but first, I would have to put that dispatch riding knowledge to good use and come up with a sponsor. I might have been changing vehicles, but the rules of engagement were the same as ever: money comes first, then you compete.

Despite all the publicity, I did not find a sponsor to support my car racing for the following season. All the hoo-ha had been for nothing, it seemed. My fallback position was to go back to racing bikes while I worked towards getting sponsorship for car racing: a two-pronged approach. Unfortunately, Mike Agostini had decided not to continue his support, despite the odd flash of promise. Now I had no sponsorship, no bike and no van. It was desperate. On more than one occasion, I found myself wondering whether the last three years had been worth it.

The winter of 1983 was pretty barren. It looked as if all my hopes and opportunities had been used up. I didn't understand how this commercial thing worked at all. I wrote, I phoned, I visited, I talked and sold myself as much as I felt I could – but came up with nothing. In order to keep earning, I returned to dispatch riding for West 1 Couriers. By March it was clear that if I wanted to race anything at all, it would have to be a bike. Because I would be forced to fund everything myself, the programme would have to be limited. I decided to go back to square one and just enter club races. If I couldn't win a club race, then I'd have my answer. I bought my friend Christian's Yamaha TZ 350 and then a cheap Ford Transit van off a guy called Bill 'The Fish' who worked in Wembley market. Because he was a fish merchant, the van was rusting from the inside out. I decided to race only at Brands Hatch, given that it was the closest circuit to home. This would be budget racing. But the stars must have realigned themselves when I wasn't looking, because things were about to get much, much better. There is no shame in going back to the bottom of the class. Many a career has been killed off early

by biting off more than can be chewed. It was a little hum-
bling, but it wasn't as if anyone was watching how I was
doing. In many ways, the pressure was off. I was my own boss,
spending my own money; the master of my own ship.

Early one morning in 1984, I got ready to head off to Brands
for the first race meeting of the season, eager and pumped up
as ever. I told Georgie it was time to get up if she was planning
on coming. She had set the alarm for a later time, but I was
ready to rock and didn't want to hang around, so I pressed
her harder. This she does not like. Actually, she threw the
alarm clock at me when I expressed dissatisfaction with her
lack of urgency, so I stumped off on my own, in a deeply
determined 'bollocks to all of you' mindset. The thing that
had really ruined a lot of my races was the starts, or rather,
the lack of them. I'd done a bit of work on the carburettors
and fitted something called Lectrons. I'd seen them on Kenny
Roberts's bike, and they looked cool. Someone had recommended them as being much better at firing up a dead engine.
They were amazing. All it needed was one 'bump' and the
damn thing lit up like it had an electric starter. I was really
keen to try them out.
    My experience of car racing had taught me that you don't
just turn up on the day to race; you can actually do some
testing. I had been out on the bike, experimenting with different riding styles. I really liked the look of Ron Haslam on a
bike, so copied him, with my head right down on the tank
behind the screen. It felt much better, even if I was on the
lanky side for my bike and struggled to get all of me hidden
behind the fairing. But with this new style, combined with my
almost religious determination not to give up and the feeling
that I had nothing left to lose, plus the extra adrenaline from
the argument with Georgie, I was about to enter a totally new
dimension in my racing career. I did practice and sat alone in
my rusty van contemplating life. The time came to go to the
collecting bay and get ready for my first race. We took our

places on the grid in total silence, as we always did: just the sound of my own panting inside the helmet and the feeling of my thumping heart trying to leave my chest via my mouth as I focused like a hungry panther on the man with the flag.

When the flag dropped, the bike started first time. I whacked the throttle wide open and slipped the clutch to produce maximum acceleration. A beautiful, pure scream from the exhausts that hardly changed pitch indicated I had it exactly right, and I shot into the lead. I can still feel the rush I got from seeing a completely empty track in front of me. Mine! All mine! And I can remember the total focus I had on pushing this thing as fast as I could. I was not going to let this one go; I was in no mood to play games.

I kept my head right down behind the screen and never lifted it up. It stayed right there, over the headstock, my eyes focusing on the invisible line I needed to take to maximise the apex speed. I shifted my weight around on the pegs as skilfully as a gymnast, letting the handlebars float in my hands. I could feel the bike as if it were just a few grams in weight, yet it was as frisky as a frightened racehorse. I rode that bike to the max, like I cared about only one thing in the whole world: winning. It seemed to me that all my questions would be answered and all my hopes for the future depended on this one action, this day, this second. I became wholly and totally invested in riding and I rode like the wind. Lap after lap went by; no one near me. I never allowed myself to look back: I wasn't going to let in any negative thoughts. I literally had a one-track mind. All I thought about was going as fast as I could. Eventually, the man with the flag appeared and dropped it as I flew past. I looked back. There was no one behind me. I was first. I'd actually bloody won something! I'd won! There is only one word that is appropriate at a time like that: *YES!*

'Aha!' I thought. 'So that's how it's done.' The secret had been revealed. All the disappointments were banished from my past. I had the knowledge, and I never, ever forgot what that first win taught me. It's not technique. It's not bravery. It's not hunger or anger. It's gathering up all the energy into one place in your body and directing it towards your one goal. Of course, it helps if you have a blazing row with your girlfriend on the same morning, but something had broken free in me. I had been true to mine own self. If I hadn't gone to Brands that day, I would never have become a F1 World Champion. During that year, 1984, I went on to win every race I entered. I became champion of Brands Hatch. I have only ever won two championships; that and the F1 World Championship, and part of me is just as proud of that little accolade as I am of the more famous one. Georgie must have felt a bit guilty about what happened because she came down on the train. She arrived after my first race win. I suppose I have to thank her for getting me in such a foul mood. Now I bring her tea in bed and let her lie in. She's earned it.

I went on to win the two remaining races that day in similar style. It was only club racing at Brands Hatch, but it was newsworthy enough for Brands to plug my victory in the local newspapers. Naturally, they made the connection with Graham Hill clear to their readers, but that was OK by me: it was all good stuff. I felt vindicated. I *was* vindicated. I was the victor! I could do no wrong in 1984. It was a nice feeling after all the disappointments, and it banished my doubts about myself.

John Webb liked what he saw, and asked if I had a sponsor. In return for a contribution to cover the running costs, the deal would be to carry the Brands Hatch name on my bike. It was a no-brainer. But there was a small issue that arose from being sponsored by the track that I was racing at: because John had taken an interest in my progress, people assumed there was something a bit 'special' about my bike. Even I was beginning to wonder if there was something fishy going on. I was totally unbeatable!

And then, during practice one day, the bike seized up and broke the engine. I was stuffed. I went to find John and tell him that I couldn't race. He was in his favourite spot at the bar in the Kentagon, so named because the restaurant had eight sides and was in Kent. He simply said to the lady behind the bar, 'Give me £100.' She gave him the money, which he handed over to me, saying, 'Get someone else's bike.' I was amazed. First, that he was that keen for me to race; and second, that he thought any right-minded person might give up their racing for a few quid, even though £100 was a lot of money in those days. John added, 'Don't try anything funny!' – meaning, don't try to pocket the cash. That also amazed me, because it never occurred to me to do something like that. I was too honest and too naive. I persuaded a guy to lend me his bike for the next three races – and I won them all. This was incredible. It wasn't the bike. Ergo, it must be me . . .

Later in the season, I entered a national event with big names of the National Championships racing at Brands. It was wet: very wet. It was so wet that the bike was aquaplaning. There was a river running across the bottom of Paddock Hill Bend. The bike squirmed around and the revs climbed as the rear wheel started to act as a very fast paddle. It was an extraordinary experience, requiring a far greater level of concentration than riding in the dry – but I won that too. This was getting serious. I thought I'd better try another track, just in case I had become a circuit specialist, but I won at Snetterton as well, and against different riders. I began to walk a bit taller and believe I had a distillation of something that I could take with me wherever I happened to be racing. It had taken a long time to get there but maybe I was like wine and getting better with age? Maybe time would be my friend, rather than my foe? I certainly hoped so.

The 1984 season was vital for me because it fixed in my mind the experience of being dominant and on top of my game. At least I now knew what it was to go to an event expecting to win. Instead of believing I *could*, if things were right, I knew I *had* already. This should be a transferable skill, should I ever get another crack at car racing. The intangible self-belief was given material form and that, in turn, fuelled more self-belief. Naturally, Georgie was excited and pleased that things were going well. She enjoyed watching her boyfriend flying past on his bike, clearly happy as could be. She was always pretty relaxed about my racing, but we had the benefit of youth and naivety. For my mother it was very different. She was a woman who remained angry and shocked about how her life had changed. I think she was actually very upset with my father for having left her to clear up the mess and raise his children. I'm not sure if she still felt any responsibility for me or not by this stage. On reflection, she may have felt a little left behind when I went to live with Georgie and moved on with my life. Mum was fifty-eight, still looking good, but she had not formed a new life for herself. She had not met anyone else – or even seemed as if she was going to. With me, the only man in the house, having left, and Brigitte living in Hong Kong, Mum's world must have been a little frightening, or at the very least, even more lonely than before.

If my mother came to a race, her competitive spirit sometimes became mixed up with her anger and frustration. She could be very short and quite tactless at times. Many a commentator, journalist and team manager found themselves being ticked off for having the temerity to question my performances. I don't think Mum realised how intimidating she could be.

I'm sure she felt that I would be safer in the cockpit of a racing car rather than astride a bike, but we never really communicated these things in detail. Either she was too distracted, or I was too inarticulate or unable to express my feelings, while trying not to be over-mothered. Throw in a bit of unresolved grief, and it had become something of a powder keg. Sometimes I was concerned that having her around could negatively influence my career; racing people do not enjoy the presence of parents. They can be too emotionally involved, and we don't like too much emotion in motor sport when we are trying to work.

But it must have been difficult for her, having had the best times of her life with her husband and seeing her son going on the same journey, but realising, yet again, that she wouldn't be wanted all the time. It was always difficult to escape the ghost of my father completely, both for me and for my mother. Perhaps that was because we never really wanted to. For Georgie, who hadn't met him, it was different; she could see all this afresh.

The amazing year continued when I pulled a sponsorship deal to enable me to start racing in Formula Ford 1600, the first step to F1 stardom. The compliment slip I picked up from the company at the back of Euston Station finally produced a return. Ricoh Copiers are still the world's number one photocopier company, employing over 100,000 people, but when I came across them, I had never heard the name. Neither, it seemed, had most of Britain. Now they have the Ricoh Arena in Coventry and are a little higher-profile. John Goodwin, the MD of Ricoh, thought I was worth a chance. I owe John an enormous debt of gratitude for sticking his neck out for me.

My winning habit on bikes was indeed transferable and found expression in a few Formula Ford races. I only managed to compete in the last half of the 1984 season, but I was always in the battle for the lead. I made enough of an impression to be awarded a commendation in the end-of-season 'industry' Grovewood Awards for upwardly mobile young drivers. It appeared very much as if I had arrived.

As I write, Max Verstappen has just won his first Grand Prix at the age of eighteen. By modern standards, I was an old man. In fact, by any sporting standard, I was an old man. I was always slightly on the wrong side of the timeline, but I knew certain things would never go against you in this sport. If you were a convincing winner, they'd have you, no matter what. This small crumb of comfort kept my hopes alive – and besides, Hill Snr didn't get his first F1 drive until he was twenty-nine. In my mind, there was still plenty of time . . .

The 1984 season ended with me racing my bike on Saturday, Formula Ford on Sunday and working as a dispatch rider during the week. My life expectancy must have been lower than ever, but with my winnings from the Champion of Brands, which came to £2,000 and hardly covered costs for the year, I took Georgie off to Saint Lucia for our first holiday to be paid for from my winnings as a semi-professional sportsman. The following season, I would make the jump to becoming a full-time professional, factoring into the overall budget a fee to allow me to devote all my time to racing. Finally I didn't have to compromise and spend all week riding around London on my bike in all weathers. This was going to be a better winter than I'd had for a very long time. I was on my way at long last.

12 » BUT IT'S GONNA
TAKE MONEY

If you want a manual on how not to carve a career in motor sport, my story is a good place to start. I had no idea how to do all this stuff: find the money, negotiate, do PR; all of that. What I was good at was the driving and the racing, which I did because I loved it. It gave me a way to express myself. In 1985, my performances on the track and the potential I had shown had convinced Ricoh to give me enough sponsorship for a full season of Formula Ford 1600. This would let me have a crack at winning a national championship, which was essential if I wanted to be taken seriously in motor sport. I would give up the bikes, as well as the day job as a dispatch rider, and go full steam into four wheels. It meant 1985 would be the first year that I would not be racing bikes since I left school, five and a half seasons before, which was ironic because I had just started to get the knack of bike racing. But even I could see that it would only be a matter of time before something nasty happened.

During my quest for sponsorship in 1984, I had roped in Leisure 10/12, an artist management company in the music business. The company operated from Curtain Road near Hoxton Square and was owned by Richard Boote and Kasper de Graaf; two entrepreneurs with absolutely no experience of motor sport. This suited me fine as I had decided that I didn't like the very corporate and more typical IMG approach, and they weren't interested in me in any case. I didn't want to become just another well-drilled driver spouting all the carefully calculated but boring sponsor spiel. I had a better idea, or so I thought. Having seen motor sport as an expression of free spirit, or even slightly anti-establishment, I thought that the music business, where image is almost everything, would be a good way of conveying an alternative kind of personality to the one ordinarily associated with motor racing. I may have had the right basic idea but it makes me cringe to think how misguided I was. At the time, however, I had no inside track on the sport, nor did I trust anyone. Any new culture is difficult to break into, but motor sport was especially hard given the hierarchy and the long-standing codes between team and sponsors, and everything was alien to me. I was so out of my depth that I found even *Autosport* impenetrable to read.

You could be forgiven for thinking that succeeding in our business is a simple matter of being the fastest, but to show you are the fastest, first you have to find money to get in a car. In the mid 1980s, most of F1's money came from cigarette sponsorship, as smoking was seen as an expression of liberty: the right to do what one wanted to with one's life. James Hunt was a prime example of a driver with this type of sponsorship, and F1 wanted more characters like him. The sponsors had become hugely powerful, and as a result, drivers had become so desperate to get a drive that they would do anything a sponsor wished. I found this an affront to my romantic idea of a racing driver being someone who did not kowtow to anyone: someone like my dad. F1 drivers of his era were a fairly wild and unruly bunch, which, in my naivety, I felt was an appealing model to follow. Sir Jackie Stewart was the exception and he knew which side of the bread was buttered, realising early on the importance of giving yourself the right image. After fifty years in the sport he is still an ambassador for top brands such as Moët and Rolex, and a very wealthy man. But I wanted to be 'different' and to have a certain style. It took me a while to realise that the key to style is to be a winner. In the absence of a free-spirited sponsor, and as desperate as the next person to get a ride, I was very happy to promote probably the least glamorous product made by man: the photocopier, but it got me a foothold in the game.

Unlike a lot of other drivers I didn't have a manager or adult mentor to guide me but Sheridan Coakley, Fay's son, had a shop right opposite the offices of Leisure 10/12. Sheridan is ten years older than me and like the elder brother I never had. I went to him for advice on almost everything. When I wasn't testing or racing, my life revolved around Leisure 10/12 and Curtain Road, where I spent most of my free time as they had a desk and a phone I could use. They also drew up the contract with Ricoh for me, and were instrumental in getting me to the next level of the sport, Formula 3, which would require raising the terrifying sum of £150,000. In my quest for sponsorship, I would arrive from Wandsworth every morning, sit at the desk and go through *Yellow Pages*, noting on an A4 pad who to call back in a couple of weeks 'when they were looking at budgets'. I used to spend the day making phone calls to marketing directors responsible for anything from antiseptic hand wipes to oil companies and camera brands. This is just the sort of area where Dad would have been able to give me some good advice as, to start with, my cold-calling consisted of little more than asking for a donation to my career in return for 'exposure'. I never had the confidence, as others had done, to say: 'One day I'm going to be F1 World Champion and you'll be sorry you missed this chance,' even though I was convinced that I had what it took. As a result, most of my conversations ended with a 'thanks, but no thanks'.

The 1985 season was another step in the right direction. I did about forty races within the Townsend-Thoresen RAC British Championship and the P&O Ferries Championship. Along with my extensive racing programme and all the testing I had to do as well, I was giving myself the best possible chance of catching up with the guys who had been racing since childhood: people like Johnny Herbert, Mark Blundell and Bertrand Gachot. Gachot was a Marlboro-sponsored driver, which meant he was regarded as future F1 material, but he had a pivotal, if unwitting, role in getting Michael Schumacher his first F1 drive in the Jordan at Spa in 1991. Gachot was a fiery individual with an almost insane lack of fear for himself and regard for the safety of his fellow competitors, which almost had dire consequences when he nearly ran Blundell into a marshals' post at 120mph on the Castle Combe circuit in Wiltshire. Around the same time, Marlboro commissioned James Hunt, of all people, to mentor their drivers, and he decided to get a report done on them all, including Gachot, over whom concerns were growing because of his temper. The story goes that the sports psychologist regarded Bertrand as a bit too impulsive and too sensitive to criticism. When James told him the result of the report, Gachot reacted furiously and lost his temper, proving their point. His impetuosity got the better of him when, in a traffic incident in London, he used a mace spray on a taxi driver and was sent to Wandsworth prison – thus leaving his Jordan seat open for Michael.

Throughout the 1985 season, I won six races or more and battled against these desperadoes week after week, making a name for myself as a competitor. David Tremayne, a future F1 journalist, was a junior at the time and remembers my performances, saying I developed a 'reputation for speed and boldness that occasionally bordered on the reckless'. I finished the season third in one championship, pipping the cheeky, diminutive Johnny Herbert at a Silverstone race in the fashion of my father against Jim Clark in the 1962 Daily Express International Trophy at the same circuit. Dad had actually passed Clark on the line – while going sideways. Johnny passed me on the line but, on this occasion, the timing beam was before it, so I won by one-hundredth of a second. At the end-of-season Formula Ford Festival, Herbert thrashed all of us in spectacular style. He'd come from last place after crashing in qualifying, leapfrogging us in the heats and eventually recording one of the most amazing feats in the history of the

Festival. I was the bronze medallist. Johnny was probably the most talented English driver since Stirling Moss, who also never won a world championship. Like Moss, Johnny had his meteoric career tragically derailed by a serious accident when he nearly lost both feet in a massive Formula 3000 crash just as he was on the verge of breaking into F1. Although he would go on to win three Grands Prix, he always had a disadvantage because his feet were so badly damaged – that and having Michael Schumacher as a teammate.

Despite the success of the 1985 season, I had not managed to secure a sponsor to help my move up to Formula 3 for 1986, which was frustrating, because I clearly had the ability to do well. I had impressed in an F3 test with Eddie Jordan's team, for which Eddie charged me the very reasonable sum of £2,000 for twenty laps. Along with my good results in FF1600, the F3 test was good enough to earn a chance to race for West Surrey Racing, which was the top F3 team of the time, and the same team that won the 1983 F3 Championship with Ayrton Senna. That connection gave West Surrey Racing a mystique that no other team had. If I was to race with them, I would have to be the second driver to Bertrand Fabi, a Canadian fresh from winning the FF2000 Championship and a favourite to take the F3 title. That was fine by me and it meant that I could spend a year learning the ropes and then win the championship in 1987. All I needed was £150,000.

The sponsor-hunting mission had so far raised precisely nothing. Undaunted, I tried some desperate methods. First, I went to my grandmother and asked if she would sell her house. 'I can't do that, dear. It's my house. Where would I live?' I didn't have an answer to that. Working my way down the Hill family tree, I went to my mother to see if she would countenance taking a big risk with the family finances, such as they were. There had been some money painstakingly salvaged from my father's estate, but this was all we had left to live on; it would have to last my mother the rest of her life. But when you are young and crazed with ambition, you have no concept of what it is to be middle-aged with no job prospects. It would be wrong to say I didn't care, but at the time all I could think about was how to get the ride I needed to catapult me into the big time. There was also another influence on my thinking. I had read Niki Lauda's book *To Hell and Back* in which Lauda explained the logic behind him borrowing money to race in the junior formulae: if you want to race, he reasoned, you have to believe you will win. And if you believe you will win, there is no risk to borrowing the money – this is the classic mindset of a true winner. So, it was OK to borrow to race *provided* you were a committed racing driver, and only the faint-hearted did not borrow money. By this logic, I would have been bottling out if I didn't expose myself to a huge debt, and I convinced myself that borrowing was almost a guarantee of success in and of itself. Now all I had to do was convince the accountants and my family, and the Hill family survival fund would put up half the money. Then I just had to find the other half.

I reached the deadline set by West Surrey Racing without the rest of the money having been found and, morose at the thought of failure, Georgie and I went out for the evening, thinking it was game over. But when we returned, the phone rang and Georgie answered it to hear a softly spoken man with a Liverpudlian accent say, 'Hi. It's George Harrison here. Am I too late?' This was a bit of a surprise, as you might expect, but not a total surprise, because George had been into motor sport since he was a small boy in Liverpool at a time when the British Grand Prix took place at Aintree. As a boy he would have seen Moss, Fangio, Hawthorn and all the great drivers of the day. I think he secretly hankered after being a racing driver, and he loved to mix with motor sport stars. He had known my father and was often with Jackie Stewart and Gerhard Berger at F1 races, and I had written to see if he would take an interest in my highly speculative career. By his nature, he was very welcoming to people he felt right with, but being a Beatle he had developed a highly attuned antenna for detecting whether people were, in Beatle-speak, 'cool'. I must have passed muster, because he looked kindly upon me and arranged to meet so I could tell him my sad story, and he and his wife Olivia agreed to help with part of the budget. Much later, after finally making some money from racing, I offered to pay it back, which they refused point blank. Over time I came to see them almost as surrogate parents. To know that they wanted to help for no material gain for themselves was like a blessing, and I also took their support as a show of faith in me as a person. It restored much of my belief in the better side of human nature, notably absent immediately after my father's accident. The Harrisons even commissioned some Krishna monks to chant for me when I was going for the Championship. Their philosophy influenced how I wanted to approach my career at a later stage, when the chips were down and I had some powerful options open to me.

I had the money I needed just in time for the start of the 1986 season and I was with West Surrey Racing, the best team around. It should have been perfect, but things got off to a dreadful and tragic start when we went to Goodwood for a pre-season test on a freezing cold February day. It was not the best weather for testing, but we would probably have to race in similar conditions early in the season, so no one thought much of it. I didn't care, as I was just thrilled to be part of the team, albeit in the number two role. Bertrand Fabi, the number one driver – who was so good that Dick Bennetts, the owner and team principal, later likened him to Senna – would be my benchmark. I would never have the chance to compare. Late in the afternoon, just as we were about to pack up after several hours of testing, the track went eerily silent. Bertrand, who was still out on the track, had gone almost straight on at top speed into the frozen earth bank at the first corner. The cars in those days were made of aluminium honeycomb, but they might as well have been made of aluminium foil. We went to see what had happened and Bert was in a dreadful state, semi-conscious and groaning as if he was dreaming. There was little we could do. I gave him my coat, but he was beyond help.

Probably because I was so obsessed with my career and could not devote enough time and thought to Georgie, we had split up earlier that winter. I'd gone off to live with a friend in a bachelor pad in Wandsworth. It must have been a sign of how close we still were that I called Georgie up, and she came over. I'm sure the emotional stresses of sport, especially dangerous ones, mean that relationships become deeper despite the superficial frictions. It gave me an insight into what my parents must have endured and how they were able to stay close despite the obstacles that my father's life threw in the way. But if we thought this was hard, we had no inkling yet of how much harder it can be. The trauma of the crash affected Dick Bennetts so badly that he decided he couldn't carry on with the team in F3. This was the closest I had come to seeing death on the track and, inevitably, I asked myself the same questions everyone did: why did we do it and was it right to continue. Sadly, there would be more occasions when I would have to ask myself whether it was morally excusable to carry on. The toughest test within motor sport is as much about whether one can cope with the emotional punishment of seeing others being hurt and killed, as about dealing with the fear of physical damage to oneself. Big boys don't cry, I told myself, and after some serious soul-searching, and reminding myself that my father had coped with all this, I looked to place my budget with another team, Murray Taylor Racing (MTR).

Since the arrival in Europe of Bruce McLaren, Denny Hulme and Chris Amon, there had been a steady stream of New Zealanders embarking on the long trip in the hope of making their own name in motor sport. Dick Bennetts and Murray Taylor were of that Kiwi tribe and I would have some good times with MTR thanks to respectable results, as well as learning a

huge amount about the methods of a bigger, more professional team. Murray set me up with an engineer called Kevin
Corin who was great for me and kept things fun. He would
make any change I wanted to the car and then simply say,
'Yep! Give it 'eaps!' After all the grimness, this was how I
wanted it to be: fun, positive, an adventure.

From the position I was in now in my career, the road map
to F1, where every driver wanted to be, was very straightforward: you had to win in British F3. It was as simple as that.
As a result, the F3 championship was always chock-a-block
with the best talent around, which meant I was getting properly tested. Martin Donnelly and Julian Bailey, both of whom
made it to F1, were there, and also the by-now-obligatory
Brazilian hotshot. Ours was Maurizio Sandro Sala. The 1985
season was dominated by Britain's Andy Wallace, who went
on to success in endurance racing with Jaguar. My highlight
of the year was when I outqualified him for a race at Silverstone and got pole position, which caught Andy by surprise as
he had dominated all season. On the day it poured with rain,
and because we hadn't raised the ride heights the car hit a
puddle and I was off, straight into the barrier. That aside, there
would be some great races, such as at Zandvoort in Holland,
where I was at the front of the pack, for a while at least,
although frustratingly I was, as yet, unable to finish the job.

Midway through the season, with the title race heating up, I
was racing Perry McCarthy (who would later become the
first-ever Stig on *Top Gear*) at Silverstone for sixth place and
the last point. I slipstreamed him on the Club Straight. Then
we were alongside, with me ever so slightly creeping past –
and he waved at me. Right, I thought, let's see how he can
drive one-handed. So I jinked towards him and he was so
startled that he overreacted, swerved and got his car stuck half
on and half off the track. It was just enough for me to pass
him and get the point. He could have been very angry with
me, but we laughed about it afterwards, at least I did. At the

end of the season, I was invited to race in the Macau Grand Prix. The trip was a big adventure as well as a chance to catch up with my sister Brigitte in Hong Kong, who I had not seen for years. The track was a challenging street circuit made up of two distinct sections. The top half followed the cliff line above the seafront of the Portuguese Protectorate (until developers eventually filled in the sea to make a harbour area). It was thrillingly twisty and hilly, whereas the lower part of the course was flat and fast. Our F3 cars would reach 160mph, the highest speed of any track we had raced on, and the exhilaration of pushing the car to its limits was intense. Ayrton Senna had won the Macau GP before going to F1, so it was a massively significant event. Alas, I picked up a puncture, probably from touching a wall, and parked the car against the wall at the next corner. Even though I crashed out, which is not untypical on that track thanks to there being absolutely no run-off area, it was another lesson learned.

One of the many mistakes I made early in my career was to have jumped over Formula Ford 2000, the stage between FF1600 and F3, unlike the flying Ulsterman, Martin Donnelly. Not having had any karting experience, my race craft was lacking. Martin had been racing since his teens in FF1600, but I was already twenty-five when I started in F3 and I needed to push on. There is a part of every racing driver's brain that says 'you are an exception' and, if all had gone well in 1986, I could have leapt from F3 into F1, just as Senna had done and Jenson Button was later to do. But I didn't dominate as they had, and by the end of the season the decade of racing driving that I lacked was really starting to show.

There was another financial problem hampering progress. I had envisaged being able to sell the empty space on the car to sponsors but, despite all my phone calls, I had found absolutely nothing. This meant I couldn't offset any of the £120,000 debt or have an income. I was broke, in debt and single. At one point, I had no money to get to a race in

Belgium. Out of desperation, I had been signing on to get enough to pay my rent, but the money had not come through. I made a vow to myself that I would never borrow any more money. I had learned another lesson the hard way.

When it came to race day, in order that the car should not look blank, giving the impression I was an unwanted driver, Leisure 10/12 created a distinctive livery: a fluorescent orange camouflage. With this design, there was no way I was going to disappear into the background. It certainly helped me get noticed, but it didn't help bring in any money. Fortunately, however, James Hunt's younger brother, David, had done an amazing deal with Cellnet, a division of BT and a new company that provided the infrastructure for the nascent mobile phone they were developing. David, hoping to follow in his brother's footsteps, had created this deal for himself, but he was beginning to realise that he didn't have the right stuff as far as driving went, so he decided to think bigger instead. For the 1987 season, Cellnet were going to sponsor a two-car team with all guns blazing on the competition and promotional side. Through David, they asked me to drive for them. Jim Wright, who had been with Eddie Jordan, was responsible for managing the whole operation and he played a key part in convincing them to put me in. They may have wanted me in the team because of my extra media value, but I flattered myself that they also wanted me because I could drive. I would be teamed up with Martin Donnelly, who, no doubt, was seen as the more likely front runner. The deal was a lifesaver and I was back in the game with the best-funded F3 team ever. Now I stood a chance of being able to pay off the debts, even if I wouldn't be able to write out a cheque for the full amount just yet.

I have gone on record as saying that Martin was the hardest teammate I ever had, with the emphasis on the word 'hard'. But if you consider where he grew up, it's hardly surprising. His parents sent him at the age of twelve to a boarding school run by priests in the Republic of Ireland to get him away from the Troubles in his native Belfast. When his mother visited him one Sunday during the first term, he told her how homesick he was. She said, 'Give it three years, and if you still feel like that, we'll pull you out.' Martin was not about to give me any quarter and, in doing so, he raised my game. I knew I had to beat him, or I would be a washed-up number two, which is as good as totally washed-up in our sport. Throughout the season we slogged it out, both aiming to be the best driver: not just in the team, but the best overall. We both knew what was at stake for the winner and the loser, but there was never any animosity; it was just frustrating how good he was. Sometimes it boiled over on the track, and when we let our rivalry get out of control at the 'Cellnet Super Prix' at Knockhill in Scotland, we were both given a dressing-down by Peter Waller, the Cellnet marketing director. I had refused to back off going into the first corner, as had Martin. I went off rather appropriately into 'Duffer's Dip' and nearly took him with me. Peter thought the racing programme was all about selling the network. For Martin and me, it was about career life or death, regardless of our friendship.

I tried to avoid bad blood with my teammates, feeling that as racing drivers we had more in common than we had differences. My attitude was influenced very much by my father's reputation as being a hard but fair man, both on the track and off it. The context for my rivalry with Martin was established by watching the tension that built between Nigel Mansell and Nelson Piquet throughout the mid-1980s, since young drivers tend to look up to and take their lead from what is going on in F1. The relationship between the Williams teammates was not exactly a love-in, and took a turn for the worse when Piquet publicly insulted Nigel's wife and then called him an 'uneducated blockhead'.

The animosity between drivers had slowly been escalating since the end of my father's era. Alan Jones had no love for Carlos Reutemann when they were together at Williams in the early 1980s. When asked if he wanted to bury the hatchet after their last race together, Alan reputedly replied, 'Yeah. In his back!' But bitterness took on another dimension when Didier Pironi and Gilles Villeneuve fell out after a disagreement over team instructions when racing for Ferrari at Imola in 1982. 'I'll never speak to him again,' Villeneuve fumed. Gilles died in qualifying for the next race: some say because he was still furious about Pironi. However, nothing compared to what was to come in the conflict between Ayrton Senna and Alain Prost.

The rivalries aside, the emergence of Nigel Mansell was also an inspiration. Towards the end of 1985, I had stood at the approach to Paddock Hill Bend, Brands Hatch, watching him hammer past at 186mph, lap after lap, willing him to score his emotional first-ever Grand Prix win. I also witnessed another a poignant victory at the same circuit for both Nigel and Williams in the 1986 British Grand Prix, the first race Frank Williams had been able to visit since becoming a quadriplegic in a road accident the previous March.

Nigel's breakthrough – maybe even more than my father's achievements – had given me hope that I could do something similar. Nigel was part of the same generation as me, while my father's career seemed aeons before. Nigel was also coming good at age thirty-three, and would win the World Championship aged thirty-nine and the IndyCar title a year later. As sporting moments go, Nigel should have a whole chapter to himself, because he was fantastically entertaining. In November 1986, we stayed up late and had a party while willing him to close his first World Championship in Adelaide. We watched dumbfounded as a rear tyre exploded at 200mph. Only Nigel could create such extreme drama. 'Colossally! That's Mansell!' screamed Murray Walker. We stared at the television screen with our mouths open, not quite able to comprehend that Nigel was out of the race when only moments before he had looked certain to become World Champion.

Impressed as I was by F1, by mid 1986 there was something

within convincing me I could emulate those F1 heroes. Much as I admired them, I was beginning to unravel the mystique of it all by starting to relate to what they were up to. In my mind, I was already racing an F1 car. All I had to do was get through this mid-career phase of proving myself to be a winner in F3 and then find £350,000 for Formula 3000, the last level before F1. Simple.

My breakthrough with Cellnet in 1987 came when I won the two prestigious international events at Spa-Francorchamps in Belgium and Zandvoort in Holland. David Hunt had cleverly created an exclusive deal for F3 drivers whereby we were given grey 'yuppie brick' mobile phones, free calls to anywhere in the world, plus £5,000. The free phone calls came in handy for sponsor-hunting, even if I did get cut off after about five minutes – unless they had actually hung up? Returning with friends on the M4 from a biking weekend in Wales, I was giving a lift to a guy from New Zealand. He was impressed by the phone, and I told him he could use it for free to call home. He looked at his watch – it was about 3 a.m. in New Zealand – and he thought, 'What the hell.' His mum answered, obviously delighted to finally hear from her long-lost son despite being dragged from her slumbers. 'Hey, Mum, I'm on the motorway talking on a mobile phone!' he proudly boasted. 'Oh, really? What's a motorway, son?' Obviously, the mobile phone was not even dreamt of in most people's minds at the time.

On another occasion, the marketing director organised for a conference call to be made to the racing car from the boardroom as the car was going round a track. These are just some of the daft stunts you get up to in the quest for 'the Budget'. It was snowing but, at the appointed time, I was sent into the blizzard with the F3 car on three wet tyres and a dry-weather slick. I had to cruise round and wait for the phone to ring in my helmet and then say, 'Hello. I'm driving a racing car.' Halfway through the call we lost contact, but despite the questionable success of the demonstration the Cellnet board agreed to sponsor the team for another year, by which time I would be twenty-eight. 1988 was looking like my last chance to have a crack at getting into F1. I was already well behind the curve. By then Martin Donnelly had already won the Macau Grand Prix and Johnny Herbert had thrashed us all in the F3 Championship – and they were both four years younger than me. By the start of the new season in 1988, Herbert was F1-bound after being spotted by the Benetton F1 team and Eddie Jordan, who signed him up to drive the Camel Reynard Jordan F3000 car. Johnny won his first race and confirmed his potential yet again, cementing his reputation as Britain's next great F1 hope, but it was short-lived. At the start of the new season he tangled with Gregor Foitek, an overambitious Swiss driver, in a Formula 3000 race at Brands Hatch. Johnny's feet were so badly damaged in the crash that a marshal who rushed to his aid fainted in front of him, and later Johnny would say that he knew it must be bad from that reaction. But he had survived, and they fought to save his feet. As Johnny described it, his contract with the Benetton F1 team was literally hanging by a thread – by which he meant 'tendon'. He would take all year to recover, although his feet would cause him pain for the rest of his life. Amazingly, he somehow took his place in the first Grand Prix of 1989 and finished an emotional fourth.

The accident triggered a chain of events that is sadly all too typical in our sport: the rush to take the seat vacated by the hospitalised Herbert. But even before Herbert's accident I had already been knocking on Eddie's door for an F3000 drive. Not long before Johnny's accident Eddie Jordan had wanted to replace his teammate, Thomas Danielsson: a quick but crash-prone Swedish driver. Thomas unfortunately had a problem with his eyes and the word was out that he was going to lose his seat. I knew Thomas well, having raced against him in F3, but this was motor racing and you don't feel too sorry for the other guy. So when the seat became available I thought I had a genuine chance to get the drive and I phoned Eddie who suggested I flew to Enna in Sicily with my helmet and overalls. But at the last minute, he gave the drive to Alessandro Santin, an Italian driver who, I strongly suspect, had one key quality I didn't have – money.

Originally, Eddie thought the Cellnet money would come with me if I raced his car, but I had never considered this and certainly had not mentioned it to Cellnet. I was contracted to them for F3; that was the priority. EJ knows some fundamental truths about motor sport. Number one: you need 'da money!', as he is keen to express it. Number two: you need a quick driver. But in this case, nationality was a third reason and one that is a huge factor in any sport. Being Irish, what else could Eddie do but sign Martin? In fairness, Martin had shown better form by winning Macau in fine style, but, in discussions with EJ, he kindly said, of the F3 drivers at the time, he placed me in the same bracket as Martin and Johnny, but clearly not enough to overcome the pull to help a driver from his homeland. Martin jumped at EJ's offer to leave F3 and race the F3000 car, even if this would upset Cellnet. Johnny recovered from his dreadful injuries enough to take up his drive in F1 and Martin would be picked up by Lotus, leaving me to lick my wounds in F3. It was only when I watched first Johnny and then Martin come as close to being killed as is possible, during qualifying for the Spanish Grand Prix in 1990, that I thought that I might have been lucky to have missed the boat this time.

Stuck in F3, while my friends and rivals had made the leap to F1, I finished third in the championship and won a spectacular wet race at Thruxton when the heavens opened at the start and then the sun came out. I made a perfect getaway from pole to leave the rest of the field lost in a massive plume of white spray. I think it was one of my best drives: very similar to the Brazilian Grand Prix in 1996. I also won the F3 support race to the British Grand Prix, but it wasn't enough to satisfy my growing desire to race at the highest level. If there was to

be any consolation, I at least knew how I compared to Donnelly. He was very fast, but I had beaten him regularly enough
and he'd raised my game enormously. I watched his F3000
progress keenly, using him as my yardstick. The better he did,
the more I thought I could do the same. He more or less
matched Herbert's performance on his F3000 debut, winning
twice and being signed up to drive for Lotus in F1, so I figured
all I needed was one more chance. To get that, I had to find
the £350,000 – give or take – necessary to do F3000, but at
that point I had no money and no drives in the offing for
1989. My last race in F3 was the Cellnet Super Prix at Brands
Hatch. The race itself was a disaster, but that's not why I was
in tears during the slowdown lap. I cried because I thought
I might never do this again.

The Brands Hatch Grand Prix circuit was a beautiful work
of art flowing like an asphalt river through the Kent countryside. To hang onto the kerb on the inside of Paddock Hill Bend
as you drop down towards the spot where, a only few years
before, I sat helpless and terrified while looking up at fellow
Formula Ford hopefuls hammering down on me; to accelerate
out of Druids and plunge through Graham Hill Bend, along
the short Cooper Straight before nailing it round the outer
kerb of Surtees; to catapult up the hill and onto the back
straight, reaching top speed as you plunge down Pilgrims
Drop (where Johnny had almost died) then rise back up
through the magnificent almost flat-out sweeping curve called
Hawthorns, before exiting like a bullet along a short wooded
straight to then lightly drift past Westfield (where Jo Siffert
had been killed) and down into Dingle Dell before swooping
like a swallow up towards the blind flick at Dingle Dell itself
where there the car slingshots into the banked (and ever so
lovely) Stirling's Bend; to then emerge in a rush onto the stage
of the magnificent natural amphitheatre of Brands Hatch,
floating round Clearways to the finish line; to think that I
might never do that again was unbearable! I loved it so much.
But however bleak the future looked, 1989 would eventually

mark the turning point in my life: the point where things started to fall into place and doors opened instead of closing. But first my career was about to take another cathartic plunge into the void, but from this void I would emerge a much better and more rounded person: a more formidable competitor, as if to prove the adage, 'What doesn't kill you, makes you stronger'. Which is just as well, because I would need all the toughness I could muster for the battles ahead.

13 » DOWN'S UP SIDE

There is such a thing as a happy accident. One evening late in 1986, I went to a restaurant in the King's Road with Mark Leveson, who owned the flat in which I was renting a room, and I spotted Georgie across the room having a drink with her girlfriends. Something in me went 'pang'. It was an awkward moment. Should I say hello? How do you remeet someone you've split up with? Say, 'Hi! Remember me?' Evidently Georgie saw me too, but apparently I was shaking my head, which she interpreted to mean, 'Oh, no. Not her.' But disaster was averted by another twist. A few weeks later Georgie's best friend, Hannah, was having a party and thinking about who to invite. To tease Georgie, she pretended to dial my number, but the call connected and I picked up too quickly for her. I must have been sitting on the phone, for some reason. Not able to think of an excuse fast enough, Hannah carried on and invited me to the party – much to Georgie's dismay. And that was that.

Georgie had got on with her own life after we split up earlier that year. Putting her degree in fashion from Kingston to good use in the rag trade, she was working for Inchcape. Life without her had not quite been what I had expected. I never really found anyone else who had the same empathy as her, and I had little to offer. I was probably quite a confusing person for many people to understand. Here I was, a twenty-seven-year-old doing a strange job, the son of a deceased famous racing driver; ex-dispatch-riding ex-motorcycle racer; apparently with no other plan for life and totally obsessed with getting to the top in a sport that looked crazy from the outside. I think this might have frightened off possible life partners. There is no doubt that I had also missed out on learning the normal social skills that come with working in groups. A racing team at that time was nearly all male, and I was the driver and before that a one-man bike team, so even though I loved it, my life was pretty lonely. When most of my friends were getting on with careers that could last them a lifetime, I was looking at arriving late into one that would eject me for being too old by the time I was forty – only twelve years away.

Georgie looked very attractive to me in her new guise as a young executive in the clothes design and manufacturing industry. Her job was to negotiate with factories and suppliers and to choose designs: a role that required her to travel to places like Hong Kong, where she had lived for a while when her father was in the army, and Korea. Her role may have been quite intense but Georgie is a match for any man and can hold her own in a negotiation. Maybe this was another reason why I was attracted to her. I think I was intimidated by certain men, powerful men; men who might have reminded me of my father. Georgie was not daunted by them in the least. Perhaps I thought she could teach me a trick or two. We had gradually begun to see each other more regularly, but continued to live apart, and she started to come to a few races, including one in August 1987 when I had a meltdown in a Zandvoort hotel room after Martin Donnelly had been faster in qualifying. 'It's over!' I ranted. 'You can't ever be outqualified by your team-mate! I'm finished!' Such is the fragile state of mind of the madly competitive, but it is part of the psyching-up process; hugely exhausting and stressful. However unprofessional it might have looked, it worked for me because I won the race the next day.

Before the 1988 season got under way, I had my first-ever F1 test at Paul Ricard, which was the same circuit my father had set off from on that fateful November day in 1975. I must have been in a reflective mood because, while waiting for my big chance, I picked up a quartz stone, thinking it was rather beautiful and that I would turn it into jewellery for Georgie. I believe that was the moment when I decided I should ask her to marry me and start a family together.

The test was an eye-opener and I had bought some Gary Lineker shin pads because I had been warned that the steering rack went across the top of the driver's legs. I would only be allowed twenty laps in a Benetton Ford B187 with the turbo-boost turned down to 2.7bar to simulate the power of the coming 3.5-litre normally aspirated engines. Even so, the thing took off like a rocket and I had trouble keeping up with the manual gear changes. I absolutely loved it, but the grip was staggering. After about fifteen laps, my neck gave up and I knew I was finished. I felt I had done a good enough job but realised I would need to toughen up if I were to be ready for F1. Both shins had massive bruises for about a week – Lineker had obviously not intended shin pads to be put to this use. But it was another reminder that to have any chance in F1, you needed to be extraordinarily fit, as I was to learn in the F1 tests at the end-of-season races. The cars were more powerful than anything I had driven before, and their grip on the road was ferocious. The races were longer too, and the thought of driving one of these things around undulating and bumpy circuits such as Interlagos or Suzuka was beyond anything I could imagine. I vowed never to get in an F1 car unless I could wring its neck for an entire Grand Prix, so I joined a gym and began to punish my cardiovascular system. To strengthen my neck, I bolted weights to the sides of an old crash helmet and I would do neck exercises while lying on the floor watching television, with Georgie looking on in bemusement.

In 1988, a few years after my grandmother had died, the house I had asked her to sell to pay for my career was sold and the money distributed between her grandchildren. Georgie was now pregnant with our first child so I put a deposit down on a house and told Georgie we were going to move in together and start a real life. Along came the mortgage, the marriage and the pregnancy all at once, just in time for my career to come to a grinding halt. Adding salt to the wound, this was at the start of the property boom in the UK. Prices may have been going up weekly but lending seemed a just about manageable 8 per cent. We found a sweet little Victorian terraced property in Wandsworth. But almost the moment I bought the house, interest rates rocketed to 17.5 per cent. Then the front of the house started to separate from the back, evidenced by a hairline crack that ran right down the middle of the house. Every night I'd climb the stairs to bed and see it had grown microscopically until it was about 1 centimetre; just wide enough to smell the cooking from next door. The insurance company's loss adjuster came round and tried to pretend it wasn't there, as if I was really pushing to have the house underpinned.

There is never a 'right time' to have children, but this was the most inspired decision of my life, even if I was not conscious of the reasons why that might be. I'm sure I was following my instincts. Georgie would be the right person to start a family with, I was certain of that. Inevitably, I was mindful of my own experience growing up with a racing driver father, and I didn't want to have children when I was too old to enjoy doing things with them. I may not have wanted to be as absent for my children as my father had been, but the way things were going, there was a good chance I would be around all the time. That said, having a family and being a racing driver is a controversial combination. Enzo Ferrari claimed that a family man was a second a lap slower than a single man. That may be so, but a look at past World Champions might indicate that one more reason to survive may actually be the making of the man. After all, as Sir Jackie Stewart often repeats: 'To finish first, first you have to finish.' Maturity, perhaps more than fearlessness, makes a good F1 driver.

We settled into the new house in Wandsworth, painted the interior sky blue, pulled up the carpet and sanded the floorboards for that 'natural' look which left you with splinters and tumbleweeds of dust that came through the cracks in the floor. Domesticity took priority as I was now a freelance racing driver with no work on the horizon, a mortgage, a baby on the way and subsidence. If all else failed, I would have to go back to dispatch riding. A friend advised me to think about getting a proper job. No doubt he meant well, but I took a different view. For as long as I was alive and kicking, I'd never give up.

On 4 March, Oliver marched forth into our world. I'd driven Georgie to the hospital in Hammersmith, a short enough journey – if you're not in labour, and your husband doesn't have to fill up with petrol on the way, which did not impress her much. The birth experience was something of a brutal awakening for me. I was there throughout, which put me one up on my father, and I think Georgie appreciated it, even if it was only to have someone to yell abuse at. The little chap was taken away, washed and weighed. I had an inkling that something was going on, but left the hospital thrilled at the idea of being a dad and didn't think too much about it. I'd come back the next day and collect Georgie and this new person in our life.

When I arrived at the hospital the following day, Georgie was in a secluded bed and clearly distressed. Georgie and I knew nothing about Down's Syndrome when Oliver was born, nor that it was named after the Victorian doctor Langdon Down, who identified the obvious genetic differences such as the single transverse palmar crease, poor muscle tone and excess skin on the nape of the neck, and set up a home to provide for the Down's children of Victorian society. In 1965, the World Health Organization recognised Dr Langdon Down as being the first to clearly identify the syndrome; thus 'Down's Syndrome'. Later research showed that it was caused by having forty-seven rather than forty-six chromosomes. Dr Down was a very well-intentioned and highly respected doctor who made the life of his Down's Syndrome people as comfortable and fulfilling as it could be, paying particular attention to their typical love of music and drama.

'They think there's something wrong with him,' Georgie sobbed, but the moment I saw Oliver, I connected with him and his plight as a helpless baby. He needed us. No one else would do, so, to my mind, whatever the doctor had to tell us didn't really make any difference. We were told they had to do tests before they could be sure, although it was clear that they knew exactly what it was. The disappointment was that they behaved like it was a tragedy. Here was Oliver, a new arrival to the world. Either we gave him the best reception we could, or we didn't. Thankfully, we had some good friends who supported us and our new arrival. Very rapidly, we were put in touch with the Down's Syndrome Association and they have been there for us the whole way through. Now, 27 years later, Georgie is the chairwoman of the DSA, and Oliver is in supported living near us and couldn't be happier. The doctor's prognosis was that he might be able to recognise his immediate family and perform menial jobs in later life. Frankly, I reckon Oliver could do a better job than them. At least he's got a sense of humour. For his twenty-fifth birthday, he made a guest list of about 150 people, only a small handful of whom were family.

At first, being a new father was fun and easy, and required little more than wrapping Oliver up and carrying him around wherever we went, and between sleeping and eating there wasn't much to it. The trouble would only start once he was able to move around under his own propulsion, but in 1989 that was a little way off. The problem would be progressing from unemployed twenty-eight-year-old racing driver with a wife, new baby and a rapidly inflating mortgage (to add to the debt incurred to race in 1986), to a seat in F1 where I could win some races. I had to reset the approach and resolved that I would drive anything I could get my hands on, but on the understanding that I would get paid instead of trying to bring money. This reverse logic had a quite extraordinary and unexpected effect. Perhaps if I had applied it earlier, I would already have been in F1. Why didn't I think of it before? Instead of begging sponsors for money, I kept my ear to the ground for any kind of possible drive. I drove a front-wheel-drive Turbo Saab saloon car as a guest in the Saab Championship, which, mysteriously, I won; shared a 500bhp Ford Sierra Cosworth Turbo with Sean Walker in a two-driver round of the British Touring Car Championship; and took part in the Le Mans 24 Hours race with Richard Lloyd in a Porsche 956.

The Le Mans experience was especially good, as we used the old Mulsanne Straight prior to the installation of the chicanes you see now. The previous year, I had taken Georgie across the fields at night to get close to the famous 3.7-mile 250mph stretch. It is strictly out of bounds because a car taking off on that straight will go clear over the barriers, but right then we found the most dangerous things to be the cows – their dark shapes against the midsummer sky were all that you could see. During the race you could hear the cars coming onto the straight and staying flat out for an entire minute. It's equally impressive to see their headlights burning through the woods like a comet. I had no inkling that I would be doing exactly that the following year.

The sister car in our team was being driven by Le Mans legend Derek Bell, along with Tiff Needell and James Weaver. My car was only for lanky drivers: me, Steven Andskär and David Hobbs, all of us over six feet. I must have been a bit wide-eyed waiting for my stint, because David kept teasing me that the car was coming any second. 'Here it comes!' he'd say. Then, no car. He'd see me relax. 'Here it comes!' he'd say once more. All great fun, except for the fact that these things were 220mph petrol bombs made of aluminium. Given that my godfather Jo Bonnier, along with countless others, had been killed in this race, I had good reason to be a bit jumpy, but the driving experience was sublime.

When it came for my turn at the wheel, I attacked my first stint with too much aggression. Going onto Mulsanne for the first time, I got the car into a massive 'tank-slapper', which is an unintended oscillation where the car wags its tail like a dog. That woke me up, I can tell you. After that I calmed down a bit, although by the time I climbed out I was dripping with sweat and had a pounding headache. 'Oh, my God,' I thought. 'Another twenty-one hours to go! What have I done?' During the race you didn't wash your overalls; you just stuck them in a tumble dryer put there for exactly this purpose. I took some ibuprofen and tried to recover in the motorhome. About two hours later, a knock on the door. Time to go again. This time the sun was going down. I drove off in my little pod into the twilight at over 200mph, which pretty much sums up the amazingly surreal experience that is racing at Le Mans.

The next stint was in the middle of the night and patches of mist started to appear on the straight from lap to lap, and it is impossible to tell if there's anything like a stopped car or a deer in the middle of it. Slowing down is not a good idea, because you could get hit up the backside by a car behind. So you have to keep your right foot planted until you pop out the other side, hopefully still on the track. It reminded me very much of flying into clouds in my father's plane. At the end of this insanely long straight is the Mulsanne kink. Every time you get there, you hope the damn car will go where you want it to go when you turn the wheel for the first time in over a minute. It's a hell of a great corner, exiting into a gradual climb to crest this beautiful rolling hill and down the other side before standing hard onto the brakes for a very slow right. At this point I was supposed to read the fuel meter but, since it wasn't lit, I had no idea what it said. The cardinal sin at Le Mans is running out of fuel. So the next time I was on the Mulsanne Straight, I had to turn on the interior light, take a quick peek at the fuel usage meter and try to extrapolate whether or not I was on target for the hairpin checkpoint coming up! But, of course, when the light was on in the cockpit I couldn't see out! I had this picture in my head of the marshals by the side of the track seeing me lit up like an alien in a spaceship whizzing down the straight at over 200mph. The next section is more twisting but just as fast and very narrow, followed by the quick corner, Indianapolis. During my night stint, a car had crashed on the straight before it and caught fire, totally obscuring the track in smoke and flames and making marshals scurry around on the side of the track to deal with it all. I crawled past, had a quick look, hoped everyone was OK, and pressed on once more. To think, my father would have raced past the place where his best friend and my godfather, Jo Bonnier, had been killed, too. Motor racing is a very brutal game.

To refuel us they were using gravity-fed fuel pipes and shoved them into a special 'leakproof' valve right behind the driver's neck, on the outside of the car. On this occasion, the leakproofing hadn't really done its job. A spillage immediately turned into a substantial conflagration, and when petrol ignites it goes *whooumpah!* because it's the vapour that burns, not the liquid so it expands a huge amount of air very rapidly, rather like a massive subwoofer. I could hear this explosion sound which kicked off a lot of shouting and people running around so I looked at Richard Lloyd who was standing calmly in position in front of the car, headphones on, one hand on the transmission switch. Normally he would give me the signal to re-join the race. But clearly I couldn't leave if I was still on fire! Our eyes met. Mine were probably on stalks, while his were relaxed as could be. I had my hand on the seat belts and the door handle, ready to leap to safety. Richard must have sensed that I was about to eject, but his cool, reassuring tones over the radio made me hang on for a few seconds longer and they put the fire out and sent me off into the rapidly returning daylight.

The famous eccentric motor racing journalist, Denis 'Jenks' Jenkinson, who navigated for Stirling Moss when they drove flat out on 1,000 miles of Italian roads to win the 1955

Mille Miglia, reported on the 1958 Le Mans, and recounted a rather unusual refuelling stop. He wrote that he was perplexed by the sight of a man sauntering towards a car during a pit stop and pouring in fuel at a leisurely rate before sauntering back to the pit wall, for all the world as if he was oblivious to the race going on. Amazed at his abnormally relaxed pace, Jenks sought the man out for a chat. The man told Jenks that he had worked out that the quickest speed the mechanics could change all four wheels would give him more than enough time not to rush and risk spilling the dangerous liquid. That man was my father. I love that tale.

A few laps into my next stint, as a beautiful dawn was breaking early on Sunday morning, the engine gave a death rattle on the Mulsanne Straight and that was the end of my one and only Le Mans experience. I would not emulate my father at Le Mans and I never raced there again. But I wouldn't have missed it for the world. I jumped into my road car and drove all the way home. I was so pumped with adrenaline that I didn't sleep until Monday afternoon. Then I slept like a baby.

For the rest of the year I did a few races in the British F3000 series, thanks to the relative cheapness of the deal and the fact that I had wangled a few pounds from Ian Dickens, a friend who was the marketing and PR man for Olympus Cameras. Years later, he gave it all up to sail round the world. He came to Japan to see me win the Championship, too. Thanks to Ian, I raced a lovely blue-and-white Olympus-decaled Reynard F3000 at Oulton Park six weeks after Oliver was born. Georgie came with Oliver, because we were a racing family now. Two years later at the same track, and in the same category, Derek Warwick's younger brother, Paul, was killed instantly when his car went straight on at one of the fastest corners.

Increasingly desperate to find work to put food on the table, I was searching high and low for any kind of ride. The word was out that Footwork, a Japanese F3000 team, were looking for a replacement driver to help develop the car they had entered into the International F3000 championship. Footwork had the same sponsor as the Arrows F1 team, but otherwise they were not connected. It may have been a well-paid drive but the car was totally uncompetitive: dangerous, even, and it was a job for only the most desperate and fool-hardy. Just two drivers fitted that description: me and Perry 'The Original Stig' McCarthy who, like me, was simply trying to survive in the sport. If it meant taking the bread from the mouths of each other's family, so be it. Let battle commence. Perry became a notorious racer when he made it to the front page of the *Daily Mail*. The photo showed him flying through the air in his Formula Ford at Oulton Park. He made it to F1 eventually, driving for the Andrea Moda team. Just before they disappeared in a puff of smoke, he managed to get the car over the line on the exit of the pit lane. Technically, he took part in pre-qualifying for a Grand Prix. In reality the car stopped eighteen metres past the line and he never actually completed a lap, but that is not important. Perry had made it to F1 and could call himself an F1 driver forever.

But in '89 Perry and I were both last-chance-saloon racing drivers, and a Footwork drive was a potential lifesaver for us both. We went for the test and were duly assessed. Perry's approach was to pick an argument with the engineer, who he found to be 'wrong'. The guy's name was Alan Langridge, and the upshot was that I got the drive. Perry took it very well, and only cried for a week. I make no apology for my ruthless-ness; I was a racing driver and I competed to win.

The Footwork car was another eye-opener, as the car offered hardly any lateral protection, being modelled on an old McLaren MP4/2. Since then, manufacturing techniques for carbon fibre had moved on and chassis were almost sculpted around the human form, offering a huge amount of extra protection. But in the Footwork, I was extremely exposed, and the car was awful to drive, too. I threw the thing at the corners and drove out of my mind to get the car into races. I think we did actually qualify for some: something this car had never done before. So, another Hill first. It would be a foretaste of the opportunity in the F1 Brabham in 1992 but, for now, I was getting credit for at least trying and giving it all I had.

Following the principle of reward for risk, I was now being paid a respectable retainer with which I could pay the 17 per cent interest on the mortgage. In addition, by moving up to International F3000, I had triggered the David Hunt Cellnet contract, which was still in effect, and was also due a nice bonus. The contract extended all the way up to F1, where it was worth a staggering £100,000 in my favour, which would come back to bite them when I finally made it to F1. I'm not sure whether Cellnet had taken out insurance, or whether they'd never expected to have to pay out the full amount, but my invoices to them went unnoticed. I had to seek legal advice and engage Robert Gore, a lawyer. Robert was recommended to me by Henry Taylor and his father, Simon Gore, who had known my father. But Robert was a busy man and passed me to an Ulsterman, Michael Breen. Michael would become part of Team Hill in the coming years thanks to his ability to pro-tect me from the inevitable legal problems and get people to cough up. I'm not sure what Michael wrote in the letter to Cellnet, but they duly paid. This impressed me and I came to trust him implicitly. It was extremely useful finally to have a capable confidant and someone who seemed genuinely inter-ested in helping with the plan. Once we had worked things out with Cellnet they became my longest-standing personal sponsor. Sadly, David Hunt died too young just like his brother James, aged only fifty-five, in 2015.

My sterling efforts in the Footwork paid dividends when Mark Blundell gave me the nod that there was the chance of a paid seat in F3000 for the following year. Mark was about to leave Middlebridge to become the Williams test-driver. Because I had been giving my all, right under their noses, Middlebridge knew what I was capable of. At that time, the team was being run by John Macdonald, a famously hard man, who had run RAM, his own F1 team which had folded in 1985. First I would have to convince John to his face that I had what it took. Towards the end of the 1989 season, I went to Milton Keynes to meet him.

John has a red face at the best of times and talks through a fine set of clenched white teeth, as if he is a terrier with a bone you want to deprive him of. He can be a little intimidating if he wants to be, but if you are going to make it in F1, you cannot afford to be intimidated by the team manager. There are plenty of others you need to worry about. I sat there and made my pitch. 'Yeah, Damon,' he snarled, pointing his finger at me, 'but do you WANT it?' I was confused. I thought I had made myself clear all season and I had driven all the way up the M1 to see him personally. He growled the question again: 'Do you REALLY wan' it?'

'Yes,' I said. 'I really want it . . . please.' I was enjoying the absurdity of it all. But this drive would be a fantastic opportunity. John arranged for me to meet Dennis Nursey, the man who ran the team. Dennis had worked for Scimitar Cars when it was bought by Middlebridge, a Japanese company. The Japanese like English-sounding names and, apparently, Middlebridge was a literal translation of the Japanese founder's name, Kohji Nakauchi. This improbable company would be my stepping stone into F1. They put me on their list and I set out to convince them I was their man. In the absence of any other option, they were my team, too.

After what seemed like an age of waiting around for the phone to ring, they said they wanted me to come up to the factory to negotiate terms. Terms! I'd do anything they asked! I took a friend, Paul Newman, as back-up, figuring he'd know if they were trying to stitch me up. To our utter amazement, Dennis simply said they wanted me to be their driver in F3000 – and they were going to pay me £50,000 because they wanted me to be happy! I was completely dumbfounded. They gave me a Scimitar to get around in, too. This was ridiculous, but

I never missed a beat and shook his hand. I had a plum drive in the bag for 1990. I was on my way.

There had to be one small hiccup, though. I had not entirely given up bike riding, regularly going on off-road trials riding trips in the Brecon Beacons and Exmoor with my friends Paul, Lance and few others. In January 1990, we were on Exmoor looking at the map, trying to find the nearest pub for lunch. They were taking rather a long time over it, so I playfully hit Paul on the helmet with the map. He reacted with a rugby tackle that made me topple over. I couldn't move my legs to stop the fall, put out my hand and broke my right wrist. Thinking I had sprained it, I rode to the pub, but the wrist was clearly broken. My face was green, so they decided to take me to hospital. With my arm in a sling, I arrived home feeling quite relaxed thanks to the Valium I had been given. Georgie answered the door and I proudly showed my plaster. What *had* I done? For the next six weeks, until the first test, I had to conceal my broken right wrist from Middlebridge for fear they would cancel my contract. I continued to go to the gym and pulled weights with the wrist in plaster because, at the time, you had to change gear with your right hand. The first test was a bit painful. I vowed never to go biking, skiing, or do anything that risked my career ever again.

The 1990 season was fantastic because the car was a peach and this complete stroke of luck would be my saviour. Designed by Mark Williams at Lola cars, and powered by a unique Tickford-tuned Cosworth, it was quick everywhere and I was able to run at the front in nearly all the races. Even though the car kept stopping when I was leading! Nevertheless, I was able to show my pace with three consecutive poles at Monza, Enna in Sicily and Hockenheim. The Hockenheim pole brought me to the attention of Patrick Head at Williams because the F3000 race was supporting the F1 Grand Prix. These bigger, more powerful cars were to my liking because I felt I could stabilise the car on the throttle, and they slid around a lot when the tyres went off, which I also liked. One of the things I had done in my 'gap year', 1989, was indoor karting. Because I hadn't done karting as a boy, this part of my training was missing. As I had nothing else to drive, I took indoor karting very seriously, using it as extra tuition. I think this seemingly trivial experience gave me an insight that had previously been missing, because it transferred so well to F3000. Things were beginning to click into place. But the key thing about F3000 was that it was the last stop before F1 and I had impressed enough to be in line for the Williams testing deal currently occupied by Mark Blundell.

Mark had told me that he was off to race for Brabham in '91 and possibly test with McLaren. He said I should go for his vacated testing job at Williams. This would turn out to be crucial. McLaren were top dogs in F1 at that time and looked like the place to be, thanks to Ayrton Senna cleaning up on his way to the second of three F1 titles, which is no doubt why Mark wanted to be there. But the right place to be for the future was at Williams, even though they looked slightly forlorn compared to their Honda glory days of the '80s. All the action seemed to be happening at McLaren, but the Renault engine in the Williams was beginning to look good and there was a magic ingredient on its way in the form of Adrian Newey, a then little-known young aerodynamicist and designer.

In July, Adrian's cars had caused something of an upset by running at the front in the French Grand Prix and finishing ahead of Senna's McLaren. I could see a new era coming for sculpted cars shaped for aero-efficiency, and the man ahead of that shapely curve was Adrian. Patrick had been quick to poach him and I reasoned that the first Newey Williams would be something to behold, so I saw no great advantage for anyone leaving them to go to McLaren. I would be more than happy to be at Williams, and besides, they were a very British team, and I liked that. I reasoned right. Williams were at the start of an upturn in form that would last for seven seasons and would take four drivers to the top of the world.

Being taken on for the test-driving job with an F1 team was not seen as the right thing for your career in the 1990s. It was a siding, you were considered to be the monkey: the man who hadn't got enough to be a full racing driver. You were the understudy, just in case a driver caught a cold, and even then, they would probably take someone else. But what did I care? I wanted to be working with the best guys in the business, and it would be like old times being in the inner sanctum of an F1 team, just like I had been with my father's team. I looked up to Frank and Patrick, too. I knew they were hard men, but I had lived with Graham Hill as a father. I thought I could handle whatever they dished out.

The F3000 season came to a close and deals had to be done for the following year. Georgie was pregnant again, too. We had decided that Oliver needed a pal to bring him on, since the development curve for people with Down's Syndrome is slower than other children, so we figured there would be a point at which a brother or sister would be on a par with Oliver and they could grow together. It was a good idea but it would mean less sleep, more family to look after and more reason to work hard. But things were definitely on the up. It was difficult to see how I couldn't make something of my limited success now, whatever turned up. I had continued to seek sponsors during the season but, fortunately, I had impressed enough for the Barclay tobacco brand to involve me in their marketing. Barclay were a division of R. J. Reynolds, who had the Camel brand, already prominent in F1 with Lotus and due to come on board with Williams in 1993. The key thing in our sport is to know your value. I happened to know that Barclay wanted an association with me, which meant I was holding the cards to some degree. However, the irrepressible Eddie Jordan was keen to have the deal for himself. He was about to embark on his first-ever season as an

entrant in F1 and wanted Barclay for that, but I knew that
this deal was crucial if I wanted to keep racing. I couldn't just
be a test-driver, even if it was for a top F1 team. I still had
to be racing and, hopefully, winning.

If Middlebridge were to stay in F3000, they too would
need the Barclay deal because all their own money was going
to be sent in another direction. During 1990, they had pur-
chased the Brabham F1 team from administration and would
need every penny for that. Companies like Middlebridge often
appear in F1. We don't know much about them and we can't
work out where the money comes from. As racing drivers, we
have learned not to ask too many questions and not to look
gift horses in the mouth, but Middlebridge were making life
very difficult for themselves by buying an underfunded F1
team that had had its day in the sun years before.

Meanwhile, Eddie was trying to convince me to drive for
his team in F3000, and I knew that if I did that, he might
eventually kick me out in favour of a driver with more money.
I decided to call his bluff and signed for Middlebridge. If
Barclay really did want me, I would soon find out. In a crazy
deal with Dennis Nursey, it was agreed that Middlebridge
should become Barclay Eddie Jordan Racing. I didn't mind
what they called it; the important thing was that my contract
was with whoever was in control of the driver, so I would keep
my job, be with the team I liked, get paid and have the Williams F1 testing job. It would be a busy year. Especially as on
9 January 1991 a brother for Oliver was born.

Joshua Damon Hill was dragged from the safety and
comfort of his mother's womb in her namesake's hospital,
St George's, Tooting. He was two weeks overdue, and he
wouldn't come out. I thought the doctor was going to pull his
head off. It was an agonising few seconds before he took his
first breath and went from death blue to pink as a little piglet.
It was amazing to see. Less than ten days later, I had to get up
to feed him at about 2 a.m. Sitting with him in my arms and
watching the news, the announcer said he had just seen a

cruise missile go down the street in Baghdad. Welcome to our world, Josh. And good luck, son.

My first test with Williams was a bit of a disaster. It was the beginning of the era of the semi-automatic gearbox, which would mean no more red-raw hands and blisters from trying to change gear with a manual lever, no more driving one-handed, no more over-revved engines because of driver error. The computer would take over, but the technology was still under development and I had the job of doing a few laps in a modified FW13B. Unfortunately, they had assumed too much. As instructed, I did a lap of the circuit, keeping the revs to what I thought was the right level, only to return to the pits with the car on fire. I thought I'd been going slowly! Apparently, the digital rev counter had two stages and I hadn't made it past the first stage, which meant the revs were far too low. F1 cars have no fan and require air to be passing through the radiators at sufficient speed to cool the multi-thousand-pound engines. They put the fire out with extinguishers and I felt a proper twit. But it wasn't my fault, really.

I first sat in the Head/Newey FW14 for a few laps around the short loop at Silverstone. It was absolutely staggering. I was blown away and loved every split second. When I came in, Patrick asked me what I thought. I said, 'Fantastic, Patrick! Really amazing!' But he was looking for criticism. He had to explain that they were trying to improve on what they had, so that was my new job: to criticise the best car I had ever driven. Everything is different in F1, especially the way people think. In time, I would be tasked with developing the FW15 active suspension Williams and working with Paddy Lowe, who went on to become technical director with AMG Mercedes F1. Of all the things I loved about my time with Williams, one of the best aspects was working with the brightest minds in the business; it was such a pleasure.

But back in F3000, the 1991 Lola was a disaster. We never discovered why it handled like a balloon full of water. You never knew what the car was going to do next. We tried every-thing to fix it, including fitting a ten-inch housing between the engine and the gearbox to make the wheelbase longer. This was known as 'the sewer pipe'. Eventually we gave up and got hold of a Reynard for the last race – much to the irritation of Vincenzo Sospiri, my teammate and an emotional Italian who was stuck with the bad Lola. When I came to lap him, he ran me off the road – so now I knew he didn't like me any more. I was also castigated by former Renault and Ferrari driver René Arnoux because I had had the temerity to overtake one of his drivers. He called me 'the worst driver he had ever seen in his life'. I thanked him for his kind words. But the 1991 F1 season had been significant for two events that now look like precursors for two later events that would have a life-changing effect on me.

Senna's third title was won in controversial circumstances at the end of 1991. Because I was racing the next day at Dijon I should have been asleep, but the penultimate round was coming from Japan, so I set the alarm for 3 a.m. The race ended after ten seconds when Ayrton committed his worst act as a driver by hitting the back of Prost's Ferrari. This was going downhill and into the superfast first corner with twen-ty-four other drivers right behind, in cars full of fuel. Disgusted and disappointed, I went back to bed annoyed that there was now no race to watch. I remember thinking that was no way to win a title. Regardless of Senna's beef with Prost, it was inexcusable. How could I ever have expected I would one day have them as teammates at Williams? Ayrton was a contradic-tion. Less than a month before demolishing Prost's car, he had been helping Prof Watkins, the FIA's chief medical officer, to save Martin Donnelly's life at Jerez.

Martin had been looking good in his new life as an F1 driver with the Camel Team Lotus. Then, going into a fantas-tically quick right-hander at the bottom of a gradual descent at Jerez during qualifying for the Spanish Grand Prix, some-thing must have broken. The car never turned and he went full pelt into the guard rail, the chassis exploding, dissipating some of the impact but throwing Martin into the air and onto the track where he lay, twisted and motionless, still strapped into his seat. It was a pathetic sight. He looked like a child sleeping, and people stood around not knowing what to do. They could be forgiven for thinking he was dead. Overcoming drivers' natural aversion to witnessing the full meaning of what they expose themselves to, Senna arrived on the scene to help Sid Watkins rescue Martin. In another life, I think Ayrton would have liked to have been a doctor.

At the FIA prize-giving in Monaco a few years later, one of Ayrton's guests suffered a heart attack. Ayrton leapt into action and applied whatever knowledge he had to save the man. As Georgie and I were leaving, we saw Ayrton and his girlfriend rushing off to the hospital on his motorbike: Ayrton in black tie, no helmet, the glamorous Adriane Galisteu clinging to his waist for dear life. We struggled to comprehend Ayrton: demon one minute, saint the next.

Donnelly's accident should have frightened everyone off racing an F1 car, but it didn't. Ayrton went back out and put the car on pole. While I was shocked and concerned for Martin, I remembered everything I had learned from losing my father. There may be a million ways to die, but isn't it worse to live not doing what you love best? Who knows.

In my last F3000 race I finished third, which was the only time in two years that I had managed to step onto the podium. But things were about to get much more exciting, because in just a few months I was to take the momentous step up to F1.

14 » PASSING MY DRIVING TEST

The winter of 1991 was going to be one of the first winters I could remember having no race drive for the following year – but not really caring. Test-driving for Williams would keep me busy, with increasing developments coming through for FW14, the car with active suspension that would give Nigel Mansell his one and only F1 World Championship in a totally dominant season. My biking trips with the boys to Wales would have to go on the back burner. This was too important to cock up by larking around on a misty mountainside.

By now F1 was heavily into the start of the computer age. To help them understand the complexities, Williams had hired a young computer genius called Paddy Lowe. Paddy and I would be given the active car to play with at out-of-the-way racetracks like Croix-en-Ternois in Northern France, and Brands Hatch, which was no longer licensed to hold F1 races. I used to lap the short circuit in about thirty-four seconds. That made your neck seriously ache.

I also spent the winter in Portugal going round and round and round doing tyre-testing for Goodyear, as well as development work with Renault and other suppliers to the team. It was very hard work, but I loved it. I was in the epicentre of the F1 world with race winners all around me. I learned a great deal about how characters such as Riccardo Patrese and Nigel went about working with their engineers, and I came to discover exactly what Patrick and Frank expected of me. Basically, Frank just wanted us to do as many laps as we could from the moment the track opened until the chequered flag came out at the end of the day. It was completely exhausting, mentally and physically; but it was a proper education and toughened me up considerably. The computer on the active car was connected to a rudimentary handheld personal computer, called a Psion, onto which we downloaded the data when we came into the pits. The key thing about the active car was that it could control the ride height of the floor, which is where all the aerodynamic downforce was generated. Imagine an eight-foot by four-foot sheet of inch ply on the roof of a car going at 70mph. Now imagine trying to lift up the back of the sheet as the car is going along. You could never do it. That is roughly the principle, with a few more twists. The computer on the active car was so accurate that it could control the ride height, front and rear, to within half a millimetre. And the grip generated was also insane. If the FW14B was already cleaning up with the mighty Nigel, the next car, the FW15C, would be untouchable. Add to that the other elements the engineers were working on – traction control, active brakes, ABS, autoshift, and it would give Williams the most advanced racing car in the history of the sport. And I would be the driver.

It didn't end there. It seemed every time we went to a test, Renault gave us another 200 rpm. The car was so quick that my name would quite often be at the top of the times at the end of the test. I couldn't help but think: 'All I need is for that to be a qualifying session, and I'm ready to race,' but, of course, the car was being developed for Nigel. Nonetheless, I felt that it would be no bad thing if could somehow get a few F1 races under my belt. My old F3000 team, Middlebridge, were persevering in F1 with Brabham, but it was a budget operation with little development and a poor engine, and it was clearly a team on its last legs. I learned through Dennis Nursey exactly what was going on and knew that, although they had signed Giovanna Amati, all was not well behind the scenes with finance. Eric Van de Poele was to be the other driver and the extremely likeable Belgian had sponsor money – so he would be staying. But Amati's promised money didn't arrive, which ensured a vacant seat, and Brabham decided to give me a go. I didn't have any sponsorship but, if they were offering me the drive, then this was a chance to prove that I could cope in F1. You can do as much testing work as you like, but actually racing in F1 in the heat of competition means you are under the noses of the people who matter. Otherwise, they hardly know you exist.

Everyone said I was mad. They pointed out that this was a dangerously underfinanced team. The car was worn out and Middlebridge weren't going to be refreshing parts properly, but I simply thought, 'I don't have a choice. The time has come in my career when I have to show that I can actually drive an F1 car in competition. I'll be getting good experience of the whole F1 procedure: going to the drivers' briefing; showing I can deal with being on track with all the big names; learning how to work with F1 engineers, the press. I have to do this.'

I hardly fitted in the car. My head and upper body were sticking so far out of the cockpit that it appeared I was sitting on a cushion, and my legs were crammed in as far as they could go and crushed against the sides of the chassis. It was so tight that the gear-lever gate was almost under my right leg. I could only use four of the six gears because it was so cramped; not what you need at Monaco, where neither Eric nor I qualified, as had happened at the previous races in Spain and Italy. The engine in the back was a Judd V10 badged as a Yamaha. It wasn't bad but the power curve was quite violent, and then a bit like a tractor at times thanks to me being unable to use the lower gears. There was no power steering and yet, despite these handicaps, it was strangely exciting to drive a no-hope car.

The more you can drive in competition – no matter what the car may be like – the more you learn. Eric was very competitive and gave me a run for my money. My sixth attempt at qualifying would come at the British Grand Prix at Silverstone, for which the car had sprung some sponsorship and a very questionable purple-and-pink colour scheme. I had an engine failure during practice and Van de Poele's car had a water leak. In those days, even a team as hard-pressed as Brabham would have a spare car, but with our various problems, Eric and I had to share the spare for qualifying. I went first and was supposed to do two laps and hand over the car. I went out and thought: 'It's the British Grand Prix; possibly my first Grand Prix. I can't give this car back until I'm in. Sorry!' I did one too many laps, got the car in the race, and then gave it back. By then there wasn't enough time for Eric to produce a good lap, but at last the team had qualified for a Grand Prix.

I was at the very back of the grid, 7.4 seconds behind Mansell who was on pole, but I was in the race, and at the moment that was all that mattered – which is just as well, since Nigel lapped me four times on his way to victory. It may have been an emotional day for him but, in its own small way, it was the same for me as I actually managed to finish my first Grand Prix, albeit sixteenth and last. I spent most of the race looking in my mirrors, but enjoying the show because I wasn't really racing anyone. It was amazing to witness all the banners and the madness as 150,000 Mansell fans enjoyed a beautiful day and got the result they wanted. When Nigel crossed the line, the crowd immediately invaded the track, forgetting that I was coming along behind him at that moment. One bloke, busy watching Nigel, ran right in front of me, clearly with no idea that I was there. The cooling-down lap was getting slower and slower until eventually the huge number of people on the track meant we all had to stop at Club Corner. The organisers came to collect Nigel and eventually picked up the rest of us, so we had to leave the cars to the souvenir hunters. It was an incredible buzz to be in the thick of it all.

It had been a strange feeling during the race each time Nigel passed me, driving a car I was so familiar with. Given half a chance, I knew I'd be up there as well if I was driving that Williams. It confirmed my feeling that no matter the quality of the driver, success is hugely influenced by the car you have. The teams with the best equipment choose the best drivers, and it was our job as drivers to impress the team enough to warrant the chance. I was working on that principle, knowing that if I was good enough, I'd eventually get the opportunity. In the meantime, the Brabham would make the starting grid just once more when I managed to qualify in Hungary. It would be the last time a Brabham ever raced, because the plug was about to be pulled and the Brabham name consigned to the F1 history books.

The chance of a full-time drive in F1 came sooner than I expected – and with my favourite team. No one could have predicted what happened at the end of 1992. Despite, or perhaps since, becoming World Champion, Nigel had had enough of playing negotiating games with Frank. Unbeknown to Mansell, Frank signed Alain Prost, which was the final straw for Nigel and he agreed to go to the States and race Indycars in 1993. Thinking Nigel would be staying and with Prost now arriving, Patrese believed there would not be a place for him, so he signed to join Michael Schumacher at Benetton. When the music stopped at Monza in September and Nigel revealed he was off to Indy, Frank suddenly found he had an empty seat to fill. At which point, I put my hand up and more or less said, 'If you're looking for someone, I'll be happy to take the drive.' From then on, it was a question of who would be acceptable to Prost as a teammate and who the team would feel comfortable to have in the car; someone who knew how everything worked and who would not upset the apple cart. But it was not a clear-cut decision by any means. Martin Brundle was in contention but, as an experienced driver, he also had a price tag. If there's one thing Frank doesn't like, it's paying what he considers to be too much for drivers. I fitted the bill on two counts: I was cheap and I was available. In order to remind everyone, I flew to Adelaide for the weekend at my own expense and hung around at the final race of 1992, making sure I was right under the noses of Frank and Patrick.

There was more testing to be done later in November and
it became clear Frank had to make a decision at around that
time. During a test at Paul Ricard, Patrick had a word with
me in the hire car and gave me a warning about how much
pressure would come my way in a team like Williams. With a
protective arm around my shoulder, he said something along
the lines of, 'We could actually end up having you in the car
and I think I ought to warn you that there's a lot of pressure
in Formula 1. There's a lot of media interest and I just want
to make sure you're happy with that.' I remember saying, 'I
can deal with that, Patrick. It's not a problem.' But his warning came from bitter experience and I would come to realise
that I had no idea about what he was really saying. Wanting
me to jump through a few more hoops, Williams said I was to
come to a test at Estoril in Portugal and they would reach a
decision after that. Frank would be there to cast his critical
eye over me one more time.

I was due to fly out of Heathrow on the evening before the
test was scheduled to start. I spent most of the day trying to
be relaxed at a lunch hosted by Paul Newman, who lived in
Wandsworth, and it being a Sunday, and airport security being
much more relaxed than nowadays, I allowed myself forty
minutes – an hour maximum – to get from Wandsworth and
onto the plane. I set off in what I believed to be ample time
but, as I crossed the Thames, I discovered that Chelsea had
been playing at home and the whole place was gridlocked.
'Who plays football on a Sunday?' I thought, not knowing
much about it. I was sitting in a little side street of Victorian
terraced houses, going nowhere. It was blocked every which
way with hordes of people streaming past. By now I'm pan-
icking, looking at my watch and thinking, 'This is the biggest
test of my life, and I'm not even going to catch the plane.'
Having eventually got clear of the traffic, and with about half
an hour to go before take-off, I decided, 'If necessary, I can
drop the car on the ramp outside the terminal and simply leg
it. If I cause a bomb scare and they have to detonate my car,

I don't care. I'm going to jump every hurdle and get on that plane.' I actually managed to throw the car into the short-term car park and run like the wind, making it to the gate just as they were about to close the doors. Sweat was dripping off me; I was stressed to the max. It occurred to me that this was not great preparation for what was about to happen at Estoril. As I caught my breath I suddenly realised it was 29 November. I was sitting on a plane on the anniversary of my dad's accident.

Compared to that experience, test-driving the car in Estoril was easy. I just got back to work and I knew exactly what was going on with everything associated with Williams and how the team worked, although it was the first time I had worked with Alain Prost. He was very easy-going. I think he knew that, as long as he didn't totally cock up, he was going to have his fourth World Championship, because his car promised to be the class of the field. Everything gelled during that test. I had done my bit; now it was up to Frank. Because I wanted to keep my options open, at the same time as I had been jumping through hoops for Frank I was trying to keep warm an offer from Ligier, but it had got to the stage where they were telling me they couldn't wait any longer: I'd have to sign or let it go. I thought, 'I haven't come this far, though all the trials and dangers, to get this close to a winning car, only to opt for second best.' If I ended up with nothing, I'd find another way to look after the family and the mortgage, but I could never live with myself if I didn't hold out for the best. So I bade farewell to the French team, and waited with bated breath and an anxious heart.

Frank rang late on a Friday afternoon, saying he'd like me to come up to Didcot. Trying to be cocky and cool, I said, 'Frank, it's Friday evening, a load of traffic; it had better be worth it.' He said he thought I should come up. When I got to Didcot, Frank said simply, 'We'd like you to drive for us.' I said something like, 'Oh, good. Thanks.' Two chronically emotionally constipated Englishmen trying not to show any feelings, but I was thrilled. We had to do a bit of negotiation, as I had expected, but I was so over the moon at the thought of having finally made it into the big time with F1, and on my own terms, that I actually videoed the contract as it came through the fax machine in my home office in Wandsworth. There were some discrepancies over the terms we had discussed, but I was being paid more than I had ever been paid in my life, so I didn't bring it up. At last, after five years, hundreds of thousands of pounds' worth of debt would start to come under control.

As it happened, I also brought some money to the team after doing a deal with Sega, a hot new computer games company. In my complete naivety, I hadn't really understood that I was actually in quite a good position thanks to connecting Williams with one of the biggest technology sponsors of the day. Philip Ley was the marketing director of Sega Europe, and was unfazed by the egos in F1. When he met Frank, Philip jokingly proposed that Sega put their cartoon hero, Sonic the Hedgehog, on the wheels of Frank's wheelchair, which jarred strongly with the sober image that Williams liked to portray. But Frank liked his spirit and the money was good, so they settled on a livery that made it look as if the drivers had Sonic the Hedgehog's legs and feet on the pedals.

It had been a tense few months but there was no way in the world I was going to let the Williams drive go until I felt I had done everything I could. When the news of my arrival at Williams was made public, the reaction reminded me of my first-ever car race at Brands. The media resurrected stories of my dad, the resulting massive coverage coming from this and off the back of Mansell Mania. Frank had to soak up criticism for being biased and signing an English driver. Other drivers thought they were more deserving and clearly had their supporters. I was put on notice that I'd have to show I was worth the chance. This is exactly what Patrick had warned me about. I would need to show the world that I hadn't got here on a magic carpet, and they had to see that I had my own gifts to display. I'd gone from being Nigel's understudy to being teammate to a three-times World Champion. I was under no illusions that this was a big deal, but I thought, 'I'm ready. Let's do it!'

15 » ZEROING IN

With South Africa staging the first race of 1993, Georgie and I reluctantly left Oliver and Josh at home, in the safe hands of her mother. In view of what had happened to my dad, Georgie and I had made an agreement never to travel in light aircraft together, but from the moment we landed in Johannesburg and immediately climbed aboard a waiting helicopter, our best intentions went out of the window. The flight was spectacular, taking us to the Palace of the Lost City, a themed hotel next to the Pilanesberg National Park in Bophuthatswana. A visit to the park showed us a world which could offer no greater contrast to the madness of F1. You could hear the animals chewing grass; it was the quietest and most tranquil place I've ever been. The trip was part of a promotional campaign set up by Camel, a sponsor of Williams; we had to be put on parade for the media to help generate column inches. This build-up to the season was new to me, but any sense of enjoyment was quickly forgotten in a race that went horribly wrong.

Traditionally, the reigning World Champion carried the number 1 on his car but, because Mansell had left Williams, they gave me the number 0. Frank was keeping a careful eye on me, being protective of his new driver and trying to reduce the pressure by telling me not to push too hard in qualifying. From testing I had expectations that I could challenge Alain but compared to Alain I was a novice and by far the more vulnerable of Frank's two drivers, although it transpired that Prost was equally nervous about the season ahead. During the year that Prost had been away from F1 on sabbatical, Ayrton

Senna had upped his game on the track as he wanted the Williams drive for himself. However, Prost had managed to outmanoeuvre him, which only served to increase the pre-existing animosity between the two, and put Alain on edge going into the South African Grand Prix.

Alain didn't seem to be someone who went out of his way to create situations, and yet trouble seemed to find him. I don't know why, because he was a lovely guy to work with: always very charming and I never had any sense that he was going to try and make my life difficult. I was the British guy in the team with a British chassis and he was the French guy with the French engine, all of which made the combination of drivers even more intriguing, but no reason for one to dislike the other. I think Alain treated me with respect because I knew how the active car worked. During testing, he had admitted the Williams was complicated and not something he had any experience of. He was not going to get too deeply involved trying to understand it because he knew the car would be good enough. All he had to do was keep it simple and get a balance on the car – make it nice to drive – and he would be World Champion for the fourth time. For my part, I was keen to learn from Prost.

In the engineering debrief following a qualifying session, I said to him, 'Alain, in Turn 4, my car is doing this' – indicating the movement of the car with my hands. 'What's your car like through there?'

'Yes,' he said in his quiet, famous nasally French-accented voice, 'my car does the same.' That was all I got out of him. Even if he did know what to do about the car, it was clear he was not – in the nicest possible way – going to say anything that might help me be quicker. But it was a good relationship nonetheless. I was always a huge admirer of Alain's driving, as was Ayrton – but for the fact that he could not accept being second to anyone at all.

Alain had qualified on pole, with his nemesis Senna along-side in the McLaren. Everyone was waiting for fireworks since it was the first time these two had been side by side since the 1990 Japanese Grand Prix – when they collided at the first corner. I don't know if that affected Alain, because he made a slow start. I made a good one from the second row and found myself slotting nicely into second place, right behind Senna, but being in such a position for the first time in an F1 race caught me out. While I might have done a lot of testing, going round and round in my own space, I had not gone wheel-to-wheel with anyone. It is possible I was affected by the turbulence and was too close to Senna's car. What is sure, though, is that one second I was going forward; the next, I was going backwards, spinning through 180 degrees – right in front of my teammate – and looking straight at the rest of the F1 grid heading towards me. Somehow, Alain avoided me and saved what would have been a painful interview with Frank and Patrick. I got going again in the midfield and lasted for sixteen laps before being hit up the back by Alessandro Zanardi's Lotus.

Once I had abandoned, the tenor of the race was set by Senna, viciously chopping Prost just like old times and giving him absolutely no quarter before Prost eventually made a brave move stick. Senna then immediately lost his place to the new pretender, Michael Schumacher. Senna got the place back during the pit stops, but Michael reeled him in – only to have Senna chop him too, making the Benetton spin out. Considering his later attitudes to uncompromising defences, it was ironic that a furious Schumacher wanted the stewards to take action and disqualify Ayrton, but I had too much to contend with to care much about Michael and his indignation. I didn't help myself by sitting near the edge of the track with my head in my hands, looking as though my world had just fallen in. I had yet to learn that people who want to put on pressure will use such a situation to do just that. It's an uncomfortable feeling seeing newspaper pictures of yourself looking demolished. I had completely bodged my first race and provided critics with the ammunition they needed to say to Frank, 'You've picked the wrong bloke. He doesn't know what he's doing: he's got no experience.' The pressure told immediately, and I knew that I was better than this, although the criticism, when it came, inevitably stung. I had to put the episode behind me and prove them wrong.

Chastened but still employed, I went to Brazil determined at least to bring the car home. Prost outqualified me by a whole second. In the race, we had to deal with a typical local rain shower while running slicks, which makes Interlagos a very difficult track at the best of times. It goes anticlockwise, which is not the norm and means the predominant number of left-handers is tough on your neck, the muscles being accustomed to tracks running the other way round. In 1991, Ayrton had used a neck strap to help hold up his head, but the strap had cut off the circulation to his left arm. By the end of the race, he was in agony and driving almost one-handed. The physical exertion was so great that I'm sure some drivers actually prayed for rain, since a wet race would substantially reduce the G-force. The rain, however, made choosing the right moment to change tyres – if at all – paramount because you could gain ten seconds in one lap if you got it right. Or fail to make it round the next lap if you got it wrong.

I was first to stop for rain tyres. Alain was following me and there was some confusion over his radio message; he thought they were telling him to stay out because I was in the pits. He carried on just as the rain was getting worse and slid into the gravel at the first corner. Now I was leading a Grand Prix for the first time. When I stopped a few laps later to return to slicks, Senna had been in a lap earlier and got the jump on me, but I managed to stay on the road and finish second on a day when the three-times World Champion had dropped it. I had redeemed myself a little and earned a bit of breathing space as I stood on the podium for the first time, next to my teammate's adversary in his home Grand Prix. Juan Manuel Fangio, the five-times World Champion, presented the trophy. This was heady stuff for the new boy, and an experience that I would not forget in a hurry. Meanwhile, for Prost it had all gone horribly wrong. The crowd liked it a lot, there not being much love lost on the Frenchman in Brazil, and it put into a new perspective the fierce pressure that I had felt two weeks earlier. For Alain, though, it was only going to get worse.

The third round, the European Grand Prix, was to take place in April at Donington Park. This was a pre-war Grand Prix racetrack owned by Tom Wheatcroft, a wonderful Dickensian character with big bushy sideburns. Tom had been a successful property developer and paid through the nose for the privilege of getting a Grand Prix back to Donington, but it didn't seem to bother him. Even if he had put his entire life savings into it, some say this was the race of Senna's life. I was very familiar with Donington, thanks to racing there many times on bikes. But it was really narrow and tight for F1 cars, particularly at those speeds, hemmed in by concrete walls around the track and very few run-off areas. This race would have intermittent drizzle, making conditions a fine balance between being damp enough for wet tyres and just dry enough for slicks – if you were brave. The conditions oscillated either side of that line throughout the entire race, and Alain and I seemed to be on the wrong tyres at every crucial moment. On one occasion, I came through the pits without actually stopping because Alain was already being attended to in the pit box. Williams were in the habit of letting the driver make the call as to when to change tyres, but Prost was not yet clear about the team's way of working. The whole race was a catastrophe for him and hugely embarrassing, and this same misunderstanding had probably accounted for the incident in Brazil.

Nonetheless, Senna's brilliance made *everyone* look stupid. He started from fourth on the grid and was leading by the end of the first lap. I didn't put up much of a fight – which still irritates me – but I didn't want another moment like South Africa, and as a result we never saw the McLaren again.

Ayrton took it upon himself to make all the decisions about when he would come in and when he wanted to stay out. On top of that, he was able to keep going on slick tyres at times when the rest of us lacked the confidence to do the same. That was the genius of Ayrton.

Alain was a bit anxious about staying out on slicks, which was how I managed to get ahead of him. All the pressure was on him as team leader and senior driver, and although both of us were on the podium, it had been a total fiasco for us as a team. To add to the humiliation, the event was sponsored by my personal sponsor, Sega. The trophy was a ghastly silver effigy of Sonic the Hedgehog which looked ridiculous. After the ceremony, we trooped into the post-race press conference. Ayrton spared Alain nothing, using the occasion to make him very uncomfortable, thanks to a few well-aimed cutting remarks about Alain having the best car and yet still being beaten. I remember wishing I could disappear into the ground because, clearly, they continued to dislike each other intensely. And if that wasn't enough, just to round off his miserable weekend, Alain was savaged by the French press. It demonstrated that life is not necessarily rosy simply because you have the most competitive car: if anything, expectation triggers the pressure. Prost may have been on his way to another championship, but he was being made to pay for it.

From my point of view, I always felt that I was in a strong position. If I could do a good job backing up someone like Alain Prost, then I couldn't go wrong. No one was going to pretend that, at my age and never having won a Grand Prix, I was going to be a front runner against Prost and Senna. Maybe my father would have told me to buck up and not give an inch to anyone. Perhaps I shouldn't have allowed Senna to pass me so easily, and I made a note to myself that survival in this game would require me to harden up considerably, which I made good at the very next race, much to everyone's surprise – including my own.

In April we went to Imola. Senna was pumped after two

wins in a row. He was one of the biggest names in world sport and, as such, he had enormous negotiating power, which he wielded like a whip. Ayrton had held the sport to ransom during the previous winter as he decided whether or not he wanted to continue in F1. This didn't please Bernie Ecclestone, who was trying to sign up TV deals. The television companies were probably asking, 'Well, who have you got? Prost versus Senna?' When Ayrton finally did decide to continue, it was on a race-by-race deal with McLaren. He was definitely the biggest fish in the pond, calling most of the shots and still very much in contention for the title. But it was this kind of behaviour that could win you enemies.

Regardless of the politicking that was taking place way above my station, my confidence had started to grow. At Imola, I was quickest in Friday's qualifying session and I started from the front row of the grid and led the Grand Prix. I had completed so many miles here on my own during testing, I knew exactly what to do when I had an empty track ahead of me, and I felt very comfortable out front – more than I had done during that difficult race in Brazil. In some ways it was like being back out on the bike again.

People imagine racing to be about chasing someone in front. But leading is a completely different game. You have to decide the pace, since no one can tell you how fast is fast enough. Even though this was a Grand Prix and not a national bike race, it was the same deal: once you get in front, put your head down, push all the way and hope you don't see anyone coming up in your mirrors. My mechanic, Les Jones, used to joke about our tactics before a race. He would say, 'Get in front and improve your position.' Nice and simple – at least in theory.

While Alain and Ayrton fought over second place, I started to pull further and further away from them. The race had started on a wet track but after about eight laps we started to think about changing to slicks. I was the last to stop and rejoined to find Senna and Prost bearing down on me. I held them off on the fast run into Tosa but, coming out of the left-hander, I went wide slightly on a damp patch, and suddenly I was third. My frantic attempts to regain my position lasted ten laps before I spun off after having trouble with the brakes, but still – I could now say that I knew how to close the door on Senna. After the race, his manager, Julian Jacobi, came to the Williams motorhome and said Ayrton wanted a word. I thought, this will be interesting. I was going to be given a lecture by the master himself.

When I went into his motorhome, it was like having an audience with the Pope. He sat there, not looking at me directly but clearly thinking carefully about what he was going to say in that slow and rather deliberate manner he had. And all the time, I'm thinking, 'Come on, then. Let's be having it . . .' So he starts off saying, 'You're young.' And I'm thinking, 'I'm the same age as you!' But he goes on, 'You're new to the sport, you should be careful; think about things, about the way you drive: it's a dangerous sport.' I listened respectfully and, when he had finished, I said, 'Thanks, Ayrton, but I don't think I've done anything that I haven't seen you do.' I thanked him for the chat and said I would bear it in mind. Off I went – feeling slightly pleased with myself. I couldn't help but think I must have done something right to warrant a quiet dressing-down from the great man. I had made a mistake at Donington in being too respectful towards Senna, and the veiled threat did nothing to dissuade me from closing the door on him again the next chance I had. It happened in Barcelona at the Spanish Grand Prix, where I was starting from the front row of the grid. There was a bit of confusion when the starting lights played up by flashing orange instead of green. I wasn't sure if this meant the start had been aborted but, when I saw the red and white of Senna's McLaren coming at me in the mirrors, I kept my foot down. Alain, on pole, had been slow away and I was leading again, with Senna right behind me.

A few laps later, Alain, having got past Ayrton, gradually closed in on me and slipstreamed by to take the lead after ten laps. Initially, I was quite happy to let Alain set the pace, but then I began to think I could beat him when I backed off to run in clean air for a few laps – and he did the same. So I closed in and pushed him hard for about twenty laps, and it was clear to everyone watching that we weren't playing about, until suddenly, my engine started to vibrate like hell and I could see smoke and debris pouring out of the back. As I was finding out to my cost, engine failures were more common then than now because there were constant developments as they tried to improve at every race. Another race, another lesson learnt.

After he had won, Alain said he wasn't sure he could have kept up the pace when I was pushing him, but it was pretty clear that I wouldn't have been allowed to overtake him, even so. There was an agreement about us being permitted to race each other, but only until the final ten laps, when we would then have to hold station. I had always been reminded by Frank that Prost was the main man and I was there to support him. This diktat would be difficult to adhere to if my pace continued to improve and my confidence grew, as I was starting to feel very comfortable in the car. Meanwhile, the media were having a great time with what was going on in front of them. In the search for headlines, it was pointed out that if I had won, I would have had the distinction of taking my first victory earlier than any other British driver, in terms of the number of races. Added to which, it would also have been twenty-five years since my father had won the same race.

Of course, no one needed to be reminded of my dad's statistics when we got to Monaco, a race he had won five times. It is an awesome place to drive any racing car, never mind an F1 car. Throw in a wet track – which it was, during first qualifying on the Thursday – and you have all you need to allow a driver to show what he can do. The surface was beginning to dry towards the end of the sixty minutes and I timed it just right, beating Alain to provisional pole by 0.6s, a result I was both surprised by and thrilled with. This being

Monaco, with practice starting on Thursday and a day off on Friday, I was on pole for a full forty-eight hours, before the final qualifying race on the Saturday. With journalists looking for something to write about in the absence of track action, I was the story, and I was happy to oblige.

Monaco is a stressful place for every driver because it's easy to throw it all away with even a light touch on the barriers. The pace of the event is also exhausting. If you miss a practice session for whatever reason – an accident or a problem with the car – then you lose vital track time, and of all the tracks out there Monaco is the one where you need all of that to get up to speed. It is one of the very few tracks that require a kind of winding-up of the brain, a familiarisation process where you have to keep driving, lap after lap, until, eventually, driving the car quickly become almost an unconscious thing. The first-ever lap you do at Monaco seems to last for thirty seconds, but by the time you do the last lap, it seems to take half an hour. Your brain has expanded its consciousness to the point where speed seems slow and the track seems massive, which of course is exactly the state of mind you want to be in. By contrast, if you mess up during qualifying it's very difficult to leap ahead after that, and if you try too hard, you end up having an accident. Sometimes it can happen through no fault of the driver – as I was to find out during free practice on the Saturday morning.

As I came out of the tunnel at full speed – about 175mph – the left-rear suspension collapsed. I spun and careered down the hill towards the chicane. There was a traffic island separating the track from the escape road at the bottom of the hill, and if you hit the end of the island, as Karl Wendlinger was to do one year later, you would come to a stop very quickly. Fortunately, I just missed it and went down the escape road at high speed. Regardless of that setback, from which I quickly recovered, Prost proved to be the master of qualifying by going more than a second faster than me. I didn't get it together and ended up fourth, Alain and I split by Schumacher and Senna. But then it all went wrong for Alain in the race. He had clutch trouble, stalled during a pit stop and had a stop-go penalty for moving prematurely at the start. He felt all of this was very harsh and made things even more difficult for him. He seemed to feel disappointment acutely, which brought to the surface the vulnerability that was easy to spot in the garage, but which he was usually able to conceal on the track. Meanwhile, I finished second as Senna scored his sixth win at Monaco. At the press conference, I thought it would be the honourable thing to congratulate him on behalf of my father for beating Dad's record – which he gracefully accepted and reached across to shake hands. I said I was sure my father would have been delighted that a driver such as Ayrton had beaten his record, but I remain just as sure that my father would not have been so supportive of all of Senna's actions on the track. Ayrton was a brilliant but occasionally very angry driver. In an interview with Ayrton at the Australian GP in 1990, Jackie Stewart famously challenged him on his record of accidents with other drivers, claiming Senna had had more of those than all the World Champions put together. Needless to say, this did not go down well with the enigmatic man himself.

We were to be in a battle for second place at the next race in Canada as I fended Senna off and Alain got away in the lead. Then a pit stop took far too long, thanks to Prost's tyres being brought out instead of mine, and by the time they had sorted it out, I was down in fourth place and only made it to the podium thanks to Senna retiring. Despite putting a brave face on it when I talked to the press, I was pretty hacked off about losing what should have been second place.

Sometimes Williams appeared more as an engineering company that went racing rather than the other way round; a race team that did engineering. That sounds harsh, but very often they were all at sea during pit stops, and neither were they as sharp as Benetton would become under Ross Brawn at thinking tactically during a race. In 2016, Williams often won the DHL Pit Stop Award for ridiculously quick stops of just over two seconds for all four wheels, but in 1993 the Canadian incident was another demonstration that communication continued to be the team's Achilles' heel. A couple of weeks later in France, I wouldn't have blamed Alain had he chosen not to communicate with me. I had taken pole at his home Grand Prix and I was determined to make the most of it – as Alain was only too aware. I liked Magny-Cours and had a feeling my first pole position was coming. I shot into the lead with Alain on my tail. It stayed that way until the pit stop, when I came in first and got delayed by Michael Andretti's McLaren in the pit lane. Alain saw his chance and put the hammer down for two laps before making his stop and rejoining in the lead.

In the closing stages, I was stuck to Prost's gearbox. I was right on top of him when I got a radio message saying that Alain had asked if I could slow down. I took the opportunity to say I was going as slow as I could, which got a laugh in the garage. We had a pretty comfortable margin over Schumacher's Benetton but I was not allowed to overtake Alain, since this was the French Grand Prix, and halfway through the season Alain was only leading Ayrton by five points. It made sense to give him the space to claim the maximum ten points for the race. Even so, this was a good result for me and for the British media's speculation about my next race: my home Grand Prix, Silverstone.

There may have been team orders for the race, but there were no rules about qualifying. Prost outqualified me this time by 0.13s; we were ahead of Schumacher and Senna. The race looked pretty much sewn up, Silverstone being one of our strongest tracks, and we were working well together as a team. Going into the race, there was a lot of stirring of the pot. If people wanted me to win, I wasn't going to argue. Alain knew the score and Williams, having gone through the Mansell experience a few years before, were not going to be pushed around or phased by tabloid newspapers. Equally, Ann

Bradshaw, the wonderful PR officer at Williams, was on hand to keep a lid on events.

Having shown I could race, I went into this one thinking I had every chance of winning it – provided I could get ahead. Which is exactly what I did when Alain made a poor start and Senna helped me by jumping ahead of Prost. Never mind trying to beat me, the one thing Ayrton wanted to do was trounce Alain. By all accounts, they really went at it, with Senna chopping his old rival more than once before Alain finally got by after six laps, by which time I was eight seconds down the road. If Prost wanted this win, he would have to press on a bit and take it from me. I couldn't see Williams asking me to wave him through in front of the British fans. Everything seemed under control as I more or less maintained the gap until the pit stops. This time, I was in and out without a problem, but Alain was better in the traffic and closed right up. Then the pressure really came when a safety car closed up the field for three laps. At the restart, I managed to pull away slightly and, just as I was working on maintaining the lead, the engine erupted in a plume of white smoke, accompanied by a massive and collective groan from the crowd. Only moments before, I had been out there in true Mansell style, giving the fans something to cheer for. When I rolled to a halt in the infield, I thought I'd better show that I was really cheesed off. I stood by the barrier and made an attempt to kick the car, Basil Fawlty style, which later prompted Patrick to say in his best booming fatherly advice voice, 'Look, Damon, I really don't think it's a good idea for you to be seen kicking the car.' I knew, though, that I was only one stroke of luck away from claiming my first victory.

16 » ZERO TO HERO: A GRAND PRIX WINNER AT LAST

From Silverstone, it was off to Germany. Formula One is a small world, and people tend not to forget, as I discovered during free practice for the German Grand Prix at Hockenheim. Having been a former Ferrari driver, Michele Alboreto was probably finding life less attractive driving a Lola for the small Scuderia Italia team – it's hard going up, but it can be just as hard coming down. In my desperation to get pole during qualifying for the French Grand Prix a few months before, I'd pulled up on Alboreto at the last-but-one corner at Magny-Cours, and as I went through, I banged wheels with the Lola by mistake, leaving him with a damaged car. In the excitement of having got pole position, I'd forgotten to apologise, but it hadn't slipped Michele's mind.

We crossed paths again going into Hockenheim's Sachs Kurve during practice. When he left the door open, I took that as a sign to go through, and he ran me clean off the road. I couldn't believe it. I was staggered that he'd done this and marched down to his pit afterwards to have a word, until it dawned on me that he was still upset about the incident in France.

By this stage in the season, I could sense a shift in the media's mood. With twenty-two points to my name, I was starting to look less like an understudy and more like a possible winner. This belief was further enforced at Hockenheim when Alain made a bad start and I jumped into the lead. I stayed there for a few laps until Alain came past, but he didn't remain in front for long. On the first lap, Prost had taken to the escape road but, according to the stewards, he hadn't rejoined in the proper manner and received a ten-second stop-go penalty. He was absolutely livid, feeling once again that he was being unfairly picked on. By the time he rejoined and worked his way back to second place, I was about fifteen seconds in front and feeling pretty comfortable, but I wasn't sure what the team expected me to do: carry on or allow Alain to catch up and take the lead? I got on the radio and was reassured to see 'P1 OK' on my pit board. All I had to do was keep going. The laps counted down and I was told later that the British newspaper journalists were already formulating their reports with lines such as my maiden win coming thirty-one years after my dad had won the German Grand Prix. For my part, I felt everything was under control and I backed off slightly. On the penultimate lap, the puncture warning light came on in the cockpit. Initially, I wasn't too worried because the light would sometimes appear if the tyre temperatures and pressures dropped because you weren't pushing too hard. It was only when I came out of one of the chicanes and the car started to oversteer that I started to worry. A few seconds later, the left-rear tyre blew as I accelerated down the straight – something sharp had gone right through the tread. I crawled into the stadium on three wheels and came to a halt on the infield, leaving Alain to pass me on the way to his fifty-first win. I dressed it up as best I could as a test of my resilience, but I was massively disappointed to have got so close, just like at Silverstone, only to fall at the last.

I was in a fortunate position at Williams; not only did I have a top car but I had Alain Prost as my benchmark. At least I had a means to show my potential. One of the best ways was through qualifying, which is a pure test of out-and-out speed. I had outqualified Alain, so I knew it was possible; I'd overcome my first race and the nervous start; I had led races and had proved I could handle it. Now I simply needed everything to come together; that and a bit of luck.

I have always loved the Hungary Grand Prix track. This, after all, was one of the two circuits where I'd managed to qualify the Brabham; the Williams FW15C was a walk in the park after that. It's a bit like a giant kart track, which means that it's very physical, tight, bumpy and slippery. From the moment I got in the car, I felt I could hustle it and roll it into the corners and drive through using the throttle. People have been disparaging about this track but I always felt I could get the best out of myself there. To win, I needed to start from the front of the grid, overtaking being almost impossible here. I duly managed that, with Alain taking pole by a couple of tenths of a second. Sadly for him, his efforts would be wasted on race day. The Williams clutch caught Alain out again and he stalled, meaning he would have to start from the back. I suddenly found myself leading the field to the grid. I might have had the front row all to myself but I knew that Schumacher's Benetton would be just over my left shoulder, starting on the cleaner side of the track. And Senna's McLaren was right behind me. If ever I needed to make the perfect start, it was now.

Not only did I make one of my best so far, but Schumacher and Senna both made enough errors on that first lap to allow me to finish it nearly two seconds ahead, which was a sufficient distance to make overtaking impossible. Now all I had to do was stay there – for another seventy-six laps. That would take almost two hours, in searing mid-European summer heat. Hungary is dry and hot; the track surface uneven. It sucks the energy out of you and bashes your head over every bump.

I was helped by Senna and Schumacher both retiring and Alain starting from the back, but this race was all about concentration, not letting up for a moment and, just as important, trying not to think about winning my first Grand Prix before I had crossed the line: the golden rule of racing. I developed a technique eventually to stop this premature thought: I would add a number of laps to whatever was shown on my pit board. If it said '10 remaining', I thought, '20'. But with a few laps to go, I admit I was already thinking about what to say. Winning my first Grand Prix would be an emotional moment, all things considered.

By the end of the race, I had lapped everyone except Riccardo Patrese in his Benetton and Gerhard Berger's Ferrari. In fact, I was more than a minute ahead of Patrese when the chequered flag finally appeared, making this probably one of the least pressured race wins in history. But nothing was going to diminish the moment, not even a dead leg I had acquired. Once I had levered myself from the cramped cockpit it was a while before I could actually walk, let alone celebrate with the team. When the announcers called out my name as winner, I hopped onto the podium and, not really knowing how to react, I took a bow. Tradition says that you should leap up and down and punch the air like a champion, but my British public-schoolboy awkwardness came out, right on cue. It had taken just under ten years to come from a no-hope novice to Grand Prix winner. After a lot of graft and heartache, I'd finally done it: the Hill name was back. In the press conference, I dedicated my first win to 'Hills, past, present and future', and I was proud to have achieved something only a very few racing drivers can ever do and added another victory to the family tally.

To avoid the terrible traffic jams associated with this race, we were taking a helicopter to the airport and then getting onto Frank's jet. I thought, 'This is it! I've arrived!' But any hopes of travelling in style were dashed the minute I saw the chopper. It was a Russian make and had been on standby as the air ambulance. It looked like a child's drawing of a helicopter: an ugly machine that appeared to be made of corrugated iron and had clearly been painted a few times by hand; the paint-work was all chipped and rough, like on a cross-channel ferry. So we all climbed aboard – me, Patrick, Frank, Adrian Newey and Frank's nurse – effectively, the nucleus of Williams Grand Prix engineering in a single aircraft, just as in my father's accident. The thing vibrated and shook as it struggled into the air, and it occurred to me that, in Grand Prix terms, this was quite a precious cargo sitting in a helicopter that was built to last, but that none of us was convinced was built to fly. Patrick pithily commented, 'Frank, in future, it might be a good idea if we didn't all fly together.' As a warning, it was of limited value: we had already landed.

The offer of the trip home proved I was at last in the team's good books, not an easy thing to achieve in an organisation like Williams where the expectation is always to win. The result didn't really sink in until the following day when I opened the newspapers and read about it. The only reservation I had was the relative ease with which I had won, but I would make up for that two weeks later at Spa-Francorchamps when I had tremendous pressure all the way, fending off Schumacher and Prost not only to win for a second time but also to pull it off on a truly fantastic circuit: one that everyone respected. It was Renault's fiftieth Grand Prix win and there was no doubt they wanted Alain to win it. They had been through a lot together, including more difficult times in 1983 when Renault ran their own team. The expectation of a first French World Championship had been incredibly high at the time and, when they failed to win all those years ago, Prost had been made the fall guy. For this race in Belgium, Renault had produced a big placard to celebrate the moment and I remember Frank being amused by the fact that they'd now have to swallow a British winner.

After Spa, there were four races left in 1993. Until then, I'd not given any thought to the championship; it was, after all, Prost's to win and I was under no illusions about my role. But the two victories, while perhaps not giving me cause to think about the title, at least allowed me serious consideration of challenging Senna's second place on the table. We were separated by just five points when we headed for Monza –

another of my favourite circuits. I loved the speed and the atmosphere of the circuit and I'd gone really well there in F3000. In 1990, I had qualified on pole and was flying during the race until my car had an electrical problem. So with that in the memory bank, plus the two F1 wins in succession, I felt confident going into the Italian Grand Prix. That feeling would continue when Alain and I filled the front row, beating Jean Alesi's Ferrari in front of the home crowd. Alain was on pole by a fairly large gap of 0.32s. At the start, Senna was right behind me as we braked for the first chicane. Ironically after the Imola ticking-off, he clobbered my left-rear wheel, sending us both off the road. Recovering from ninth place, I began to climb through the field. An engine failure on Schumacher's Benetton-Ford helped me into second place – by which time Alain was eighteen seconds in front and heading for the win that would guarantee his fourth championship.

I was catching him at quite a rate and the team began to worry that I might be going to cause trouble, so they came on the radio and asked me to confirm that I would not race Alain. I was absolutely flying and so wound up that I replied, 'Tell Alain I will race. I will race.' They came back and said, 'Thank you.' They must have misheard me, which left me in a predicament. What would I do when I caught him? Even I didn't know. There had been an agreement not to change position less than ten laps from the end of a race, but it had been spoken about quite some time before, and I wasn't sure if the arrangement was still active. As we peeled through the laps, I was hunting Prost down, getting closer and closer and closer until the gap was under five seconds, when suddenly his engine went boom in the middle of the Curva Grande, the white smoke making it temporarily impossible to see where I was going as I came through the long, fast corner. I never got to find out whether I would have tried to pass him; Renault had answered the question for me. I was on my way to win number three.

A hat-trick should not have been surprising because the

car was so dominant, but I was pushing myself because I could not afford to be seen to sit back and let it all come to me. My contract was for one year and already there was media speculation about my future with Williams, thanks to rumours that Frank was talking to Senna. I had to show form, otherwise I knew they would sign someone else without a second thought. But with three wins, Williams could now think, 'OK, we've got a driver here who is quick, can take pole positions and win races.' Surely I was past the shaky-start phase in South Africa by now? As ever, it was all down to Frank.

I had come a long way since the beginning of the season. Wins do something irreversible to your mind and I was not the same driver at all as the one who had started the season. They also do something to the minds of others, solidifying your credentials to a degree. But F1 is brutal and relentless, and even the very best get a grilling. It was helpful being pitched against someone as successful as Prost so early in my career, as he showed me I still had to improve but I was not too far off a four-times World Champion. My good form continued to the end of the season with a pole position and a couple more podiums. In the end, Alain did win the championship and I finished a few points behind Senna. But it was 'job done', from my point of view; whether Williams would think the same remained to be seen. Whatever they decided, my first full season as an F1 driver was under my belt at thirty-three, the same age my father had been when he won his first World Championship.

17 » SENNA AND IMOLA: THE PERFECT STORM

With my first full season in F1 nicely concluded, Frank was sufficiently impressed to open the door to his office again. Except for my final two years with Jordan, I only ever had a one-year contract in my entire racing career. Motor sport is not for those who like security and the prospect of long-term employment. As the saying goes, you are only as good as your last race, but it serves as good motivation.

Being in F1 therefore involves a perpetual process of navigation through the minefield of team principals, press, managers and the ringmaster himself, Bernie Ecclestone. It also involves doing deals, and while some people absolutely love this game and Frank Williams is one of them, I found the whole thing unnecessarily time-consuming, stressful and occasionally just plain daft. Because these games are a constant in our business, whatever you do will be interpreted as part of a negotiation, like it or not, and as a result there is a continual presumption of untrustworthiness. I worked out quickly enough that it was better to get other people to do the negotiating for me.

The problem with this method is that key men such as Frank and Bernie do not like dealing with minions. For my first contract with Williams, I was mindful of this and agreed my retainer personally with Frank, knowing that I was in a weak position and the only thing that mattered was getting the drive, whatever I was paid. Now, however, with three Grand Prix victories to my name and a greater degree of leverage thanks to the media coverage, I was what they call a 'commodity' with a more tradable value. The question was, what was that value now? So I sent Michael Breen in to see if he could get a better deal from Frank for 1994.

Meanwhile, Frank had been busy doing business with Johann Rupert, a large and very direct South African whose company owned the Rothmans cigarette brand, and had made a fortune out of inventing the king size filter cigarette. Their company also had a few offshoots in the luxury goods sector, including Cartier, Alfred Dunhill, Baume and Mercier, Piaget and Montblanc, and they were about to tempt the world's greatest living racing driver, Ayrton Senna, away from McLaren, a team where he had been for most of his F1 career and which was sponsored by their main tobacco rival, Marlboro.

At thirty-three, and having bagged three world titles already, Ayrton Senna simply wanted to keep winning. Based on what he had seen in 1992 and 1993, it was obvious Williams would dominate F1, at least for a while, and if Senna moved there, he could win a few more championships and then retire at Ferrari, where he had talked about wanting to end his career. But even Ayrton had to negotiate money, and the rumour going around Williams was that Frank had been prompted by Ayrton to ask Johann if he could increase the offer, to which Johann apparently replied, 'I pay the organ grinder. Not the monkey!' Clearly Ayrton's demi-god status cut no ice with Johann!

Prost, on the other hand, probably knew his time was up but had cleverly done a two-year deal at the start of 1993. Since their bitter times as teammates at McLaren, and after Senna refused to yield at the first corner of the Japanese GP in 1990, resulting in them both going off at high speed, he wouldn't countenance driving with Ayrton ever again. Frank had to fly to the south of France and agree to buy him out of his contract, and Prost quietly left the stage, with his four

World Championship titles and only Fangio above him with five titles.

Patrick's cautionary words about F1 taking no prisoners had proved truer than I had the capacity to appreciate at the time. But if I thought I now knew the score, I was about to find out there was no end to just how serious things could get. As Bill Shankly famously said about football, 'Some people believe football is a matter of life and death . . . I can assure you, it's much, much more important than that.' The difference with F1 was that the risk of dying, or apparently not being afraid to die to get what you wanted, meant racing drivers and the teams had a ruthlessness bordering on callousness when it came to winning.

I thought I was pretty serious about winning, but nothing I had experienced had come close to the intensity of the rivalry between Senna and Prost. At Suzuka the previous year, in 1993, I had accompanied Prost to the helipad because the Japanese fans made the short walk from the track utterly impossible. When we arrived, there was Senna standing in the queue for the helicopter on his own. We could easily all have made the one-minute trip together, but he and Prost didn't even look at each other. Senna took the next ride alone, while we hung back for the helicopter to return, and Prost gave me a wry smile that might have said, 'Welcome to my life.' But in 1994, Senna was to lose his old foe and a new unknown quantity was about to emerge to challenge Senna's status as top dog.

Since his sensational debut for Jordan in 1991, Michael Schumacher had been lurking just below the surface of F1 like a great white shark. From the moment he arrived in the sport the new players in the game of F1 had pounced on Schumacher: Flavio Briatore, Ross Brawn and Tom Walkinshaw. The latter two, having won Le Mans with Jaguar, were the racing experts; Briatore had come from marketing within the huge Italian knitwear company, Benetton, which now owned an F1 team. Bernie had noted that Michael put 20,000 extra fans on the gate at Spa that year, and with the German economy becoming one of the strongest in the world it was obvious that Michael was box-office gold. While Senna was coming to be seen by some as a troublesome Brazilian causing embarrassment, Schumacher represented a powerful new piece on the F1 board. Bernie and Max Mosley, the new President of the Fédération International de l'Automobile, worked closely to ensure the future of F1, and there was no doubt a Senna–Schumacher rivalry would fit the bill nicely.

Max had also wasted no time in challenging certain technical regulations to improve F1 as a spectator sport. In 1993 he had pushed through the implementation of narrow rear tyres as an attempt not only to slow the cars down but also to make them slide around more, and make racing more thrilling to watch. For 1994, we also had the reintroduction of in-race refuelling, which had been a regular part of Grand Prix racing in the early 1950s. The Brabham team tried it in the early 1980s, leading to a dangerous phase of the sport with teams force-feeding fuel at high pressure into their cars. In 1984, they decided to ban it before something really awful happened. Ten years later it was back, but with gravity-fed fuel pipes only.

Max's big ambition was to use F1 and the FIA to promote road safety improvements. When it was decided in 1994 to introduce a pace car to lead the field when necessary, calling it 'The Safety Car' emphasised this goal. The thinking was that, in the event of an incident where caution needed to be exercised, the field would be slowed behind this car rather than having the race stopped. In principle, it was a good idea. In practice, it required further work.

In Brazil, the first race of the 1993 season, the safety car was a Fiat Tempra. A sudden downpour when it was deployed made it immediately obvious that this car was completely unsuitable. Even when the F1 cars were in first gear, the driver of the safety car was having enormous difficulty staying on the track. Ayrton said it was not acceptable because we couldn't maintain the all-important tyre pressures at such slow speeds. This became a bone of contention between Senna and Mosley. F1 now uses an extremely high-performance Mercedes-Benz GT S safety car with a professional driver rather than some local man at the wheel, but in 1994 they were years away from that level of sophistication. All this was in the mix for the start of the 1994 F1 season. I thought I would be a bit player but, as things turned out, I would be smack in the middle of this new drama. It would change my life forever.

During the pre-season press hype, I was repeatedly asked if I was psyched out by the thought of having Ayrton Senna as a teammate. 'Why?' I asked. 'What's he going to do? Put me in a Vulcan Mind Grip?' In my book, we all put our trousers on one leg at a time and I tried to convince myself that Ayrton was a normal human being, just like the rest of us. But the press were right, and he cast the same sense of awe over the other drivers as he did over the fans, and the whole nation of Brazil. He was Ayrton Senna and I had better get used to it.

Michael Breen might have negotiated a few improvements to my Williams deal but I would effectively remain a number-two driver, even though Ayrton never stipulated that he had number-one status. His contract simply said that he would receive 'not less than equal equipment', but he would have to take into account the FIA's banning of active suspension, which had given Williams such a huge advantage over their rivals. Ironically, this had come about partly through Senna's own doing.

At the end of 1992, Ayrton had accepted an invitation from Penske to visit the Firebird Raceway in Arizona and drive an IndyCar. At the time, he was losing enthusiasm for F1 and made remarks about IndyCars being 'more human'; meaning you had to change gear with a lever and the cars were not using driver aids. While he was definitely playing games, I understood his point. The effect was to turn the tide against the pre-eminence of Williams in this particular field, just in time for Ayrton to join the team! For 1994, cars would return to 'passive suspension', which was more or less the old suspension system, although, thankfully, the semi-automatic gearbox would stay. Meanwhile, Williams were working on power steering: a new and welcome development. Losing active suspension was a retrograde step technically, but taken in the interests of 'the sport' and to reduce costs and complexity. The truth was that the other teams were not up to speed with active and campaigned loudly for a ban on the perceived Williams magic ingredient. The resulting levelling effect was such that Ayrton found himself with less of the huge advantage that had been enjoyed by Prost, but he was big enough to deal with that.

During the 1994 pre-season testing, the car's feel was unfamiliar to Senna and also to me, since I had spent the majority of my time at Williams in an actively-suspended car. Adrian Newey had done another fantastic job and the car generated massive downforce, but we wondered if it was all too much and responsible for creating what is known as 'porpoising', a phenomenon caused by the car's downforce attaching and releasing in an uncontrolled oscillation. During a test at Imola, the car bounced wildly on its tyres, and we only finally started to get on top of it by adjusting the damping, which made the car much better to drive. It goes to show how much of an impact apparently minor changes in the rules can have: it would take almost half a season to get to where we really ought to have been at the start.

In the garage and out on the track, I watched with fascination as Ayrton applied all of his famous intensity and attention to detail. Having been with McLaren for six years, he must have found the people at Williams and their culture and way of working strange. He stalked the garage looking serious as he scrutinised everything, in striking contrast to Nigel Mansell who would gather all around him and entertain because he loved the attention. Prost, on the other hand, would work quietly and unobtrusively with his engineer and talk to carefully selected journalists. From the moment he arrived, Senna seemed perpetually pensive. He gave the impression of someone carrying the mantle of being the best of all time while embodying the hopes and dreams of the entire Brazilian nation. On a few occasions, he wanted to know what I thought of the car. 'Does it always feel like this?' he asked. I couldn't say because I had less to go on than him, and I was rather hoping he would tell me. As the season beckoned, Ayrton would never have believed that he would fail to finish a single race.

It was a measure of Senna's brilliance that he put that car on pole at Interlagos, which was a horrendously bumpy and twisty circuit. I was fourth fastest: a shocking second and a half down the grid. In the race, Ayrton led for a while but then the car got the better of him when lying second and trying to catch Schumacher. Senna spinning – on his home track – said everything about how hard that car was to drive. I finished second, one lap down. I was physically destroyed after seventy laps, and I could not imagine how Ayrton had managed to get as far as he did. I had six points and a lot of thinking to do. Ayrton had none and the weight of the world on him.

It got worse when we went to Aida in Japan for the Pacific Grand Prix. Senna was on pole again; this time I was 'only' half a second slower in third place. Going into the first corner, Ayrton was tapped by the McLaren of Mika Häkkinen, and the Williams went into the gravel – where it was hit by Nicola Larini's Ferrari. Two races, two retirements: both races won by Schumacher. Despite retiring with mechanical trouble, I stayed ahead of Ayrton in the championship.

As we flew back from Tokyo to London, Ayrton reflected on what had gone wrong, as there had been rumblings about whether or not Benetton were doing something clever with the butterflies on their engine as a means of circumventing the latest rule banning traction control. According to Ayrton, the Ford engine sounded different as Schumacher accelerated out of the first corner. It was probably also dawning on him that this season was going to be tougher than he had bargained for. He was sitting directly behind me on the plane and I wanted to get to know him better and find out what he made of Schumacher, who had taken the season by storm, but I never had the nerve to disturb him, as he gave the impression of a man who wanted time on his own. He was a thinker, and a devout Christian. He had enormous compassion and was a fighter for what he believed to be right. As we were later to discover, there was a lot going on in his personal as well as his professional life.

Going into the San Marino Grand Prix in Imola, two weeks later, the team had made enough progress during testing to feel more optimistic, and we believed that we were starting to get a proper handle on the car. Meanwhile, the headlines in the press were asking, 'Senna: can he take the heat?' and 'Schumacher 20: Senna 0', referring to the championship race. Ayrton's private life was undergoing increasing turmoil, the Senna family reputedly not liking Ayrton's new girlfriend, Adriane Galisteu. Combined with his suspicion that Schumacher was taking his victories in a car that might be bending the rules, and the Williams car not being as competitive as he had hoped, Senna had a lot of distractions going into the first practice session at Imola, where Rubens Barrichello, a twenty-one-year-old fellow Brazilian, had an enormous accident coming into the penultimate chicane. We all watched in horror as the monitors showed the car running along the top of the tyre barrier and, for a moment, looking like it might flip over towards the grandstand. It came to rest on its side and when the marshals shoved the car back onto its wheels you could see Rubens's head give the side of the cockpit another whack. If he wasn't unconscious before that, he probably was now. Professor Sid Watkins was on the spot and overseeing everything once they got Barrichello to the medical centre, and Ayrton went to check on him. Rubens regained consciousness to find his fellow countryman weeping over him, a clear sign of Ayrton's emotional state. Rubens would be a bit concussed but otherwise OK. The marshals fixed up the barrier and we continued practice.

The press, meanwhile, sensed a story. I bumped into Bernie after practice, just as the journalists were pummelling him with questions about the chicane kerbs being too big and responsible for launching Barrichello's car. Bernie was throwing the question back by saying something like, 'Yeah, why do we have kerbs? What are they there for?' – and then looking at me to respond as if it was something to do with me! All of which confused the journalists because they couldn't move the debate on, but it was evident there were worries because it had been a spectacular shunt and the kerbs had nearly launched the car into the stands. Bernie's evasiveness aside, after that weekend the height of the kerbs was reduced almost to the point of being flat.

Although startled by the accident, I continued to take my dad's stoic attitude, which was: 'It's dangerous. You know it's dangerous. If you have a problem with that, you should sort out your concern before you get in the car. Once you step into the cockpit and go onto the track, you have accepted the unwritten conditions.' But I also needed to avoid hitting the kerbs. Over the next forty-eight hours, that stoic attitude was about to be put to the test in the biggest way imaginable.

Feeling a bit better about the car going into qualifying on the Saturday, we looked competitive against Benetton. Ayrton had just gone quickest when the session was suddenly red-flagged as the Austrian driver Roland Ratzenberger, attempting to qualify for his second Grand Prix, had gone off on the 200mph approach to Tosa. I drove past the scene slowly, marshals' flags waving, and saw this had been a huge accident with not much sign of life in what remained of the Simtek. It was the fastest part of the track, but I had seen big shunts before in which the driver was knocked out but later recovered, and I returned to the pits to wait for qualifying to eventually resume. What followed was one of those horrible moments when the track goes silent and you are in the garage watching television pictures of the medical people at the scene doing all they can. Ayrton was out of his car immediately and was clearly affected by what he was seeing. On the monitor we could see that Sid and the team were working urgently on Roland while he was still in the car, which was one step beyond Barrichello's accident. When that happens, you know it's pretty serious.

Ayrton got an official's car to take him to the scene. It was typical of him to do that: to take the initiative, because he never saw himself as simply a competitor. As a World Champion and senior driver, he took responsibility for everything that was involved in his life. His view seemed to be, when you go onto the track, you need to understand as much as you can about every facet of what this game involves, or you don't have the right to call yourself a racing driver. Many drivers choose not to know, but I had seen, in my father and in Jackie Stewart, the same willingness to go right to the heart of the most difficult and unpleasant aspects of this sport. I had witnessed Bertrand Fabi's accident first-hand and I had sadly seen other fatal incidents. I think Ayrton was right in feeling that he had to be aware of everything that was going on. He needed to see what could be learned, not just for himself, but for future reference and for the safety of every driver. He was clearly deeply upset by what he found, as we all were.

Roland would be the first fatality in F1 since 1986 when Elio de Angelis had been killed while testing his Brabham at Paul Ricard, and Williams and Benetton were among a few teams that chose not to continue qualifying when the session resumed after a forty-minute delay. Ayrton himself told Frank that he would not resume the session, but Betise Assumpção, Ayrton's PR manager, was told to let Ayrton know that he would be threatened with disqualification if he did not go back on track. He stuck to his principles, though, and gave the stewards a conundrum, which they dealt with by taking no action.

Saturday night was, understandably, a pretty grim affair. I didn't know Roland very well but he was a handsome man: a charmer, by all accounts. Naturally, everyone wanted to know what had happened. Roland was with Simtek, a new team that was doing its best but with a limited budget; it was his big opportunity to be in F1. It quickly transpired that the Simtek's front wing had come off and gone under the front wheels, in which case there would have been no way of steering or stopping the car at over 200mph. There was a suggestion the wing might have been damaged beforehand, possibly on one of the high kerbs. If there was a subsequent weakness, then it was going to fail when under full aerodynamic load; in other words, at top speed. We all analysed the circumstances of the accident as far as we were able, and the conjecture that the front wing failed because it had been damaged on the kerb seemed the most plausible. I made another mental note. Even though I was in a Williams, I knew nothing was unbreakable.

Ayrton was very close with Professor Watkins. He had stayed with Sid at his home in the Borders and there Ayrton confided in Sid with many of his innermost thoughts. Following Ratzenberger's accident, they had a long talk as the Prof tried to console Ayrton and to persuade him to stop racing, saying, 'You've got nothing left to prove. Give it up and let's go fishing together.' According to Sid, Ayrton thought for about a minute, then said quite simply: 'Sid, I have to go on.'

On race morning, we dutifully and soberly trooped to the track, where there was none of the usual pre-race banter. Georgie was in the team motorhome and Ayrton came in to get changed. She asked if he wanted her to leave but he gamely said she could stay and he engaged her in casual conversation, asking if she had children. As they spoke, he hung up his Senninha T-shirt. Senninha was a cartoon character of himself as a young boy, designed to inspire young Senna fans to follow his lead, always do what is right and get an education. (Before leaving Brazil to come to Imola, Ayrton had talked with his sister, Viviane, about doing more with Senninha for impoverished Brazilian children. She would eventually set up the Ayrton Senna Foundation which gives all the profits from Senna merchandise to their chosen charities.) Georgie replied that we had Oliver and Josh. He asked her about them and then said, 'Don't worry about Damon. He'll be OK. Williams are a good team.' It was an enormously generous thing to say: a measure of his incredible sensitivity to show concern for others and their feelings at a time like that.

Georgie and I had both noticed that there was something different about Senna's demeanour in 1994. He had yet to settle in at Williams and Georgie remembers seeing him arrive that weekend and poking his nose into the garage for the first time. She says no one said hello. If the truth be told, I think most of us were a bit in awe of him. But backing up the impression that Ayrton still felt disorientated at Williams, Jo Ramírez, who had looked after all the little logistical things for the drivers at McLaren, told of how Ayrton had called him that weekend to say there was no one at Williams to do all these important little jobs. As a favour, would Jo organise a helicopter to take Ayrton to the airport once the race had finished? Whatever was going on in the background, Ayrton's press officer Betise Assumpção's view was that, 'You could just tell Ayrton didn't want to race.' But there is a world of difference between not wanting to do something and feeling you have to, like going over the top in the Battle of the Somme. That comparison is not as overblown as you might suppose. I think Ayrton felt compelled not to disappoint all those who had come to believe in him. His nephew, Bruno, described his uncle this way: 'People were aware he was fighting for something more important than just winning races. It was a belief. He was convinced that he had been given a singular opportunity by God, and he had the personality to make the most of it. These are the qualities that make special people in history.' We can only imagine the emotions and thoughts that were going through Ayrton's mind that day. No one but he knew what they were. That said, he was one of the sport's greatest-ever competitors and by the time we came to race, I'm pretty convinced he had only one thing on his mind: winning.

In the pre-race warm-up, Senna was significantly fastest: he absolutely nailed it. I rarely went flat out in the warm-up because I couldn't see the point; I just wanted to get a feel for the car. But Ayrton was on it, qualifying pace, putting down a marker for the race. Everything about his attitude said he wanted to stop the rot of the past two DNFs; everything about his warm-up said he was out to stop the Benetton runaway train and score his first victory of the season. Michael was not quick, perhaps not wanting to show his hand before the race and reveal his strategy. At some point after the warm-up Ayrton even had a brief rapprochement with Prost, who had made an appearance. Ayrton had filmed a short piece for French TV, driving a lap of Imola in a road car and sending Prost this message: 'To my friend Alain. We miss you, Alain.' Prost would be the primary pall-bearer at his funeral and now sits on the board of the Senna Foundation.

On the way to the drivers' briefing, Ayrton pulled me over to have a quiet word. He wanted my cooperation with something. He said Gerhard was going to start a conversation about the safety car, criticising it for being hopelessly inadequate. He asked if I would follow on with a further question to get the ball rolling, and then he would pitch in but not appear to be the instigator.

Ever since he accused the FIA of favouring Prost at Suzuka in 1989, Ayrton viewed the organisation with suspicion and did not want to incur their wrath, because he knew better than most how political F1 could be. Indeed, they were already going after him because he had failed to attend the previous day's obligatory post-qualifying press conference. They let that one go but were back on race day, accusing him of commandeering a car to go onto the track. This incensed Ayrton, naturally enough. But rules are rules and the FIA were not prepared to make any allowances, even for exceptional people in exceptional circumstances.

Gerhard and I duly made our points, and Ayrton joined in, expressing his concern about the safety car. There was a bit of discussion about whether we should race at all in the light of what had happened during qualifying, but the default position of F1 has always been that the show must go on. Niki Lauda had also spoken with Ayrton about resurrecting the dormant drivers' safety group, the GPDA (Grand Prix Drivers' Association). At first Ayrton was not keen, but when Niki suggested a meeting at Monaco, the next race, Ayrton said maybe and the discussion was finished.

Another factor that played an important role in the events about to take place was that Williams had not yet got on top of fuel versus tyre-degradation strategy in the battle between Senna and Schumacher. Benetton had a much better handle on it because their technical director, Ross Brawn, was very sharp on refuelling strategy thanks to experience gained in endurance racing when he was running Jaguar. They understood better than Williams the consequences of tyre degradation and the balance you have to maintain between the number of stops versus fuel load and tyre performance. Put simply, the car will go faster as the fuel load burns off, but it will also go slower as the tyres wear. The rate of these things happening will give a few options for the race: one stop, or two, or occasionally three, but crucially it determines how much weight of fuel the car will have to carry at the start.

Our understanding of the subtleties of pit stop strategies was still not good, and sometimes it felt as though we were plucking a number out of the sky. From my recollection, at this stage of the season there was not a very sophisticated calculation, which meant that the strategy was based on the idea that you didn't want to come into the pits more than you needed to. We would continue like this for a few more races before Patrick Head plotted it out using graph paper. Benetton had been using computers all season, and we were way behind the curve with this one, but it is critical to understand this when considering how the race unfolded, because Benetton were about to do something completely different.

It was a beautiful, bright May day as we charged into the first lap, the race finally under way, but immediately behind the front runners the third major accident of the weekend was unfolding. The Lotus of Pedro Lamy had slammed into the unsighted stationary Benetton of JJ Lehto, who had stalled on the third row. Debris went everywhere and two wheels flew over the spectator fence, hitting a couple of people in the grandstand. Out came the safety car – an Opel Vectra.

We trundled along behind this regular road car which was trying to go as fast as it could, and our tyres were gradually cooling off, just as Ayrton had predicted. If the tyres cool, two things happen. Firstly, the contact patch of rubber gets hard and loses adhesion. Secondly, the pressure in the tyre drops, which means the car is less well supported. We weaved around, trying to increase the work going through the tyres and keep the heat up. It was better than nothing but, because of the slow pace, the weaving was not making enough difference. There was a lot of debris scattered across the start line area, which was another concern because of the chance of a tyre picking up something sharp. Adrian Newey thought Ayrton might actually have picked up a puncture, but this could never be proved. The clearing-up process took four laps, the safety car pulled in and we were off once more, twelve minutes after the starting lights had originally gone out, and the tyres now significantly cooler than they had been before the race started.

The first corner, Tamburello, was a flat-out 175mph long left-hand curve, but the cornering load was impressive. On the apex, there were patches in the asphalt created by a largely unsuccessful attempt to grind away some bumps. By staying in the middle of the track during testing, I had discovered it was possible to avoid these bumps. It was not the fastest way, but it lost very little time. Because of my concern about tyre pressures, I took this more cautious line on the first lap after the restart, the sixth lap of the race. The car didn't feel that difficult to drive, but I wanted to treat things with respect until the race settled down and optimal heat and pressure returned to the tyres. I was not the fearless competitor that Ayrton was. From the moment that we restarted he stuck to the aggressive line, right over the worst of the bumps.

As we crossed the line to start the seventh lap, I was a couple of places back and about two hundred yards behind Ayrton in the lead. He was pressing on with Michael hot on his heels. Ayrton's one and only flying lap would stand as the third-fastest time of the race. Bearing in mind he had about 60kg of fuel on board, enough for the first of three stints, and the tyres could not yet have been up to full temperature and pressure, that was mighty impressive. Senna's lead may have been a slender 0.6s, but he was looking absolutely determined to stretch it. He didn't know it, but he probably didn't need to push so hard. Having more fuel on board (probably 10–15kg more than Michael) meant he could just hold Michael up and the race would probably have been his. The restart had probably ruined Michael's race strategy, but we had no idea what Benetton had up their sleeve at that point and neither did Ayrton. To hold on to his lead with more fuel than Michael, and to have set that time on lap 6, there is absolutely no question Ayrton would have to have been right on his limit.

Coming into the start of the second lap after the restart, Ayrton didn't make it round Tamburello. After the second of two big bumps right in the middle of the corner, the Williams snapped out of control and the car left the road, hitting the retaining wall at almost unabated speed. Looking at the TV pictures after the event, it is clear that on the first flying lap Ayrton's car was really hitting the deck, creating plumes of sparks on the entry to Tamburello and over the bumps on the apex. Michael, who had the closest view, later recounted that the car looked like it was unstable and that Ayrton was having to work at it. His ultimate conclusion was that the car just got away from Senna.

I flew past as Ayrton's wrecked Williams was rebounding off the wall, the car's front wing landing just in front of me from a great height. It never occurred to me that this might be a fatal accident. I just thought: 'Oh, fucking hell! Not again!' Not just because it was yet another accident, but also because Ayrton was out of the third race in a row. But when the red flags appeared soon after, the first doubts began to creep in that this might be more serious than I had imagined.

They brought us back to the grid, where we switched off our engines and I stayed in the car. Gradually, some rather shaky messages began to come through on the radio. 'Damon . . . erm . . . just hang on. The race has been stopped because of an accident. It's Ayrton. We'll keep you updated.'

While I was beginning to feel uneasy, the guys in the garage were trying to cope with some worrying images on the television screen. From the aerial shot, the cockpit area looked relatively free of damage even though it was clear the right-front corner had taken the force of the impact with the wall. Professor Watkins and the team were on the spot in seconds and immediately went through the correct procedures on Senna while he remained in the car. Everyone at Imola and around the world was holding their breath, fearing the worst but hoping for the best. But thousands of miles away in Buenos Aires, Juan Manuel Fangio turned off his television. The five-times World Champion could just tell Ayrton was dead.

It must have been the most terrible feeling for Sid, dealing with the friend he had previously tried to persuade to stop racing. As soon as he opened the helmet visor it was obvious to him that Ayrton had suffered a severe head trauma because part of the right-front suspension of the car had penetrated the helmet. Sid knew, but then had to go through the procedures that Ayrton himself had helped him conduct on Donnelly in 1990. I can only imagine his heartbreak and distress, having to cope with two fatalities in two days. To Sid they were just boys.

In Italy, if someone is declared dead at the scene of an incident, then the whole venue gets closed down and everything must stop, including an F1 race. It becomes technically the scene of a fatal road traffic accident, so nothing could be said officially at this stage for fear of invoking this rule. The urgent action among the officials can be imagined as a helicopter landed on the track, ready to fly Ayrton direct to hospital in Bologna.

Confusion reigned. This was something F1 had never faced before in the modern era. The possibly fatal accident of the world's most famous racing driver had been transmitted into living rooms around the world. Ayrton was, officially at least, not dead. The helicopter took him away – and the countdown to the restart began.

Back on the grid, Ann Bradshaw, the Williams press officer, was the only person from the team who told me frankly what she thought was going on. She looked me in the eyes and said: 'It's Ayrton. It's serious.' When I asked how serious, she simply said: 'Not good.' From that I inferred the worst, but no one confirmed anything. I looked around and saw Michael sitting on the wall next to his car, kicking his heels as if this was just a normal day at the racetrack. Whether he understood or knew anything, I don't know. I was trying to deal with what I had just heard and it gave me some strength to know my father had been through all this in the past and had managed to cope. 'It's what we do in the Hill family; it's what being a racing driver is all about. You get on with your job. We're going to restart, so get prepared,' I told myself. The state you get into to do battle in an F1 car is icy cold; chilling. We all do it, by blanking out all distractions and only thinking ahead. It's afterwards that emotions catch up.

I got a message from my engineer, John Russell, to say that, just to be on the safe side, they were going to ask me to turn off the power steering. It was a sensible precautionary measure in the absence of any firm information about the cause of the crash but, as far as I was concerned, this was not going to make life easy. We had been using power steering all year and it had been a very welcome introduction, massively reducing the physical effort required of a driver. Without it, I would be put to the test – as would the steering column, because of the increased torque needed from my end. Before power steering, the cars had been beasts because it was really physical and unbelievably difficult to turn the steering wheel. I spent ages in the gym, constantly trying to improve my grip strength. The arrival of power steering changed all that. Suddenly, it was like having fingertip control, and it was wonderful not having to use all that force. Even when heavy with fuel, the car was a lot easier to drive. But now, going into the rest of the race at Imola, it was back to square one with steering that would be impossibly heavy. Over the years I have thought about this; if the steering column was going to break, it wouldn't break with the power steering active, as it was on Ayrton's car. It would break when we had no power steering, as it was configured on my car for the re-restart. But mine withstood the extra load exerted upon it for the remaining fifty-three laps. Something to ponder for those who say Ayrton's steering column broke.

Being an Adrian Newey car, the cockpit was very snug to help the all-important aerodynamics, but that did not leave much room to leverage the wheel. When Ayrton and I sat in the car to do the seat fitting earlier in the season, he had commented about the lack of room. At last I had an ally, I thought. No more bleeding knuckles! I was very happy that they were going to modify the cockpit and allow the steering wheel to be raised a little. To do that, they had to modify the steering column – and this modification would become one of the focal points of the investigation when it was later suggested the steering had failed at some point during the accident. Adrian

Sweet victory with the massive flag that was to get me into trouble!

My proudest day: winning the British Grand Prix and having Princess Diana present the trophy. Celebrations followed immediately.

Typhoon conditions at Suzuka 1994 – the race of my life!

Michael and I went at it hammer and tongs. Famously, it got closer than this in the end.

Michael giving me a piece of his mind, Monza 1995.
The marshals try to drag him to safety.

The colourful Jacques Villeneuve, my new teammate for 1996.

Ron Dennis advises Georgie about F1 driver negotiations.

Hello and goodbye! The last time I drive the Williams FW18,
which took me to the top of the world.

Passing without crashing!
Finally putting one over on Michael, Hungary 1997.

One more for good luck! Eddie goes bonkers with delight.

Flying home with Aga Khan's horse.

Leaving my mark on F1: team bosses Tom Walkinshaw, Sir Frank Williams and Eddie Jordan with the FIA's Herbie Blash, giving me a nice send-off!

My beautiful children (left to right, top to bottom):
Oliver, Josh, Tabitha and Rosie.

Racing in New Zealand with Josh.

admitted the modification was made poorly, but it was not proven that it caused the accident. I still believe it did not.

Despite everything that had happened, we went into race mode one more time and got on with the job. Martin Brundle was angry about the race going ahead. Speaking to a journalist in 2015, he said, 'I'm still angry today, if I'm honest. What makes me angry is that we raced past a pool of his blood for fifty-five laps. I thought that was disrespectful, and not the right thing to do.' But Martin raced, as did the rest of us. Going into Tosa on the first lap, I damaged the right-front wing endplate against Schumacher's left-rear wheel and had to make a pit stop. The rest of the race was a bit of a blur, to be honest, but I see I finished sixth; it could have been sixteenth, for all I remember.

Michael won his third race in succession with a novel tactic of three pit stops, but this time he looked shocked and ashen-faced on the podium when he heard about Senna. By then I was in the medical centre, totally exhausted and suffering from stomach cramp after having had to fight the now heavily loaded steering for fifty-three laps. As I was recovering, Dickie Stanford, the Williams chief mechanic, came and told me the latest on Ayrton. Back at the motorhome, Frank was stoic as ever, giving it to me straight. Normally, you would talk about the race that had just finished, but that was the last thing anyone wanted to do under these circumstances. A sense of utter disbelief descended as the news that Ayrton had died spread throughout the paddock.

Georgie and I were told by Ann Bradshaw that the best thing to do would be to get away from Imola. We got in the car and half-heartedly tried to eat in a restaurant around the corner from Bologna airport. Once we had checked in for the flight, we went to a place that had been cordoned off for the Williams team. The mechanics and engineers were sitting there in silence, absolutely distraught. For some reason I felt the need to pipe up, and said to them, 'I just want you to know that I will always trust your cars.' It's easy to forget the stress the mechanics work under. We totally depend on them to keep us safe, and the trust is a powerful bond. This event had hit them all very hard, understandably.

Looking back, I think this was the moment that I began to feel I had a responsibility to carry the load of whatever was coming our way, just as my father had done for Lotus in 1968. I was, after all, second in the World Championship and it was still up for grabs, and race teams exist for one reason: to win. Over the coming days, after we had got back to the headquarters in Didcot and started to come to terms with the whole shocking event, there was a growing feeling among the team that we had to give our best for Ayrton, if not for ourselves.

If getting the Williams drive changed my life significantly, the Imola weekend changed it forever. It changed F1 forever, too, while Senna's reputation as one of the fastest and least compromising drivers ever to have sat in an F1 car could never be undone. His sister, Viviane, told us later that on the day of the race, Senna found solace in the Bible. He read that he would receive 'the greatest gift of all, which was God himself'. To get into a racing car with all the thoughts and feelings that were assailing him at the time must have required an act of faith and courage beyond normal mortal comprehension.

I believe that with all the disharmony and distress in his life at the time, ultimately he got into the car because he wanted to show he was not afraid to live according to his rules. But I also think he wanted to show the depth of his empathy and compassion. Because, secreted away in his overalls, the doctors found a small Austrian flag, which, I assume, he intended to produce when he climbed onto the top step of the podium. But, like a lot of things about that weekend at Imola, we will never really know what he had intended to do, or what had created such a perfect storm.

18 » GRIEF UPON GRIEF

The question everyone was asking was, 'Why did Ayrton crash?' This was a driver who had competed in more than 160 Grands Prix, won forty-one of them and been champion three times. How could he have left the road in the way he did? Had something broken? Did he make a mistake?

The coroner's report stated that Ayrton had been killed by a piece of suspension from the front of the car hitting him in the head, but photographs had shown a broken steering column still attached to the steering wheel lying on the track by Ayrton's car. This had prompted speculation that the cause of his accident was steering column failure. During the weeks following the accident, all eyes were on Williams. I spent some time with Patrick, Adrian and the key engineers, who wanted me to look at the details of the crash and to give them my opinion of what had happened. I went to see Frank and he said, 'You've got nothing to fear, Damon. Be honest and tell me exactly what you think.' Since I had driven virtually the same car through Tamburello on the same day, clearly my observations were vital to understanding what Ayrton might have been experiencing. The most immediately obvious thing to me was that Ayrton was taking the racing line, which was backed up by the on-board camera in Michael's car. This, I imagined, would have made the car difficult to control for a number of reasons particular to that race.

Going over a bump, tyres compress with the load. They also distort with cornering load. But there is another force unique to our F1 cars: aerodynamic load, which is a vertical load 'sucking' the car towards the ground and enabling it to corner faster. This is generated in two ways: the first is from conventional 'wings' at the back and front of the car, but the second uses the underside of the car to create a 'venturi effect'. Simply put, the air is squeezed through the small gap between the floor of the car and the ground to create massive 'suck' which holds the car to the road even more. Obviously, these loads have to go through the suspension and the tyres. What you want as a driver is for the loads to be as consistent as possible, not coming and going all the time. If the car 'bottomed' (used up all the clearance under the car so that it touched the ground), this underfloor 'suck' would instantly stop. The car would then 'ping' back up until the load returned and then the cycle would begin again. This is why active suspension was so effective, because it could more accurately control this variation.

Before he even reached Tamburello, Ayrton's car was already bottoming a lot, as indicated by the sparks coming from the protective metal skid-blocks which are there to prevent the asphalt grinding away the carbon floor and the more valuable parts of the car. They were working overtime, indicating that his tyres were not yet up to pressure enough to resist the loads – but if they were not able to resist the loads vertically, they were not going to be behaving too well laterally in a heavily loaded corner like Tamburello, either.

Tamburello was a 175–180mph corner, so there was almost maximum aerodynamic load vertically, plus enormous cornering or 'twisting' loads on the tyres. The last thing you need at a moment like that would be for the car to hit a bump and lose the venturi part of the equation. On the replays from Schumacher's on-board camera you could clearly see Senna's car bottom for the first time, lose downforce, slide, rise again, grip and carry on through the corner. Then on the next bump it bottomed and slid as before, but more pronounced than the first time. This is when Ayrton lifted to 50 per cent throttle and applied opposite lock: just the kind of thing you do when you want to catch a slide. But this time, the sudden return of grip caused the car to snap back: a violent and sudden move-ment I previously described in relation to my Le Mans experience that bikers call a 'tank-slapper', where rather than returning to the midway trajectory you want it to, the car goes too far the other way. So now you are heading *out* of the corner instead of *around* the corner – and at that speed there would have been no more chances before running out of road.

We could see Ayrton's steering working, not only from the car data that had survived, providing us with graphs on a computer screen, but also from his on-board camera, posi-tioned behind his head, above and to the left. On each of the Williams cars there was a yellow button on the left spoke of the steering wheel, which was for one of the functions, either radio or neutral: I can't remember, but it's not important. The key thing is, this button shows how much lock Ayrton was applying and in which direction he was turning the wheel. As he turned into Tamburello on the seventh lap, the button disappeared out of the bottom of the frame, indicating all was as it should be. When he felt the first oversteer, the dot reappeared, again exactly as I would expect to see if he was correcting a slide. Having done that, he put on more lock and the dot disappeared once more: all perfectly normal (for a racing driver). When the car slid again, the dot reappeared, indicating another big slide, judging by the amount of oppo-site lock applied. People would subsequently look at that on-board footage and claim the actual steering column was moving. But it wasn't the steering column; it was the camera that was moving around. When you put that footage together with the footage from Michael's car and the data that was shown to me by Williams, it's clear that Ayrton was in a battle with his car, which was trying to cope with his massive force of will to win.

'There was an aura about him, something that's difficult to describe. He most certainly had a presence,' Newey said of Senna. 'I guess one of the things that will always haunt me is that he joined Williams because we had managed to build a decent car for the previous three years and he wanted to be in the team he thought built the best car – and unfortunately that '94 car at the start of the season wasn't a good car.

'Ayrton's raw talent and determination . . . he tried to carry that car and make it do things it really wasn't capable of.'

I believe the car got away from him, not that the car broke. I understand that there are those who would never accept such a thing. But Ayrton's state of mind was such that he was never going be beaten at Imola, come what may, so it is entirely plausible to suggest he went over his own extra-ordinarily high limits. This is my personal opinion gleaned from inside information and experience of that car and track, and from having been a witness to all that was going on at Imola. But most importantly, I had to convince myself that I really understood what had happened, or I would never have sat in a Williams car again. I loved my family too much for that.

For those who believe the steering failed I have these final observations: if the steering column had failed at that moment, then he would have applied as much left lock as he possibly could to try to get the car to turn. Also, in order to turn left (the correct direction for Tamburello) the steering wheel would have been under anticlockwise load. A sudden loss of torque would have made his hands almost cross over anti-clockwise with the release of resistance. None of these things happened.

I have no desire to damage Senna's reputation; it would be impossible anyway. But he was an uncompromising racing driver and he was racing flat out, absolutely determined to beat Michael. In a fast corner such as Tamburello, the car sliding happens in a split second and unleashes huge loads. I cannot imagine how I would have dealt with the amount of car movement Ayrton was trying to cope with. It would have snapped right in a flash. Even Senna would have been tested to the max. Ayrton hit the wall just as Nelson Piquet or

Gerhard Berger had on previous race weekends, but Ayrton would not have the luck to survive.

From my perspective the accident resulted from the culmination of many factors, the classic perfect storm. It started even before we arrived at Imola and gradually ratcheted up as time went on. Rubens's accident, Roland's death, the arguments about safety cars, Senna's personal life problems: all these things could be included as factors, but the accident on the start line and the debris on the track may also have been key because of the possibility of a slow puncture being picked up and the effect of the safety car on tyre temperatures. Possibly the safety car enraged Ayrton, too, and increased his mental pressure over and above all the other factors. To this can be added Michael pressing him hard, forcing Ayrton to drive at the limit without realising that it was not an equal fight because Michael had less fuel. Throw the thought into Ayrton's mind that Benetton might have been cheating, and you have a very powerful cocktail.

Ayrton always made it clear that his intention was to commit himself 100 per cent to winning, never to back off. How else can we interpret his own words about himself:

'On many occasions I have found satisfaction from beating my own achievements. Many times I find myself in a comfortable position and I don't feel happy about it. I feel it is right to slow down, but something inside me, something very strong, pushes me on, makes me try to beat myself. It is ... an enormous desire to go further and further, to travel beyond my own limits.'

He was a living legend already, but we were always scared that he was prepared to be a dead one if necessary. As his career progressed and he racked up one, two and then three World Championships, Ayrton had become an icon in Brazil, and with that came additional pressure to win. He was everything to his people: a beacon of hope; a champion who was going to fight for their rights. How could he ever back down in the face of such a powerful feeling of responsibility? All of this led to that extraordinary culmination of his life at that moment on 1 May 1994. He wouldn't have been Ayrton Senna if he had done anything differently. It later transpired that, as he was watching Senna and Schumacher at the restart, Prof Watkins, sitting in the medical car at the exit of the pit lane, commented to his driver: 'There is going to be an almighty accident in a moment.' Sid has seen pretty much everything that could happen in an F1 race, and he knew what combination of factors were needed for something terrible like this to happen. There was tension in the air; he could feel it.

It was immediately clear that the younger generation working in F1 had never experienced anything like this before; they were stunned by what had happened to Roland and Ayrton. But I had grown up with this sort of thing. It had been going on from when my dad had spent too many days going to funerals, to similar experiences during my own racing career – less frequent, of course, but something that I had to come to terms with. I never had any doubt that I or any of my friends could get killed in a racing car. Bertrand Fabi, Paul Warwick, Pete Rodgers: they were no longer with us. Martin Donnelly and Johnny Herbert had survived, but they had been smashed to bits. With the loss of both Roland Ratzenberger and Ayrton Senna, there could not have been a more profound demonstration that no one in motor sport is immune. Back of the grid or front of the grid: everyone is vulnerable. If any racing driver had previously felt safe, they certainly did not have that feeling after 1 May. Niki Lauda summed it up perfectly when he said that God had had his hand on Formula One, but that weekend he had he taken it away.

I have known Jackie Stewart all my life, and even now when I speak to him it summons up memories of my father. They were friends, they raced together and they went through all this kind of thing with far more regularity than we did. So when he called me after we had got back home his voice invoked a strong emotional response. He asked me point-blank if I would be going to Ayrton's funeral. I said I didn't know; flying to Brazil was not high on the list of things I wanted to do right then. I preferred the thought of staying at home with my family to grieve and reflect in peace and quiet, but Jackie gently persuaded me that if I didn't go, I would always regret it. He knew from terrible experience what he was talking about and so he convinced me that I should go.

I flew out with Richard West, the head of marketing for Williams, along with Frank and Derek Warwick, who had lost his brother, Paul, in a racing accident nearly three years before. As we were leaving the hotel in São Paulo en route to the actual funeral, we bumped into Bernie Ecclestone. He looked perturbed, even beyond the sense of upset you would expect on an occasion such as this. Senna's brother, Leonardo, had apparently advised him not to attend because of the strong feeling in Brazil that the race should have been stopped after Ayrton's accident. Bernie didn't seem to know what to do with himself; he was clearly affected by the family's edict that his presence would be, as they put it, 'inconvenient'.

We got into a van that was capable of carrying Frank and his wheelchair and were taken to where Ayrton was lying. He had been granted a state funeral and three days of national mourning. Presidents and dignitaries from around the world joined the estimated 3 million people who turned out carrying banners, flags and Senna memorabilia. We waited in the van outside the Monumental Hall where Senna lay in state.

It all took me back to when I was fifteen and Dad's funeral. I was trying to keep a stiff upper lip, but the emotions were the same and almost overwhelming. I couldn't help but think about how Frank must have been feeling. The greatest driver of all time had just died in one of his cars. Frank never showed a flicker of weakness, but stoic as he was, this must have hurt. He was solemn and reflective, which was his way of coping. But I wasn't, and neither was Richard West. The funeral cortège made its way to Morumbi cemetery and Ayrton's final resting place. Crowds were running alongside chanting, 'Olé, olé, Senna,' and singing his name.

When we reached the cemetery on the hillside, the sun was hammering down on us, our black suits attracting even more heat. Everyone silently dripped with sweat, the only relief coming from the dark glasses that proved their worth twice over. Most of the current F1 drivers were there – Gerhard Berger, Emerson and Christian Fittipaldi, as well as Jackie Stewart, Alain Prost and Rubens Barrichello. I did my best to play my part as we carried the coffin up the hill, and when we got to the grave we gathered around with his family at the forefront. The mood was understandably sombre and reflective – many of those at the graveside had known Ayrton almost his entire life as he blazed a trail through the junior ranks before breaking into F1. But it was a media fest. There were helicopters overhead filming from every angle, and despite the family's clear wishes, there was not a moment's peace, the beating of the rotors drowning out the ceremony. I never heard a word.

Jackie was right. I was glad I went and saw with my own eyes how much Ayrton meant to everyone in Brazil and around the world. If we had known this before, perhaps we would have understood him better. He was much misunderstood and he seemed too intense to us sometimes. But he had people to inspire, a nation to promote, and his own legend to be faithful to. He was in the same league as Ali, a sporting great who transcended mere sport. If sport has any value, it is that it throws up such people as symbols of what we can be. It was a tragic ending, but his life and funeral reminded me that this was the path we had chosen. You either lived it heroically, as Senna had, or you chose another, more moderate path. After the funeral, his sister Viviane would carry on the legacy by expanding and developing the Ayrton Senna Foundation in memory of a national icon. For ourselves, we had to do our bit by carrying on racing. I'm sure that is what he would have wanted.

19 » BACK TO THE FRONT: THE RACE GOES ON

After the emotion of the previous ten days, I was trying to put everything behind me and concentrate on Monaco, a race that requires total focus at the best of times. F1 had a short-lived existential crisis with many questioning whether a sport like ours could be justified in the modern, live TV era. There had been talk about not continuing from some of the drivers, but everyone knew in their heart of hearts they would carry on racing. After all, that's what Ayrton loved doing. If going racing is how you express yourself, then that's what you do. But I didn't feel I was expressing myself very well as I prepared for the next race, the Grand Prix of Monte Carlo.

I arrived amidst all the usual craziness, walked into the changing area in the Williams truck – and found Ayrton's Senninha T-shirt hanging up with the rest of his clothes. In all the confusion this pitiful detail had been overlooked. When a driver is in an emotionally vulnerable state, he doesn't need a reminder that, when he leaves the changing room to step into a racing car, he might not be coming back.

It was not the best start to what was always going to be a difficult weekend. But when you're trying to deal with something like this in the macho world of F1, how you are feeling is not a subject people tend to talk about. Everyone is going through the motions of doing their job and you begin to wonder if you're alone in finding it hard to carry on as if nothing had happened. Was Imola a one-off and we're back to normal now, you think?

The answer to that would come during first practice on Thursday morning. Karl Wendlinger lost control of his Sauber on the approach to the Nouvelle Chicane and went straight into the end of the traffic island I had been lucky enough to miss the previous year. Suddenly, the TV screens were carrying images of another driver sitting motionless in his wrecked car. F1 and the watching world were going into shock. Again. I could only think, 'So, it's not just me.' The massive media coverage immediately radiated a sense of outrage about what we were doing. Wendlinger was removed to hospital, where he was put into an induced coma to facilitate a slow recovery. Effectively, that also put F1's dilemma on hold, while the media did anything but stand still.

One effect of Senna's death was to bring the Grand Prix Drivers' Association (GPDA) back together for the first time in years. We had a meeting and, to my surprise, Niki Lauda came along. I had no idea about his Imola conversation with Senna. I'm not sure anyone did. Niki had long since retired, although he had been a driving force in the GPDA – particularly when he organised a drivers' strike in South Africa in 1982. Everyone respected him enormously and he had more right than anyone to discuss issues concerning safety.

The other, more immediately pressing issue was actually driving the car, which was not made easy by Patrick making it clear that he wasn't terribly impressed with what I was doing. To be fair to Patrick, he and the team were under a lot of stress thanks to the publication of pictures showing the broken steering column dangling over the side of Senna's car. People in the team were starting to mobilise and defend themselves against accusations that they were in some way responsible for what had happened at Imola. They could even be facing charges of culpable homicide. Indeed, there were a lot of worried people in the sport at that time, not just within Williams. The Italian investigation into the accident would have far-reaching powers to look at all responsible parties, from race organisers to circuit owners and promoters. Everyone was on edge. In due course I would have to give evidence to the prosecutors in Italy, too.

Since there had not been time to organise a replacement for Ayrton – an almost impossible task in any case – Williams had entered just one car for Monaco. The prospects and hopes of the entire team now rested with me for this event. Even Ayrton had benefited from having a teammate and I hope I can be forgiven for feeling that I was overloaded with this responsibility so soon after Imola.

Nevertheless, everyone was doing their best to carry on. I was being asked how the car felt, as always, but in the context of the catastrophe that we had just had, I felt like asking if that really mattered. All things considered, I thought I did reasonably well to qualify on the second row at Monaco. Then the tension cranked up a bit more before the start when the drivers gathered at the front of the grid holding a Senna flag for a minute's silence, the MC being Niki. Some people take the view that this is a bad time for that kind of thing. In Hungary in 2015, the drivers conducted a similar ceremony in memory of Jules Bianchi. It is certainly not easy to jump from showing deep respect for a recently deceased driver to showing no mercy for the living ones you are about to race. But human beings are remarkable creatures, and Grand Prix racing drivers are probably more remarkable than most in their ability to compartmentalise their thoughts and feelings.

Despite everything that had happened, and whatever others might have been thinking, I was as ready to race as ever. I made a brilliant start – but Mika Häkkinen's McLaren cut across my right front going into the first corner and we touched. He was out and I got as far as Casino Square before the damaged steering finally broke. That left me with a long and lonely walk back to the pits, where everyone was silently packing up. It was the worst outcome imaginable at a time when the team needed a decent result, and I had to soak up some of the blame, on top of everything else.

Meanwhile, the sport in general was coming under

increased pressure, and it was as close to a state of emergency as I had ever experienced. Max Mosley knew that, under the heading of safety, he could impose radical changes that could never have been brought in before, and he announced his reforms during the Monaco weekend. The fact that his 'safety car' was possibly a contributing factor in Ayrton's accident must also have been on his mind, but it didn't help matters that at almost the first test of Max's changes at Silverstone during a private test, Pedro Lamy had another massive accident, ending up over the barrier and down a spectator tunnel. He was knocked out and broke both kneecaps and his thigh. He was incredibly lucky not to be killed. This immediately put all the teams into a heightened frenzy, as well as the drivers.

Max's proposals included a radical reduction in downforce by virtually 'chopping off' chunks of the aerodynamic part of the cars and raising the ride height by forcing a plank to be bolted underneath the car, a regulation that stands today. The GPDA, with me, Michael and Gerhard Berger as directors, had our first official meeting before the next Grand Prix in Barcelona under the cloud of Karl Wendlinger still being in a coma and this latest Lamy accident. In what was in retrospect a bit of a knee-jerk reaction, we insisted on a temporary chicane made out of tyres before a fast kink on the back straight. This was a ridiculous solution, but we felt we had to highlight an issue with the layout of the track. We were going to have to crawl around these piles of tyres, but it was probably better than leaving the track as it was.

It was still early days for us and we didn't have much experience in race organisation, but we must have been right in principle because the corner was eventually altered to the one in use today. On top of this, the teams – Williams included – were threatening not to run because, they claimed, the changes called for overnight to the rear diffusers were not properly tested and might actually be unsafe. Lamy's accident had not conclusively been attributed to Max's changes, but then, as if to continue the trend, we had another potentially serious accident at the end of first practice.

Andrea Montermini, in his first F1 race meeting, had lost control coming out of the final corner: a quick downhill right-hander which was very satisfying, provided you got it right. He had smashed at high speed into the crash barrier on the outside of the track and ended up right beneath where I happened to be standing at the pit wall. It did nothing for my state of mind, particularly when I registered that Montermini's feet were exposed. It was obvious that he was not moving in what was left of the cockpit. I just couldn't believe what I was seeing. And this was the same team that had only recently lost Roland at Imola: Simtek. I couldn't imagine how they must have been feeling. At the end of the race the press gathered behind the Williams garage, waiting to speak to me. I couldn't find anything coherent to say, but my expression spoke volumes. I think I was developing a version of shell shock by then.

After we had packed up I went to the Benetton truck, opened the door, poked my head inside and saw Michael. I said this had to stop: it was getting ridiculous with one accident after another and we had to do something. There was no reaction, except for Michael looking at me as if I was hysterical. I got the impression that he was not too bothered by what I was saying, but Michael was very good at hiding his true feelings – especially from fellow competitors. I guess he took the view that there was nothing we could do about it, an attitude that contrasted starkly with that of Ayrton's at Imola over the Roland accident.

With the events following Imola, David Coulthard, our test driver, was launched into one of the best seats in F1. I now had a new, eager and quick teammate, eleven years my junior. But Coulthard was seen as a stopgap until they could pull in another big-name driver. I was hearing that Renault wanted Frank to find someone like Nigel. They had lost Senna, the chosen number one, so they thought they needed a driver who had the name and reputation. In the few years I had been with Williams I had never been regarded as a potential lead driver and there were some who did not believe I was capable of carrying the championship challenge to Schumacher. They may well have been right, but at a time when I had expected the team to get behind me, it wasn't the news that I had been hoping for. Did I really appear that incapable?

Being number one had never been my original ambition when I started the 1994 season. I hadn't expected to be leading the Williams challenge for the championship and it was only due to circumstances, many out of my control, that I had been ahead of Ayrton at the time of his death. Whatever way you wanted to look at it, however, I was now in contention for the title, since I was just behind Michael, and I felt I should be getting a lot of support to help me fight this guy, rather than having the sponsors undermining me behind the scenes. Michael was starting to become the anti-hero of the season, probably not entirely through any fault of his own, but to us he was the opposition, and I wanted to take the fight to him. But Williams' behaviour was just giving succour to Benetton. It made the most likely threat to their campaign, me, look like not even the first choice of my own team. Williams can be very strange sometimes.

Despite the circumstances, I had to do the best I could while being aware I was going to have a new challenge from Coulthard, who had ambitions of his own. I couldn't afford to be overshadowed by him, and I was on a very steep learning curve from that point of view. Previously, I had always tried to be snugly tucked in behind Alain Prost or Nigel Mansell. I'd been a good test driver and had been able to perform somewhat in the shadows, but now I was exposed. I had to become the head of the team and dig really deep within myself. In my wildest dreams I would have outqualified Ayrton Senna once or twice and had a good story to tell the grandchildren, but now I was the one in the hottest seat in F1. It's one thing to win on your own bike and to have success in Formula 3000 and Formula Three, but in Formula One, the lead driver has to give the team hope and reassure them that all their efforts will be led by you and take them to their goal. Ayrton did that job. That's what he was there for. But me? I was suddenly in this new situation and asking myself, 'How the hell did I get here?' And yet, on the flip side, I could see this was a great opportunity, however tragically afforded to me. Everything had tumbled out rather than being planned, but it was another chance. I had to grab it with both hands, starting with this race in Spain.

Just when I needed it most a bit of luck came my way. Schumacher had been in charge until his gearbox gave trouble and I was able to lead the final twenty laps. By winning I had repeated what my father had done in 1968, when he had assumed the mantle of lead driver at Lotus following the death of Jim Clark and went on to win the Spanish Grand Prix. The win gave me a bit of breathing space and reminded me what a victory will do for your confidence. It also sent out a timely reminder to Williams and Renault that they had better not underestimate us Hills.

The Canadian Grand Prix was the sixth round of the championship and the second Grand Prix for David Coulthard, but already I found I had to make a few things clear with him. He was the chirpy, fresh-faced kid who, in my view, hadn't been through the mill or paid his dues as I had. It's an age-old problem: youth and enthusiasm versus old age and bitterness! When I qualified fourth, one place ahead of David, I had a word before the start and pointed out it would be silly to take each other out at the first corner. That became irrelevant, though, when I made a bad start and had to fall in behind my teammate. Gerhard Berger was ahead of us both, with Schumacher racing off into the lead. When I saw that David was unable to overtake the Ferrari and had no intention of letting me by each time I tried, I got on the radio and said he needed to be told to let me through, which duly happened, but not before Michael was some way down the road. I remember not being too impressed by DC and, after finishing second, said as much in the press conference. Since it had been a pretty boring race, this became the lead story in the British media, and I began to wish I had never said anything. It wasn't David's fault; he had to think of himself but, tactically, it was going to be more difficult if I had to contend with David *and* Nigel *and* Michael! That was how it was going to be, however, like it or not.

Despite being second to Schumacher in the championship, I was still being made to feel as if I was not up to the job. The media began to say as much when Nigel Mansell was brought in to replace DC for the next race at Magny-Cours in France. Nigel was fantastic; I enjoyed having him in the team. He played up to the accompanying media hype but, in fact, he was very supportive towards me.

I knew then that I would be competing against someone who was undoubtedly a huge star. I was up against it, but felt I ought to be able to cope, thanks to being race fit and very familiar with the car. In an odd way, I wouldn't have minded being beaten by Nigel so much as by DC because it was Nigel who was expected to deliver. Nigel, after a year racing in the States and living well, was not currently at the uppermost fitness level required for F1, but nevertheless, I knew he was quick and a fantastic fighter. That potential problem would be resolved when, starting from pole, I stayed ahead of Nigel and he eventually retired from the race.

What would be of greater concern to everyone at Williams was the way in which Schumacher had immediately come from the second row of the grid, swinging left and then right before powering between Nigel and me as if we were standing still. Then the Benetton cleared off into the distance and I didn't see him again until the finish.

By then, I was completely dehydrated. It had been an un-believably hot weekend and we had been staying in a cheap hotel by the river, which meant the bedroom window had to stay shut to keep the mosquitoes out. The glamour of F1! There was no air conditioning and I tried to sleep covered with wet towels and with a fan blowing on me. I think I had heat exhaustion even before I had reached the track. It was so hot that the fire brigade had to hose down the crowd. During the race, my drinking bottle decided to pack up, and I was starting to suffer. Just before a pit stop, I said on the radio that I needed water. When I came in, Patrick said, 'Here's your water, Damon.' I opened my visor and looked up like a bird with my mouth open, expecting the cool, refreshing liquid to quench my throat – and he chucked it down my back before I was sent off again with water sloshing around in my car instead of in me.

Having won the race, Michael got out of the car showing not a bead of sweat. That's when I began to think, 'This guy is different.' Schumacher had creamed us, and the muttering started again – Benetton had to be up to something. There were so many places at Magny-Cours where traction control would have given a massive advantage. There was not much else at this track; it was all about getting the power down. Benetton were clearly good at it: so good that, going into the British Grand Prix, speculation about their methods was rampant.

The hyped-up media attention around me before my home Grand Prix was a sign that, for the first time in my life, I was in contention for the World Championship, trailing Michael by thirty-seven points with ninety still available. I startled the British press by arriving at Silverstone and immediately letting rip about stuff they had written questioning whether I was up to the job and capable of beating Schumacher. In my naivety, I couldn't understand why they were not giving me the support I felt I deserved. When the press briefing had finished, Ted Macauley, a seasoned tabloid journalist, ran after me and anxiously asked if I had been speaking specifically about him. 'You don't mean me, Damon, do you?' he pleaded. While we were having our 'conversation' (me giving him a piece of my mind), his newspaper's photographer was busy with his camera. The next day, the paper carried a picture of me pointing a finger at him, under the headline 'Damon's Gone Nuts!' One way or another, the point had been made, and released some of the tension that had built up, but looking back, it was a clumsy way to kick off the weekend.

On race day the atmosphere was brilliant, with bunting being hung out and barbecues fired up in the many campsites around the circuit. I was the hero and Schumacher was being portrayed as the villain. It was pure pantomime, but the crowd loved it and I played along. In testing I had stupidly set up a photo of me giving Michael two V-signs as he drove past our garage. This seemed funny at the time, but now I am embarrassed every time I see it.

During the break between the final two races of 1993 in Japan and Australia, I had been scuba diving with Michael on the Great Barrier Reef, so we had spent a little time together, although I couldn't claim to know him really well. Despite that, I felt the urge to pass on my thoughts to him when we got to Silverstone and the rumblings about Benetton cheating were gathering strength. As our paths crossed in the middle of the paddock I stopped him and said: 'Michael, are you sure you're with the right people? Because, you know, you're obviously incredibly talented but you don't want to be getting into that sort of thing.' I was advising, with the best of intentions, to make sure he had the right people around him. He said: 'What do you mean?' He pretended to have no idea what I was talking about, or else he genuinely didn't. So I thought, 'OK, I've had my say'. I just wanted to pass on my view to him. I've always thought this was about seeing how good you really were. Not just winning whatever the cost.

In any case, I had my own worries within seconds of going on track for the first time on Friday morning. The car was polished to perfection as I climbed on board, really pumped up for this big weekend. As I approached Becketts and applied the brakes for the first time, the front suspension popped out and started waving around in the air. It's the most extraordinary thing that's ever happened to me in racing, and the front of the car was suddenly bouncing all over the place. I had absolutely no idea what was going on and pulled over and got out of the car. It was only then that I discovered the suspension had not been bolted in properly.

On my way back to the pits, I happened to see Patrick emerging from the car park, carrying his briefcase and papers like a commuter arriving at Waterloo. As he saw me approaching, carrying my crash helmet and with the sound of racing cars coming from the track, you could see the penny drop as he figured I really shouldn't be there. His first assumption was that I had spun off and he found it hard to take on board my explanation. The mechanic concerned, a really lovely, hard-working and diligent guy, was absolutely mortified. There was no need for anyone to say a word but I didn't think he ever got over that incident. I forgot about it quickly enough, particularly when I won pole the next day – by 0.003s from Michael. I was pleased that I could give the media something decent to write about for a change after the months of morbid fascination in the sport since Ayrton's death. I knew our car was going to be competitive on that circuit and we just needed to make sure we did everything right. By now, Williams had started to get the hang of the pit stop strategy and we had every hope of putting one over on Benetton. In the event, Michael did that for us.

On the parade lap as we were warming up, Michael overtook me, shot off into the distance, then slowed right down and let me back in front. I thought it was a bit odd, but maybe just gamesmanship. Then as we lined up, waiting for the start, Coultard stalled. That meant another parade lap – and Michael did exactly the same thing once more. I got on the radio to inform the team that what he was doing was out of order. The driver on pole position is supposed to dictate the pace and he can't do that if the other guy on the front row has legged it. Besides, it was against the regulations to overtake the pole sitter on the parade lap. It appeared to be a precise repeat of the previous occasion, and by doing it a second time, it didn't look as if he was trying to unsettle me. None of it made any sense, particularly as he had contravened the rules. As the race started, the stewards were obviously thinking about what to do in the light of Schumacher's rather strange behaviour. They eventually decided on a five-second stop-go penalty, which should have been applied immediately but which Benetton thought they could take at the end of the race.

I had led from the start and felt very comfortable. Any threat from Michael was removed when officials then showed him a black flag for ignoring their instructions to take the stop-go penalty – which he also ignored and, by doing so, committed an even more serious offence! In the space of one afternoon, Schumacher seemed to be confirming his role as the dastardly villain driver. He would lose his second place and the team would be fined $500,000. Not bad going for one race meeting.

Meanwhile, I was the home hero as I won the British Grand Prix. The jubilation on my slowing-down lap had to be seen to be believed. A marshal gave me a massive Union flag attached to a stout piece of two-by-four about ten feet long. Picking up a large item at this stage of the race was not allowed – we would hear more about this later – but I thought, 'Sod it! My father never won the British Grand Prix and now I've put that right for the Hill family.' It was a truly fantastic feeling that would continue for the rest of a perfect summer's day.

The paddock was not the concrete enclosure we have now. The Williams motorhome had a lovely lawn bordered by a little picket fence, which Frank loved, and the two of us sat there with the trophy on the table watching the sun go down, just drinking in the atmosphere as a constant stream of people came by for autographs and photographs.

In the background, I could hear rock music starting up. Eddie Jordan had arranged to have a flatbed truck, complete with band, brought into the paddock. I wanted to join in and, after a good hour or so of signing and having photographs taken, I decided to try and slip away. I went to another motor-home, waiting for my opportunity. While I was there, a guy came up and said, 'Would you just come over to our table and sit down with us?' I said that was very kind of him but I had been signing and doing stuff for a couple of hours and now I was trying to relax. He said, 'I'm just asking you. It won't cost you anything. Come on.' He was very persistent and was starting to get slightly annoying. He clearly had thick skin and I gave him my best polite rebuff, but he didn't give up easily and got more pushy. So I had to get polite but firm with him, after which he looked at me with a slightly menacing expression and said, 'Come on, Damon, it's been a lovely day. Don't spoil it.' Considering that I'd just won the British Grand Prix, it was a bit rich to accuse me of that! But nothing was going to spoil this day for me, I consoled myself. It reminded me of the story of my dad, at the end of a similarly long day, being upset when he politely told an autograph hunter he had to go and heard him mutter, 'Miserable bastard.' My mother said that really upset him all the way home. I couldn't help thinking about the scene in *The Life of Brian* when the ex-leper tells how he complained to Jesus that being cured had destroyed his liveli-hood. 'There's no pleasing some people,' is the punchline. Thankfully most people were more than happy with what I gave them that day.

I eventually got on the stage for some rock 'n' roll with Eddie and the gang and then I jumped in the car and headed home. Just as I was turning into our road in Wandsworth, a dog shot out in front of me and I ran over it. The dog disappeared and elation suddenly turned to distress. The neighbours had put up a huge, lovely sign, welcoming the winner of the British Grand Prix home to Bucharest Road, and all I could think of was the dog. I saw the owner walking the dog the next day and stopped to see how it was. 'Oh, he's fine,' he said. 'No problem!' I think he was more excited to see me than care about how his dog was. What a weekend. It felt like the best Monday morning ever.

20 » DRIVING OUT OF MY SKIN

Things were moving on in every sense. Georgie, the boys and I were very happy in Bucharest Road, but now I was a famous racing driver who'd won the British Grand Prix. It was no longer easy living in a terraced house in Wandsworth as it was a little too accessible for the increasing number of fans who wanted to pop by for tea or just get an autograph.

While I negotiated a deal to continue racing for Williams in 1995, Georgie and I found a nice house in Ascot and moved during the three-week break between the British and German Grands Prix. We didn't know it at the time, but we were only going to be there for about nine months, which continued a familiar pattern since, in my lifetime, I have moved home fourteen times. Georgie had a similar experience, her father having been in the British army; it's very tiresome and disorientating. But finally, I had bought a house and had no mortgage; I could pay for the house outright, and I felt that I was in a position to make things good again, as I had promised myself all those years ago. Other aspects of my life had also changed. In the space of twelve months I had gone from continually begging to having to refuse requests left, right and centre, with no middle ground – it was an experience I was not prepared for, nor that I suddenly had to be in ten different places at once, meaning that I had to work twice as hard to find the time to be a good husband and father.

One demand that I couldn't refuse was the summons to Paris. Four of us, including Rubens Barrichello, Mika Häkkinen and myself, had been hauled up before the FIA World Council. Rubens and Mika had been involved in a last-lap collision at Silverstone, while Michael was up for ignoring the black flag. I had to answer the charge of picking up the Union Jack during my slowing-down lap. Although Michael's was clearly the gravest offence, by hauling up three teams Mosley could claim to be scrupulously fair by not appearing to be picking on Benetton, but the whole proceedings was a farce, as far as I could see.

The hearing was held in the FIA's grand headquarters in Place de la Concorde and seemed to me to be an opportunity for Max Mosley, the FIA president, to make a big show of things, but the press had a field day with the motor sport delegates drafted in from around the world. Bernie Ecclestone was there, which was to be expected as Commercial Rights Holder. The presence of Jean Todt, Ferrari's sporting director and a direct rival, was a sign of Ferrari's influence in the sport's administration, something we would become familiar with over the years. At that time, they had the right to sit in on court proceedings but didn't get a vote.

The court had pulled me up on a technicality because drivers are not supposed to stop on the slowing-down lap to prevent them from running the race underweight then picking up something that would nudge a car back over the limit. Regardless of the fact that I didn't actually stop, I would have had to have left the flag and the ten-foot pole in the car to have made any difference to its weight. It was quickly agreed that I had not actually broken the wording of the rules. I stepped outside the court to find the man from the *Sun* waiting with a photographer and a Union flag for me to wave.

Michael's case was much more serious. Under team instructions, he had disobeyed the black flag, which, after a red flag, is effectively the highest authority you can have in a motor race. He received a two-race ban and lost the six points for finishing second at Silverstone. On appeal, he would be allowed to race in his home Grand Prix in Germany, and the atmosphere among his fans was running at fever pitch when we arrived at Hockenheim. On arrival at the track, I was called into the Williams team motorhome by Ian Harrison, the team manager, to meet two German police officers who explained that a local newspaper had received a message from an anonymous caller who was threatening to shoot me if I qualified ahead of Michael. As a precaution they wanted to take me to and from the track in a police car via a discreet road in the woods, which felt very ominous. I changed my hotel room to one registered in someone else's name and kept the curtains closed. I even called Sheridan Coakley out from England to give me some company and protection if necessary. Although he had no formal training, he was a big guy and just having him around made me feel more secure. I wasn't going to let some lunatic dictate my plans for the race. I qualified one place ahead of Schumacher – although not on the front row, which was filled with the Ferraris of Gerhard Berger and Jean Alesi as they made good use of their V12 engines on the very long straights.

I had tried to put the threat to the back of my mind, which worked reasonably well until the drivers' parade on race morning. Standing on the back of an old car, Coulthard and I were completely exposed. There were the huge banners waving around the track, with one jokingly referring to me as Benny Hill. As we entered the vast stadium at the end of the lap, the 100,000 fans responded by cheering and waving and letting off bangers: the perfect cover for shooting some hapless racing driver. I hid behind David hoping they might hit him instead, but, thankfully, nothing happened to either of us.

The crowd did not have much to cheer about during the race, after Berger led all the way and Michael retired from second place. I probably lightened the mood for the Germans after being hit by another car on the first lap, making a pit stop for repairs and then finishing out of the points in eighth place: an opportunity lost to close the gap on Michael. But the race shall forever be remembered for the fire in Jos Verstappen's car when he stopped to refuel. Benetton would find themselves in trouble again when it transpired that they had removed a compulsory filter to enable them to refuel their cars more quickly.

With an investigation into the conflagration in Germany pending, and a two-race ban looming for Michael, Benetton had to make the next Grand Prix in Hungary stick, which sadly they did. They completely outfoxed us on strategy by having Michael stop three times, while I followed the traditional routine of stopping twice, which put me into traffic just as I needed to close down Schumacher's lead.

The Benetton team had not done much to dispel the impression that they would do all sorts to win races. The Senna fans had decided I was their man against Ayrton's nemesis, which was uplifting, but at the same time another pressure, and my mood was deeply affected before the race when I was presented with a Brazilian football shirt signed by the entire team, wishing me luck against Schumacher. This championship was never going to be just about two guys racing. Imola was months behind us but feelings were still running high, and there was still a sense that what was important was how you went about winning. I didn't want to disappoint them, but I was not Senna and I could have done with some of his inspiration.

When Michael beat me again two weeks later in Belgium, I was feeling pretty dejected as he now had a thirty-five-point lead in the championship with five races to go. When I reached Brussels airport, Ann Bradshaw appeared and said, 'Have a beer. You've won the race!' It turned out that Michael had been disqualified because the plank on the underside of his Benetton had been worn beyond the permitted limit. With much of the downforce being created by running the car as close as possible to the ground, such discrepancies – even if only amounting to a millimetre or so – were crucial to the performance. He was disqualified and I was declared the winner, and closed the gap on Michael by fourteen points – by which time, of course, Michael had gone off with the trophy. For years, I accused Michael of not handing it over, then a few years ago I visited Williams and they produced it. They had had it all the time and only just remembered!

The trouble over the plank was yet another chapter in an increasingly controversial year for Benetton since their appeal over the black flag episode was overturned, and Michael would miss two races: Monza and Portugal. Their fuel hose trick was not penalised, nor was anything found on their on-car computer that could prove they were breaking the rules, but they had been put on notice, and the world was watching them. I won both the races he missed, and going into the European Grand Prix at Jerez I was just one point behind him with three races to go. It was game on. Or it would have been, had we not suffered a mysterious problem in the race. Michael started from pole, with me alongside. I made a perfect getaway and led the race until the first of my two pit stops. Even though it was clear that Michael was on a three-stop strategy, I felt we had everything under control.

I was called in for my final stop with just under half the race to run, but when I rejoined all I could do was watch as Michael pulled away while I struggled with a sluggish car, which was feeling weirdly heavy. I couldn't work out what was going on and felt really unhappy as I stood on the podium and watched Michael celebrate his comeback with another win. Now he was five points ahead with two races to go. Frank and Patrick gave me the cold shoulder, which I could understand; I must have looked like a total tugger. But a few days later, Ian Harrison phoned me and explained there had been something wrong with the fuel calculation. After my first stop, the fuel gauge had indicated the rig had not delivered the full amount of fuel. Fearing I might run out, they had called me in early for the final stop and added what they thought would make up the shortfall, in addition to the scheduled amount I needed. In fact, the gauge had been wrong, so that I was carrying almost twice as much fuel as Michael. The extra twenty or thirty kilos of fuel were costing me more than half a second a lap in inertia, not to mention the extra work on the tyres.

I had to go up to the factory at Didcot and fight my case with Frank and Patrick. It became clear in discussions that they were completely unaware of what the implications of the faulty gauge had been. To me, it seemed they had already decided Jerez was more evidence that I was not up to beating Michael and that we would lose the championship, rather than accepting that I was trying to beat the person who would turn out to be the most successful driver in the history of the sport with one hand tied behind my back. It was like pulling teeth to extract any sort of apology from them.

Racing for Frank and Patrick is not for the faint-hearted. 'At the end of the day,' Frank used to say about his drivers, 'they are just employees,' and while I had carried this challenge to Michael all season through extra-difficult circumstances, I never really felt they had faith in me or, if they did, that they were prepared to show it. Everything was always provisional. The term 'team' is a misnomer as far as drivers go in F1. There are people working at Williams today who were there when I raced for them but the drivers are just passing through. Michael was an exception. He had a nucleus of key personnel around him who gave him everything he needed to win. He had a team all to himself. To beat a man like that, everyone would need to pull together. It's frustrating to think what I could have done if Frank and Patrick had given me 'the nod' a few more times. Maybe they did and I just didn't notice? Frank would eventually describe me as a 'tough bastard', but that was after I'd left!

In my attempts to get the best for myself in Williams, I had blundered occasionally. When we were at Monza I created a bad vibe by saying I thought I should have the lead engineer on my car. David Brown had worked with Mansell, Prost and Senna. He was regarded as the best engineer, but he was working with David Coulthard, who had no chance of winning the title. This caused a massive uproar within the team, upsetting

John Russell, my engineer, and giving people the impression that I was a prima donna. While I felt uncomfortable doing it, I wanted evidence from Williams that I was their man for the championship. Even though they conceded, I continued to feel that I was only temporarily important to the team. This was compounded by my discovery, as we headed for Japan for the penultimate race of the season at Suzuka, that they would be bringing Nigel back again.

Williams couldn't have done a better job of making me feel like an understudy to Nigel if they had tried. As good as he was, like David he was not in a position to challenge Michael for the title of 1994 Formula One World Champion – and yet they hung on his every word while he told them exactly what I had been saying all year about the improvements that needed to be made to the car. I just didn't understand what it was they wanted from me, but the truth eventually came out after qualifying.

I qualified second; Nigel was fourth. Patrick came up to me with a speed graph and said, 'Look, Nigel is 20kph faster than you through 130R [a very fast left-hander].' I said, 'I know – but I'm ahead of him on the grid.' My blood was boiling. The time gain versus risk was a poor trade because if you went off on that corner, you'd be lucky to be ready for the next season, let alone the next day. We had already lost one driver that year and I had been driving according to what my instincts were telling me. And that was good enough for a place on the front row alongside Michael, but it was not enough for Patrick, and the atmosphere within the team had been getting worse. I felt I had been putting my life on the line for them and not getting any appreciation. Then Patrick said to me, 'The thing is, Damon, you walk around with a long face; you're glum, you're never happy. It affects the team.' I listened to this personal attack and held my tongue. I think Patrick thought this would 'gee' me up, but I was actually thinking, 'OK. Sod you, then.'

It was as if Patrick had suddenly let me off the hook. I had been trying to be the good driver, to do everything to satisfy them. I gave them all I had to give and would do almost anything to get their approval – but I had been barking up the wrong tree. It wasn't about my performance; it was about my style and charisma, or lack of it. They wanted a man like Mansell. I didn't have that 'thing'; that supreme confidence that permeates a group of people and gives them hope everything will be all right. There is a lot of vicariousness going on in F1, and the frustrations of not being able to drive the car oneself inevitably come out. I needed to 'lighten up a bit', Patrick said. As a result, I decided to cut myself loose from what I perceived to be their expectations. From now on I would be out for myself. This was my car, my track, my race; I'll do what I like. It would be just like that day I set off for Brands on my own, just me and my bike against the world.

I had plenty to think about while sitting on the grid. The skies were black as we raced downhill towards the first corner, a long right-hander ringed with grandstands packed with tens of thousands of spectators. As we all poured through, the whole place lit up with the flashlights of their cameras in a spectacular starburst explosion accentuated by the gloom. I was on Michael's tail and stuck to him like glue. As the rain came down there was so much spray coming off the Benetton that I couldn't see anything. It was like having a garden hose turned on you. All I knew was, if I lost sight of the red light on the back of that Benetton, he'd be off into the distance. I hung on and, for the first dozen laps, I witnessed the most incredible driving display I've ever seen in a racing car. I lost count of the number of times Michael went off the road and yet he never lost a beat. Meanwhile, I was driving out of my skin. This was the highest level of driving I had experienced so far in my life. I knew I was on the edge of my ability, up here in the thin air with one of the very best there has ever been. But, bit by bit, Michael was starting to get away. I have no doubt Senna would have stuck with him or beaten him. Maybe Mansell too, in his very best days. But Michael was working right out there on the end of the branch, where most people dared not go.

As the race progressed the conditions got worse: so bad, in fact, that one or two drivers spun off and the race had to be stopped. By this time Michael was 6.8 seconds ahead of me, which would be crucial because the race would be split in two with the result being determined by the aggregate times from both parts. The first few laps of the restart were run behind the safety car but, when we were released, I was back on Michael's tail. Then, to my surprise, he dived into the pits. He was going to stop twice whereas I would be stopping only once, which explained why he had been able to pull away. This was a similar situation to that which Senna had been in at Imola: I had the impression that I had to keep up with him, whereas in fact he was lighter so I didn't necessarily have to. But this time, Williams' playing safe would actually work in our favour as Michael rejoined and was held up behind the midfield cars and their spray. I had the big advantage of clear vision and an empty track in front of me; everything was going as well as could be hoped. Then came my one and only stop.

The conditions remained wet enough for another set of rain tyres, but the mechanics had trouble getting the nut off the right-rear wheel which meant it was never changed, except I didn't know that. I rejoined in second place with only three new tyres but aware that Michael, now leading, would have to come in one more time. When he eventually made his final stop, I was back in the lead, but Michael would have fresher tyres and the 14.5 second gap between us was certain to come down. The leading question was: by how much? I had to be at least 6.9 seconds ahead at the finish in order to make up for his advantage at the end of the first part of the race. There were ten laps remaining.

I wasn't receiving much information on the radio and I remember glancing at a giant trackside screen while trying to learn more about our relative positions. I could see Nigel sitting right on Alesi's gearbox as they fought for third place and, even though I was driving the race of my life, I remember thinking, 'Blimey, that looks like a good fight! They're having fun.'

Eventually I caught a brief glimpse of Michael on the screen, so I knew where he was on the track, but I had no way of knowing how the aggregate time was panning out. I simply had to push as hard as I could on worn tyres. I dug deeper and deeper until, going into the last lap, I knew Michael would have me unless I could find some extra something from somewhere. The inner voice that usually urged me on admitted it was out of ideas: 'I'm completely spent. I simply can't give any more,' it told me. So I said to myself, 'Ayrton, if you're up there, I could do with a bit of a hand here.'

All I can say is that, from the moment I exited Turn 1, I did not drive the car in any normal sense until I reached the hairpin, halfway around the lap. I was possessed. I watched my hands moving the wheel, completely free to do whatever they wanted in response to the car moving around beneath me. I was removed, one step back from all this action going on. I was just an observer of something phenomenal. It was quite unbelievable: what I suppose one could call an out-of-body experience in which I appeared to have totally surrendered trying to control the car myself. Everything seemed to be happening completely by instinct. There had been flashes in the junior formulae when something happened in front of me and I reacted without even thinking about it, just like when I had fallen from the climbing frame as a child back in Mill Hill. But this lasted all through the Esses, up the hill, round the terrifying Dunlop corner, through Degner until I reached the hairpin, where I must have returned to my normal in-body state and I took back control.

I would never come close to driving like that again. All the other experiences had been poor imitations. But had it been enough to beat Michael? I took the chequered flag but then had an agonising wait until Michael crossed the line and we could tell whether or not the gap between us was less than 6.8 seconds. I had 3.3 seconds in hand. I'd overdone it! The championship was down to one point.

I had just driven the race and the lap of my life: the most pressure and drama I had ever experienced; the most difficult conditions; racing against one of the best drivers, arguably, in the history of F1. I hadn't conceded; I had won in what I considered to be a completely straight and fair fight. When I got out of the car, I had to hide in the stairwell before going onto the podium because I broke down with the emotion of it all. It was a huge pressure release to have won, but it had taken everything out of me and then this thing had happened on the last lap that I had no explanation for. I kept it to myself for years, trying to understand what had happened. It had given me an insight into another dimension I never knew existed. But for now, this result was all that I ever wanted: to know if I could do it when it really counted.

21 » TWO WORLDS COLLIDE

There was one week between Suzuka and the final race in Australia. On the Monday, I was due to leave Japan with my friend and photographer, Jon Nicholson, but due to a mix-up with our luggage being sent to the wrong airport, we had to spend the entire day waiting for the bags to be returned to our hotel. Being trapped in Suzuka after the event, I went for a run around the track. There was no sign of what had happened the day before: no indication that, for a couple of hours on a wet afternoon, this place had been the focus of the motor-racing world. It was just a windswept racetrack in the middle of nowhere. By the time the bags had arrived, time was getting short and I was desperate to get out of there. As we drove up the ramp to Osaka Airport after three hours watching this man fighting the controls of his taxi at 40mph in his little white gloves and cap, I could see he was going to take the wrong turn. I leant over and grabbed the wheel – and the man went apoplectic, thinking a madman was attacking him. In the ordered world of Japan, you do not do things like that, but the stress had got to me, and we made the flight with just minutes to spare.

After spending a few days on the Gold Coast with Barry Sheene, I poured my heart out to him on the flight to Adelaide about how badly I felt I was being treated at Williams. I thought I'd carried the main load but still been paid a number two retainer. Barry was not only agreeing with me but also winding me up, saying, 'Yeah, yeah, yeah. You gotta say something.' By the time we landed, I was in a semi-crazed state of feeling hard done by. We were greeted at Adelaide airport by

Murray Walker and the BBC TV crew, plus a number of reporters. Without prompting, I launched into an attack on Williams and said, among other things, that I was not being paid enough and shouldn't be left dangling over contract negotiations at a time when I was trying to win the championship – for me *and* the team. It came across badly. In fact, it was catastrophic: the worst thing I could have done. By the time I reached the track, the word was out and I could tell by the look on Patrick's face that he was not impressed. I said ironically and apologetically, 'You always hurt the ones you love, don't you, Patrick?'

I had a sit-down with Frank and Patrick and we expressed our views. Both sides were unhappy but they were rightly concerned that this would distract me at a crucial time. When I subsequently spoke to the media, I tried to back-pedal by highlighting the fact that this was a very exciting finale to the championship and that's what we should be focusing on. But the damage had been done, although at least I had made my point.

Fortunately, neither Frank nor Patrick was the type to dwell on something like that and we got on with the job in hand. Meanwhile, having been responsible for increasing my own stress at a crucial time, I called my friend Peter Boutwood in the UK and said, 'I could do with a mate, Pete. Could you come down to Australia?' I had met Pete when we raced in F3 together, so he understood how racing worked as well as having become a close friend. He jumped straight on a plane to Adelaide for the weekend. Pete was a lot of fun and always had a way of lightening the mood: just what I needed at this point. George Harrison had also come down to Adelaide, which meant another friendly face could join our small party. Barry knew an Italian restaurant and he organised dinner every night in the same place. Now I felt really supported.

Because people at home had stayed up to all hours to watch the race from Suzuka and witnessed the fantastic turn-around in the championship, the tension had been heightened even more for this race. In Adelaide it was spring, just coming into summer, and we had the wonderful sense of expectation surrounding a race that took over the entire city, and turned it into a party town.

Nigel, impressive as ever, took pole after being fastest on the first day, which was dry. Saturday was wet, precluding any challenge to Nigel's pole, so Schumacher was next and I was third quickest. At the start, Michael got alongside Nigel who, seeing me coming through, moved to one side and let me go after the Benetton. From the word go, it was like Suzuka Part II. Michael and I went straight at it: nose to tail, fastest lap after fastest lap, pulling away from everyone else and continuing our intense private battle. Once again, I was on his tail and thinking I could not let this guy get away. There is a photograph of the pair of us lapping a backmarker while under very heavy braking at the end of the 180mph back straight – and I am less than a foot from the back of the Benetton. I remember thinking as I hauled on the brakes at that moment, 'Oh shiiiiit!' When they checked the cars afterwards, I had double the brake wear of Nigel and he did the whole race, which should give you an idea of the pace at the front.

I consoled myself that Michael must have been finding my pressure hard to take, particularly after being beaten fair and square at Suzuka. He had to quietly acknowledge that I had upped my game. After about twenty laps, a backmarker came between us and he started to eke out a small advantage. Because it was a city street circuit, many of the corners were right-angled. Michael got far enough in front to be almost one corner ahead and momentarily out of my vision. The gap was only a few seconds but he must have been pushing like mad because, on lap 36, he overdid it coming out of a left-hander at the start of a sequence of corners. On this occasion, unlike Japan where he went off the road more than once, he did damage the car but, crucially, I did not see this happen. When I came round the corner, all I could see was Michael coming off the kerb and recovering from what I assumed to be a moment on the grass. As he weaved in front of me I thought, 'He's trying to gather momentum and, if I allow him to do that, he'll be off again. I can *not* let this opportunity go.' The next corner, a right-hander, followed almost immediately. Michael moved left and appeared to leave the door open. I stuck my nose into the gap and accelerated through. Michael moved right, either not knowing I was there or trying to close the door. He clouted me, sending his car up onto two wheels and almost right over before hitting the tyres.

I remember thinking, 'That was a bit clumsy, Damon.' It was always going to be a half-a-chance move, but I had to take it. I had come from bike racing, where you never crash into people in order to win but in karting it tends to happen more. So maybe he had chosen to collide? At Williams we had never even discussed the possibility that he might choose to win the championship by taking us both out. If it was deliberate, we must all have been innocents because at first I thought it was me that had done the wrong thing by trying the passing move.

Michael was out on the spot but, as I continued, I could see my left-front suspension had been damaged. I knew if I could keep going I might still win the championship – I only needed two points – but there seemed little hope the suspension could be fixed. When I reached the pits, Patrick tried to bend the suspension straight with his bare hands. I was shaking my head, thinking, 'That's not going to work, Patrick, really, is it? And if you think I'm going to hammer around this track at 180mph with a dodgy suspension, think again!' The car was retired and Michael was crowned World Champion.

It's fair to say there was a bit of controversy over the incident. The guys at Benetton were jeering. George Harrison was hopping up and down; everyone was in uproar. Barry came up to me and said, 'Everybody saw what happened. Don't say nothing!' I thought, 'After what happened when I got off the plane, Barry, that's probably the best advice you've ever given me.' I retreated to the office at the back of the

Williams garage and called Georgie. Just as I was beginning to do some taping for a column with Maurice Hamilton, Barry came into the office and said I should see a rerun of the incident. He got on to his TV producer and somehow got them to play the moment on a screen in the office.

I watched it and, to my amazement, I saw Schumacher hit the wall. Because his car had been obscured around the corner before we touched, I hadn't realised his car was fatally damaged. Barry was going on about watching Schumacher's head as he looked in his mirrors and obviously knew I was coming through. Suddenly, the picture in my mind had started to change dramatically. I thought, 'They can't let him get away with that.' But they did. The result stood. Michael had won his first F1 World title. It wasn't the only time a championship had been decided like that, either. Prost and Senna had their collisions in 1989 and 1990, but Alain had done it in a rather more subtle way in '89 by taking his line rather than crashing together at full speed as Senna did in '90. So the officials were following a bit of a new tradition by not enforcing a penalty for deliberate 'accidents'. Racing had changed a bit since my dad's day. No more gentlemen racers now.

I had to accept the result. But a large part of me also felt that from the moment we had lost Ayrton this had been a tainted championship anyway. We all wanted to get this season done and dusted. I could be satisfied that I had at least tried my best to win for Ayrton and for Williams. There is no logical reason why I should think of it in those terms; everyone, including Michael, had been affected by the loss of Ayrton, but there was a certain amount of relief that the season was finally at an end, as there always is: that end-of-term feeling. But this one felt particularly good to let go of. I had never been in a battle for a World Championship before and I had found it extremely stressful, especially with Imola and the follow-on from that. Some bits were enjoyable, though, and I had gone up another level in terms of my ability as a driver. But the championship hadn't happened for various reasons, and we had no idea how good Michael was going to eventually turn out to be, either. This was only the first of seven Formula One titles, which was a target way beyond anyone's wildest imaginings at that time. Probably even Senna never thought that would ever happen.

Michael and I were staying in the same hotel. The following morning, I saw him having breakfast and went across to shake his hand and say well done. I just wanted to see if he could look me in the eye. He didn't say much. I had half hoped it would be an awkward moment for him, but he's pretty impregnable.

The British sporting public responded magnificently, though. In 1994, it was necessary to fill out a form to vote for the BBC Sports Personality of the Year. Because Adelaide had been so dramatic and had come close to the end of the year, I think this was in my favour when I won it. In some ways, that defines the British: you can win Olympic gold medals, but we'll give it to the guy who is a good loser! I was in the middle with Sally Gunnell on one side and Colin Jackson on the other. And I hadn't even won the championship! But I had won this one. To be voted for in this way by the British public was stunning. I said I accepted the trophy in acknowledgement of the fact that we had lost Senna, as I felt that whatever plaudits I had received in 1994 were acquired by dint of his demise. It had been a pretty gruelling year but during the six months since Imola, I had accumulated a lot of experience and sharpened my skills enormously. Next year, I thought, I can have a clean run at the championship. But motor sport is never that simple. I should have known by now.

22 » 1995: THE GOOD, THE BAD AND THE UGLY

Events in 1994 had set up what could best be described as a convenient PR rivalry between Michael Schumacher and me. Part of me thought it was good fun playing the Good Guy v. Bad Guy game, but looking back I had picked a fight with the wrong guy.

David Coulthard would be my teammate now for the full season and I was fine with that. It would be good to have a younger charger to keep me on my toes, although it was a reminder that I was not the future any more. I had a better contract for 1995, not necessarily because of my complaints but more thanks to some serious negotiation by Michael Breen. As a result of the more favourable terms, Georgie and I had to up sticks once more. I would be earning more money so a decision was made to move to where I could reduce exposure to tax.

Georgie took a look at Monaco and didn't like it. Oliver having Down's Syndrome meant we needed to go somewhere that could provide proper support and we thought another language would be too much. We liked the sound of Ireland, and moved there at the beginning of 1995. We rented our first house, which had a fantastic view over Killiney Bay, just south of Dublin. With my contract being renewed every year, I had no idea how long this run of luck would last, especially as I was already thirty-four and could probably only count on another four to five years of being able to deliver at the level F1 demanded of its drivers. But we were to stay in Ireland for the next five years, where both our daughters were born and we made lifelong friends. The children picked up hints of accent and I had a lovely drive to Josh's school past Sugar Loaf Mountain. I went mountain biking up in the Wicklow Hills and could run down to the sea and up to the top of Killiney Hill which had magnificent views over Dublin Bay, all of which was good preparation for the new season.

Because of the change in my position to that of a driver with championship potential, I now wanted some more experienced management in my corner. I was trying to get together with Julian Jacobi, who had previously managed Prost and Senna so knew everyone and understood how F1 worked from that point of view, but each time I raised the subject with Michael he would try to persuade me not to make the move.

I think Julian would have given me better advice about how to cope with F1, but the truth is Michael Breen also had his strong points. No one likes the guy who always wants more, but you have to fight for every penny in F1 and Michael knew how to use the law to his advantage. Julian already had a good reputation, though, particularly with people such as Frank Williams and Ron Dennis. I just didn't have the experience or the enthusiasm for the business end of things. The fact was, I was already into a complex situation with Michael and could not spend the rest of the season working out how to change it as I had a World Championship to win. Compared to what Senna had to deal with, my problems were small fry, but I was starting to realise how much more complicated being an F1 driver was. My career had taken off in a massively spectacular way in a very short space of time and this had rather caught me out.

Although I was not number one in the team going into 1995, that didn't really matter. If 'not less than equal' was good enough for Senna then that was good enough for me too. Williams felt they had two front-running candidates and I knew I needed to keep David in his place if I was to keep my job. That went according to plan when I put the Williams-Renault FW17 on pole for the first race in Brazil. But having the rear suspension break while I was leading was definitely not part of the plan, particularly when Schumacher went on to win. Benetton now had a Renault engine, so their challenge would be greater than ever.

I put that right a fortnight later by winning in Buenos Aires, the first time we had visited Argentina since F1 had stopped going there due to the Falklands War in 1982. Downtown Buenos Aires was a really attractive city; the circuit wasn't quite so great, not very challenging to drive and there was a big bump in one of the corners. As one of the leading drivers, Bernie had asked me to come and meet the President, Carlos Menem. When the President politely asked if there was anything he could do for me, I suggested he could get rid of the bump in Turn 3! He said, unfortunately, that was not something he could manage. David was on pole and led the race until he had a problem with the car. Mine was perfect, and felt even better when I was able to overtake Schumacher and take that win. But David had left a marker that he was going to be a factor in the championship.

Returning to Imola was always going to be difficult. The minute you walked into the paddock, the memories of twelve months before were bound to come flooding back. The organisers had added chicanes, the most significant being just before Tamburello. These alterations might have changed the character of the circuit but, like everything else that weekend, were something that just had to be accepted as part of the post-Imola 1994 world. As a GPDA director, I had been asked to take a look at other circuits to see what else could be changed. Silverstone would also be altered but some of these changes did not improve the driving experience. There was always going to be a tension between what the drivers wanted and what Max and the FIA wanted. For better or worse, the fantastic fast flow of Imola was gone forever.

Given the emotion attached to the weekend, particularly

for the Williams team, it was quietly satisfying to win the race
– and felt even better when Schumacher spun off. For the first
time in my career, I was leading the World Championship. It
was destined to be short-lived, although for the next few races
there would not be a lot to choose between me and Michael;
it was a good contest even if he was marginally ahead on
points. Then it went badly wrong – at Silverstone, of all places
– and never really recovered.

An increasingly fraught season for me had actually started
long before the first race. At the end of the stressful 1994
season, Frank had asked me to go on a promotional tour for
Rothmans. Before the racing had even begun in 1995, I had
been to Hong Kong, Beijing, Moscow and Dubai. There were
new pressures and I really needed to manage my time better
as the season got going. I may have been running at the front
and winning races, but I did not realise until too late that I
was burning myself out. The tension would increase, as it
invariably does, at my home Grand Prix. The previous year,
the press had been critical of my efforts, which is their job, but
in 1995, Frank would provide plenty of extra fodder for the
journalists after a race that I'd rather forget.

It could have been a fantastic victory as I had started from
pole and led Michael until the first of two pit stops. Benetton
had decided to stop just once, but Williams definitely made
the right call. When I rejoined in second place after my final
stop, I was cutting massively into Schumacher's lead. Michael
knew I would have him sooner rather than later.

As we hammered through the fast right-hander at Bridge
I was right on Michael's tail. Then, considering he knew I
was right behind him, he went unusually wide on the entry to
Priory corner. All I could see was a massive open gap: an
opportunity, I thought, to stick my car right on the apex,
forcing him to yield. But I had miscalculated, not the corner
but my opponent. Instead of trying to avoid hitting me he
just came back across and slammed into me. At first, I did
the usual and blamed myself, but the more we learned about

Michael's tendencies, the more I think he was happy to collide with me rather than come second. It was like Adelaide the previous year all over again, except that this time I was the villain. Frank let slip that he thought I had been 'a bit of a prat', and it was manna for the sports headline writers. The next day the whole of the back page of one of the tabloids had a picture of me with the one-word headline, 'Prat!' Winning the BBC Sports Personality of the Year only six months before seemed a hell of a long time ago now. It had a big negative effect on my confidence and on the public perception of me as someone able to take the fight to Michael. Furthermore, not only had the team boss publicly humiliated me, he had just given Schumacher another reason to feel Williams were not a unified force. But this is how F1 works. The pressure is relentless.

Meanwhile, Georgie was about to give birth to our third child, Tabitha, who was due on the day of the race. Georgie had come to Silverstone and was reassured by Prof Watkins that the medical facilities and staff available at the track were more than capable of dealing with childbirth. She informed them that she would never in a million years be giving birth at a Grand Prix.

Georgie managed to prevent the stress of the race from getting to her and returned immediately to Ireland. I followed on later like a bear with a sore head after the PR catastrophe of Silverstone. I went with her to the hospital for the birth, trying to be as good a husband as I could, and as we waited in her room I ranted on the phone to Breen about the head-lines and the atmosphere within the team, while Georgie had to endure my fury on top of her own more important and more immediate concerns. The season was all going horribly wrong. I imagined that Schumacher must have been loving it.

Needing to cool off and give Georgie a break, I nipped out to see Plant and Page round the corner at The Point, in Dublin. 'Don't mind if I go, do you darling?' I think she couldn't wait to get rid of me. Having been present at the two previous births, I knew these things could take a long time, but sometime during *Whole Lotta Love* or *Celebration Day* my lovely Tabitha must have come into the world, because when I returned there she was! She gave me the biggest scowl. Tabitha, that is. Georgie was radiating love for her new born and I was forgiven for not being there. Actually, I was thanked.

The arrival of Tabitha was the only piece of really good news during that whole year. Having had a controversial end to my race at Silverstone, it would get no better in Germany. I really liked Hockenheim and had the car hooked up to produce a fantastic pole position lap. I jumped into the lead and, going into the first corner at the start of the second lap, the rear of the car hopped over a bump and I was into the barrier. There appeared to be no reason why it should have happened as I was not trying to brake late or do anything out of the ordinary. The car simply swapped ends, although it looked like I simply lost control. Coming on the back of Silverstone, that was all I needed. And to compound it, Schumacher won to pull twenty-one points clear. A couple of days later, to my relief, I had a call from Adrian Newey to tell me they had discovered that the differential had suddenly locked. I said something like, 'That's good to know. At least it wasn't me. Perhaps Williams would like to tell everyone this is what caused the spin?' Certainly, it was a relief to hear about this discovery, but the damage to my reputation had been done and the championship tide appeared to be turning. A few weeks later the Rolling Stones played the Hockenheimring on their Voodoo Lounge Tour. Mick Jagger quipped, 'At least we got further than Damon Hill!'

I made amends a little by dominating the Hungarian Grand Prix from pole. Things were also looking up as Frank and I had sat down at the Hungaroring and renegotiated my contract for the 1996 season. He had offered me a lot of money to stay on, so, finally, I was getting a deal sorted well before Christmas. That was confidence-inspiring: a good weekend one way or another. And Michael didn't score any points, which left the score as Schumacher fifty-six, Hill forty-five. Game still on.

The Belgian Grand Prix was not so straightforward. I was behind Michael at one point and, after weaving all over the place to keep me behind, he barged me off the track at Les Combes. We hadn't seen that sort of blatant blocking since Gilles Villeneuve and René Arnoux at Dijon in 1979. The difference was that at that time it was all good-natured racing. But Michael and I had a history now and his attitude and demeanour made him appear utterly ruthless. Meanwhile, Frank and Patrick were not impressed. They didn't go as far as complaining publicly, but after 1994 they were not big fans of Schumacher or Benetton, and it was disappointing that the FIA stewards didn't have the courage to come down on that kind of driving. Because I had finished second to Schumacher, the gap had opened to fifteen points. It would remain the same after the next race at Monza, thanks to neither of us finishing. But the reason why would be another controversy in this increasingly tense season.

It was a bizarre start to the Italian Grand Prix in the sense that David, who was on pole, somehow managed to spin during the parade lap. He damaged the car on a kerb and appeared to be out. Then, at the end of the first lap, a multiple collision at the back of the field brought out the red flag. Since the rules said it would be a completely new race, David was allowed back on pole in the spare car for the restart. You don't get many second chances like that, and he made the most of it by leading until a wheel bearing went after thirteen laps. That moved me up to third, chasing Schumacher's Benetton and Berger's leading Ferrari. It was a thrilling race on those very fast straights.

While travelling at close to 200mph on the twenty-fourth lap, I got a tow from Michael just as we came up to lap the Footwork of Taki Inoue. I went to go to the right of the

Japanese driver and Michael went left. Poor Taki must have been freaking out. As we approached the chicane, absolutely flat out, I remember feeling that Taki hadn't seen me, he'd only seen Michael. My worst fears were confirmed when he started to creep across. I knew I would have to brake really late for the chicane in order to get ahead of the Footwork because, if he jinked, we would touch wheels and that would be an absolutely massive shunt. So I braked really, really deep, getting safely ahead of Inoue. But Michael came across in front of me as he returned to the racing line – and I just could not stop in time. We touched ever so lightly and both went off. I couldn't blame Michael for this one, and it was just a shame that he appeared right in front of me and I couldn't slow down. He came over while I was in the car and started yelling angrily. Instead of defending myself vigorously and blaming poor old Taki who was dollying along in the middle of the track, which is what I should have done, I took it all on my shoulders. I felt like I had screwed up yet again and after the mess at Silverstone, this just compounded the feeling in myself and in the media that I was not up to it. It was all the press needed, as this was now the third time that, as title contenders, Michael and I had crashed.

In retrospect, I can see that I had opened myself up to Michael's attacks. Sport is all about finding the 'weakest link' and I was not impervious enough to cope with it. Therapy teaches you that humans are able to transfer their own doubts and insecurities to others, much as dogs and pigs pick on the runt of the litter and eventually destroy it. The price of being in the frame for victory is that if you don't win, you are the first of the losers. If I could have given myself some advice back then, I'd have said, 'Chin up, Hill! Try to enjoy the game! Don't let it get out of proportion. After all, it's only the Formula One World Championship.'

David's luck changed when he won his first Grand Prix and led all the way from pole at Estoril. He was definitely starting to show form, while I finished third behind Schumacher, which allowed Michael to stretch his lead to seventeen points. Not only had my crashes damaged my confidence but I had allowed David to get a foot in the door, too. All was not going to plan.

Michael, being exceptionally brilliant in all aspects of racing, had been able to create an environment in which he was never under threat from anyone in his own team. Meanwhile, David had moved into third place in the championship, but he was sixteen points behind me, thirty-three behind Michael, and so not really in the reckoning. Fighting your teammate is absolutely fine – until you get to the closing stages of the championship. Frank's reluctance to take the fight to Michael and Benetton by giving me total unequivocal support was starting to irritate me, especially as I could see that Michael didn't have to deal with the same issue.

The tension began to boil over when we went to the next race, the European Grand Prix at the Nürburgring. I had to argue my case with Frank by asking why I had to fight David as well as Schumacher. There was no question that David was getting quicker and I felt a little threatened by him within the team, which is all part of a driver's life. It was uncannily like my dad having another Scot, Jackie Stewart, come into the team at BRM in 1964. I was aware that David had to make a career for himself and had to do the best he could, but he wasn't yet fighting to win the Drivers' Championship for the team.

Once again, David was on pole and I was alongside. Any time a driver is quicker in qualifying, all complaints from the outqualified fall on deaf ears. The only answer would have to be to outqualify and outrace him. Williams, it now appeared, were less interested in the Drivers' Championship, and it looked as if all that mattered to Frank and Patrick was the Constructors' Championship. Teams get paid according to where they finish in the Constructors', but in my view they were stubbornly refusing to recognise the real value to them of the Drivers' Championship where all the real kudos resides. I made the situation worse in the race when I spun off, cracking my knee against the bulkhead in the cockpit. Michael went on to drive a superb race in the wet. I watched jealously and chastened, standing at the side of the track by my crumpled car. On his slowing-down lap, I stepped out and applauded him; we all knew that we had witnessed something special that day. Meanwhile, David had finished third. There were three races left and the situation was getting pretty dreadful from my point of view; Michael was getting away and I was feeling the pressure. It got worse at Aida in Japan when we had a bad pit stop and finished third, all of which seemed irrelevant on the day Michael was confirmed as champion for the second year in succession. It was humiliating.

To compound the misery, the team was in a sulk and I was blamed for not stopping on my mark when I came in to change tyres and refuel. I had to explain that it was impossible, sitting so low in the car, to see the line on the ground marking exactly where I should stop. I became my father's son and dragged them out to show them the problem so we could fix it. After that race, we established a procedure in which the mechanic on one of the front wheels would put out his hand over the crown of the tyre, which I could see very clearly from the cockpit, and I would stop with the wheel exactly under his hand. From that moment on, not only did Williams do this, but every single team would eventually copy us. It is one of the contributions to F1 I'm most proud of, and one of the few things of value I really contributed to Williams in 1995!

Around the same time, there was a rumour going around that I would be replaced by Heinz-Harald Frentzen the following year. I knew it had been a bad slump but I thought I had a contract. I asked Patrick if he knew anything about it and he just replied by saying I would be driving for Williams the following year. Which was technically correct. But there was a twist he may not have been completely open about.

Suzuka was a week later and I couldn't do anything right; I couldn't even drive properly. I was falling off all over the place, a sure sign that I was in complete meltdown. I couldn't take the defeat and we had already lost. I had no more tricks up my sleeve. To say that my racing driving muse deserted me in that race would be a massive understatement. I eventually slid off the track in the wet to end up parked on the exit of Spoon corner in a puddle. Suddenly, my finest performance in a racing car the previous year seemed a very, very long time ago indeed. After the race, in the team office with Patrick and Frank, I felt like crying – but I was also laughing at how bad it had been. It was a catastrophe, made worse because David had had a bad race as well. It was one of those days when everyone had performed pathetically. Patrick and Frank's mood was not improved by knowing they had signed me for 1996 and I could forgive them for thinking they had signed a broken man.

I could accuse them of having bad man-management skills, but that would not be fair. The problem was with me. I looked up to them as father figures and I was projecting onto them a role they had no desire to play. I was in dire need of approval from them and all season I felt they had been keeping me guessing or keeping their belief in me provisional, which unsettled me. They had no responsibility for me beyond giving me a car to get on with my job. I know that now, but back then I didn't understand how much the loss of my father was still affecting me. I had been the son of the team principal and as such I had enjoyed a special relationship with the boss. Part of me was trying to recreate that relationship with Frank and Patrick. Great guys though they might be, I can understand them not wanting to be surrogate parents. They had enough on their plate with running an F1 team.

My other mistake was to have made the battle between me and Michael personal when I should have just focused on my own job. It had all seemed a good game at first, but I had been humiliated by his brilliance, and the battering I had received from the press I found baffling and frightening. When you have enough doubts about yourself, you don't need everyone pointing out more. If I was going to survive in this business

I would need some help to understand where I was going wrong. What I probably really needed was my dad to tell me to pull my finger out. But he was gone, long ago. Twenty years had passed since I last heard his voice. But there must have been something of him still lurking in me, because I was about to have a bit of a turnaround in fortune and form.

There were two weeks between Suzuka and the last race in Adelaide. I went to Bali and Georgie came out to join me. Georgie could see straightaway that I was down in the dumps, and we talked the whole thing through. Georgie said I had taken the pleasure out of what I was doing. I had been full-on since the end of the previous season and gone into 1995 taking on far too much responsibility; we spent the week taking stock of the situation. Georgie and I agreed that the best way forward was to just think of myself and get on with my job – much as I had done when I said 'Sod it!' in Suzuka after Patrick had lectured me about not smiling enough. The championship was over, so there was no use crying over spilt milk. There was always 1996, as long as Williams didn't replace me with Frentzen.

I moved on to the final race of the season and met Michael Breen and Pete Boutwood in Perth. Fancying a bit of surfing, I went to a shop that hired out flippers and boogie boards. I knew nothing about the area and when I asked if it was OK to surf, the guy said, 'Aw yeah, you'll be right, mate!' I was pretty fit and managed to get past the breakers. I must have been on a rip, because one minute I was fighting like mad to get through and the next I was out the other side, heading for South Africa. I fought like hell to get back. On the way, I came across Michael, who was in real trouble and needed help. We eventually made it to the shore and I don't think either of us realised how close we had come to either drowning or being eaten by a shark. It was only later that we discovered a surfer had recently been attacked at this very spot. When I got to Adelaide, it was as if I had reset my whole mind and body.

I knew I would have one more shot at the championship in 1996 and that nothing could be as bad as this season, and I was determined to enjoy the race.

I put the car on pole, with David alongside. When he jumped into the lead, it was a bit like following Schumacher the year before. DC was really on it, pushing hard to stay in front. I remember thinking, 'This is quite hard; he's really quick!' but come the pit stop David peeled off – and drove straight into the wall at the start of the pit lane. At that stage in his career, David seemed to have the capacity to snatch defeat from the jaws of victory, which is a bit rich coming from me, but he did have real talent and was young. If he had stayed with Williams for 1996 it could well have been him who became champion instead of me. Fortunately for me, he had signed for McLaren.

It turned out to be one of the most bizarre Grands Prix of my career. I finished two laps ahead of second-place man Olivier Panis in a Ligier, the first time that has been achieved in GP racing history since Jackie Stewart beat Bruce McLaren at Montjuïc Park in 1969. After the race Frank could not understand how I had appeared to be a ruined man at Suzuka, and then turned up in Adelaide where, with a little help from David, I had blitzed everyone, as if this was something I could do every day. Finally, he seemed genuinely pleased with me.

That night we all partied like lunatics, relieved to be all in one piece again. We went to a club full of all the drivers. George Harrison confronted Schumacher and told him he could be really great if he really wanted to be. I don't think Michael had a clue what he was talking about, but he responded by pouring a pint of beer over my head. I'm not sure that was what George really meant by 'Great'. His message had clearly got lost in translation. But Michael had just bagged another F1 Championship. Only five more to go! To the 1995 runner-up; the wooden spoon. But it wasn't all over yet.

23 » 1996: THE BIG ONE

It was clear that 1996 was going to be a golden opportunity. I would, in all probability, have the best car on the grid and no Michael Schumacher to worry about. He was off to Ferrari with the key members of Benetton, Ross Brawn and Rory Byrne. They would not be championship contenders just yet, thanks to the Italian team still regrouping. Indy 500 winner and recently crowned IndyCar Champion, another 'son of', Jacques Villeneuve, was joining Williams. Because no one knew exactly what to expect of him, I began to feel the team rallying around me at last. There was the distinct feeling that they wanted me to have the best and deliver the best of myself, Adrian being especially supportive from the beginning.

Adrian Newey went to the trouble of making sure my size 11 feet fitted inside the cockpit and produced the most comfortable car I would drive in my entire motor racing career. Everything was in the right place; it was a lovely snug fit, so much so that I felt as though I could fall asleep in there, which is actually difficult not to do, even on the grid. But if the Williams FW18 was blissful to sit in, it would be heaven to drive.

At the end of 1995 I had decided to avoid the Autosports Awards, preferring to appear on a video link; I had grown a beard and I must have looked awful. I may have finished the season on a high note in Australia but, in truth, I remained quite depressed, and I decided to get some help. The BBC had done a piece on Michael Schumacher, during which they had interviewed an American woman called Mary Spillane. Mary advised politicians on interview techniques and strategies for protecting yourself in the public domain. After I heard what she had to say, I gave her a call.

On the subject of body language, the BBC had asked Mary what it was about Michael Schumacher that Damon Hill didn't seem to have. She listed my faults, which included looking haunted, holding my head down, and looking at the ground instead of looking up and at the world – which is exactly what my mum used to say about me. More to the point, her comments sounded very similar to Patrick's criticisms. In short, I was too withdrawn and did not exude confidence in the way Michael did. Michael was a game changer in many ways in our sport. The previous generation always looked pissed off; even Senna and Prost had a perennial air of being put upon, but Michael leapt into the air on the podium even if he had come second. I had made a rod for my own back by getting drawn into verbal jousting with Schumacher. The only good thing about Mary's summing-up was that there was plenty of room for improvement.

Mary came to see me in Ireland and I started to pour my heart out. She sat and listened for about a minute, then held her hand up and said, 'Stop!' She paused and simply said, 'Save it for the book.' It was as if someone had just hit me on the head and brought me to my senses. She gave me some golden rules: focus on your job; look for the positives in whatever happens; don't get distracted by what the press are writing but, if there are any inaccuracies, correct them immediately; always come across upbeat whenever appropriate; don't invite the world to pile in on top of you; don't say more than you need to. It was probably the most valuable piece of career advice I had ever had and as a result I approached 1996 in a completely different manner. I wasn't going to create a rivalry between me and either Jacques Villeneuve or Michael Schumacher. The only thing that mattered was allowing myself the space to do the best I could, maximise the opportunities I had and deliver with the car I was being given. As much as an F1 season ever can, 1996 would turn out to be a piece of cake.

Jacques was a very good driver, but I always felt I had the measure of him if needed. There was quite a bit of fuss when he turned up and I could quite easily have been destabilised by his arrival. He liked to attract attention by always doing the opposite of what was expected, but it was easy to see that this was a control technique and a bid to stand out. I could see so much of my younger self in him. He'd lost his father, too, but at a much earlier age and in a more gruesomely public way. There used to be a series of video tapes called *Havoc!* which had all the accidents one could take from across the motor racing spectrum, compiled together in one havoc-packed hour of action. One of them featured the death of Gilles Villeneuve when he crashed his Ferrari during qualifying for the 1982 Belgian Grand Prix. And I thought I'd had a difficult experience.

Jacques went for the 'grunge' look and wore really baggy overalls. He was a different generation and, like David, eleven years my junior. I thought, 'I'll play the mature old hand if that's what is needed. I really don't mind.' I was now thirty-five and it was time to grow up and win a World Championship before I was too old to chew my food.

Jacques had a good manager in Craig Pollock, a Scot who had been director of sport at the college in Villars where Jacques had grown up. Eventually, he and Jacques set up British American Racing in Brackley, which morphed into Brawn GP, the team that won the championship in 2009 with Jenson Button and later became the world-conquering AMG Mercedes Team of today. Jacques exhibited similar ambition in his driving. During testing at Estoril, he mentioned the long, 180-degree, super-fast final corner that had absolutely no run-off, just a barrier on the edge of the track – similar to the Indianapolis Motor Speedway. He bet all the engineers that he could overtake a car around the outside. 'Yeah, right!' we all thought. 'He must be nuts!' We dismissed it as bravado, but

Jacques insisted it was possible. I had him down as an over-confident kid who would either come a cropper or learn F1 was more difficult than he had appreciated. Secretly, though, I envied his chipper demeanour and the team quickly warmed to him, although he had some strange quirks. He would clean his teeth after every meal and he would have eggs for breakfast, but chop them up like baby food before wolfing them down. You notice things like that when you have a new teammate and you are trying to discover where his strengths and weaknesses might lie, but I had taken my lessons on board from Mary and I wasn't about to pick a fight.

The only issue I ever had with Jacques occurred quite early on during testing. We were in the debrief room when they brought us our lunch and Jacques started to help himself to mine. I thought, 'There's got to be a line somewhere – and I think it's right here!' I had to give him a ticking-off. We joked about it afterwards, but now he knew I wasn't just going to roll over and let him tickle my tummy like a submissive dog. Jacques was a good sportsman and teammate. We both liked fierce competition but, most of all, we wanted to have fun racing.

The pre-season training had gone better than it had ever done, and I was in the perfect frame of mind to take on the championship. Not long before the first race, I was asked to appear on the TV show *Pebble Mill at One* in Birmingham. I was a bit late and exceeded the speed limit while going up the M40. My heart jumped into my mouth when I looked in the mirror and saw blue flashing lights. I backed off, but they had clocked me at 101mph, and I knew that anything over 100mph would be an instant ban. I immediately panicked, worrying that my racing licence could be taken away as a consequence. Suddenly, the championship was hanging in the balance. I thought I might get off when they discovered who I was. Not a chance, and the officer wrote out a ticket without even a flicker. I was summonsed to appear at Bicester Magistrates' Court.

I had to hire a lawyer to get across the point that it was very important for Mr Hill to keep his licence. The court was packed with press but there was this homeless guy who repeatedly stood up while I was talking, saying, 'You tell 'em, Mr 'ill. Go on, Mr 'ill.' It got so bad that the magistrate had to threaten to eject him, which added a comical element. I didn't help myself when, thinking about the ban being triggered at 100mph, I said, 'Please, Your Honour, I was only one mile an hour over.' Of course, I had to be reminded that I had actually been 31mph over the speed limit. They did me for speeding and I received a ban – but for just one week, which was a huge relief. For the moment, I had been given another chance. 'Bad boy, Daddy,' as my son Oliver might have said. More importantly, the FIA didn't get involved. Given their mission to improve road safety, they might have made an example of me. I have since worked with a campaign called 'Safe Drive' which educates pre-driving-test students on the perils of driving too fast.

Having rebooted myself mentally, I had also changed my fitness routine, thanks to the help of Erwin Göllner, my Austrian trainer. He pointed out that I had been overdoing it and not training in the right way. Instead of pounding endlessly in the gym, he got me outside, doing more appropriate exercises, including coming to stay with him in Salzburg to climb the Untersberg mountain, famous for Julie Andrews singing *The Hills Are Alive* on top of it. I gave it a few bars and never felt more magnificent. It was all part of getting me in the right frame of mind for what I recognised would, in all likelihood, be my last chance to bag 'The Big One': the F1 Crown. Erwin's programmes helped keep my mind fresh and stress-free. I wish I'd met him earlier in my career, but better now than never.

So I felt super relaxed and totally prepared for anything when I set off once more for Australia. Adelaide had lost the Australian Grand Prix to their rival city Melbourne and would now kick off the season instead of being the finale. The Williams Renault FW18 was not only the most comfortable car I had ever sat in, it also handled beautifully and was incredibly well balanced. I could put it anywhere I liked on the track and, for once, I felt free in a racing car, not crammed in. I had room for my hands and feet and it fitted me like a glove. It was a slight disappointment, therefore, when I was outqualified by Jacques. There is no doubting that he did a good job getting pole, but I was quite happy to let Jacques have his day, which showed just how much my mindset had changed since the previous season. I knew from experience it was going to be a long year and my objective was to score the maximum points possible in every race.

I didn't make a good getaway at the start, but that didn't matter when the race was stopped after Martin Brundle spectacularly barrel-rolled his Jordan and somehow managed to scramble free. Jacques led once more, but I stayed with him. I wasn't really pushing but I could see he was all over the road and using every bit of track. Eventually he went off at the first corner – and almost collected me in his effort not to lose the lead. For quite some time, I was getting covered in orange oil coming from the back of Jacques's car. He had managed to kink an oil pipe – possibly when he went over a kerb – and the Renault engine eventually failed. It was hard luck on Jacques but I knew I could deal with his pace. I left Australia with maximum points in the bag. The perfect start to my campaign. Next stop, Brazil.

Just before the start at Interlagos, we had a typical Brazilian rainstorm that flooded everything and caused the drains to pop up and overflow like fountains. Everyone was soaked to the skin. I waited patiently in the car, staring ahead at this beautiful empty track glistening in the light of a powerful Brazilian sun, which had decided to show itself at last. This would add to the degree of difficulty for the guys behind because it would be impossible to see through the spray. Although I would have a clearer view, I would also be the first to have to motorboat through the deepest water. Provided I made a good enough start, that is.

I made a peach of a start and slithered over the puddles and rivers with real confidence. I was relishing this. It was like old times again at Brands Hatch on my bike in the wet, and it reminded me that confidence is the secret to success at this highest level. Jacques spun off and I wondered if that might be a bit of an Achilles' heel for him because they tend not to race in the wet in the US. But I was long gone, taking full advantage of the clear track and, decisively, I was the first to change to slicks. It all went perfectly, probably my best race of the year. Niki Lauda said: 'Damon drove like a god today,' which was high praise indeed. I was also reminded that this was my fifteenth Grand Prix win, surpassing my dad's total. It was not something I had thought about because comparing different eras is of questionable value. Quite apart from it being a lot more dangerous in the 1960s, they did far fewer races and had more mechanical failures. Beating my father was never what this was about; it was more to do with answering the questions I had about myself.

There was a week between the race at Interlagos and Argentina and I thought it would be a good idea to spend the spare few days surfing in Rio. I got a boogie board and went into the sea at a spot just outside our hotel. There were a lot of local kids around who kept admiring the board and asking if they could have it. When I got back to the hotel I met a Brazilian journalist, who was horrified when I told him where I had been. It turned out the beach was right by the sewage outlet for one of the biggest favelas in Brazil. I was lucky I didn't get mugged too, he added soberly. Sure enough, I picked up a bug that wiped me out for the next week. It was awful. Bright green, mostly. By the time the race weekend in Buenos Aires came round, I was completely dehydrated and had hardly slept. Nevertheless, I managed to win the Argentine Grand Prix from pole, which either meant I drove better when I was exhausted or that I still had a big advantage in reserve. When I was bike racing, the local paper called me 'Hat-Trick Hill' because I won three races a day. So, here was my

F1 hat-trick. If you counted the final race of 1995 it was actually four in a row. So things were now looking really good: thirty points to me. My teammate was next on twelve. Schumacher was still struggling with an uncooperative Ferrari.

Jacques redressed the balance slightly by winning his first Grand Prix at the Nürburgring on a day when I could only manage fourth after what could best be described as a bit of a pantomime in the pits. I reported a vibration at the rear of the car and the mechanics and Adrian checked it over when I made an early pit stop. Nothing was found to be amiss but the stop took twenty seconds, partly because Patrick, who was in charge of operations, forgot to tell me it was all clear and I could go. Added to which, I took off with Adrian's radio on the rear wing, where presumably he had placed it while taking a look underneath. I rejoined in eleventh place and, all things considered, did well to salvage three points and not take the most talented aerodynamicist in the world with me for a couple of laps.

I made amends in the best possible way by winning the San Marino Grand Prix, thanks to an excellent strategy. By now, Williams had got on top of the refuelling/tyre wear matrix, deciding to load me with fuel at the start, keep me out until the point when I was about to come across back markers and then make my first stop much later than everyone else. This depended on me leading – not necessarily a given because Schumacher had pleased the Italian fans no end by putting the improving Ferrari on pole. He ran ahead of me until his first stop – which was when our tactics came perfectly into play and I moved into a lead I would never lose. Jacques retired with broken suspension, possibly the result of having been knocked by Jean Alesi's Benetton on the opening lap. I was twenty-one points ahead as we moved on to Monaco.

Considering that this is the blue riband event of F1, plus the fact I had a great car to add to the pleasure of racing on this iconic circuit, I was out to really enjoy this weekend. I can't say the same for Jacques, who didn't seem at home on the narrow streets and qualified back on the fifth row. The only fly in the ointment was that Michael once again took pole. I was alongside and the nature of the track is such that starting from pole you really ought to win – barring mistakes or misfortune. Between us, Michael and I were about to have both.

Classically, it had rained just before the start so we were on rain tyres even though it had stopped raining. That was fine by me because I liked the wet. My start was perfect and I got ahead of the Ferrari going into the first corner. The concentration required is such that I didn't notice the Ferrari had disappeared from my mirrors halfway round the first lap. Michael had made an atypical error when he put a wheel on a slippery kerb and slid into the barrier. With my car going beautifully, I simply had to make sure I avoided a similar mistake, which around Monaco is about as easy as playing hopscotch in a minefield. Piquet once famously described Monaco as like trying to ride a bicycle in your bathroom. Now the bathroom floor was wet, too.

The stop to change from wet to slick tyres was timed perfectly. You can instantly feel the extra grip, so I was sitting pretty with a comfortable lead and pulling away. Then, on lap 41, the oil warning light came on. Having blown up quite a few engines throughout my racing career, I had got to recognise the warning sounds and knew what would happen next: I'd hear tiny little tinkles just before all hell let rip.

Coming through the Monaco tunnel flat chat in Grand Prix driver ecstasy, leading the Monaco GP comfortably, I heard the death rattle as the V10 began to destroy itself. There was nothing for it but to freewheel into the escape road, blue-white smoke trailing from the back of the car. A Renault mechanic had not tightened a bolt properly and the oil had seeped away – along with my one and only chance to win this great race.

My dad never won the British Grand Prix and I was destined never to win at Monaco, but the manner of this retirement was hard to take, although I was philosophical. There were far worse fates that could befall a racing driver and there was a much more valuable prize that was still in my sights. At least my retirement was easier to stomach than Michael's collision with the barrier. The roles were to be reversed at the next race.

I sat on pole position for the Spanish Grand Prix and looked down the very long straight that seemed more like an infinity pool at that precise moment. It had been raining hard since the morning warm-up and I was seriously concerned about conditions that were worse than they had been at any stage in the weekend. I looked across at Jacques, who was alongside on the front row, and wondered what Schumacher, directly behind me, must be thinking. Surely we couldn't race in this?

Bernie Ecclestone's TV antenna must have been working overtime as he had detected that his lucrative television schedules would be seriously disrupted if the drivers decided it was too wet to race. This had happened before in Adelaide in 1989 where the drivers refused to start. There was no such thing as a safety car start in 1996 and there was the distinct prospect of nothing happening on the track at the appointed hour. Just as I was trying to weigh up our options, Bernie stuck his head into the cockpit and said in his best terse voice, 'Race starts on time!' That was it. Before I could think of a reply he was off and over to Jacques to say the same thing before working his way through the front few rows, nipping any thought of protest in the bud. Like a load of idiots, our keenness to race overcame our fears and we went back into 'race on' mode.

This was the first season when the green starting lights had been replaced simply by the red lights going out. Within seconds of that happening at Barcelona, we all realised racing in these conditions was total madness. It was far worse than Brazil at the start of the season. Thousands of gallons of rainwater must have been lifted off the road as we all slipped and aquaplaned towards Turn 1. I went off the road a couple of times before finally losing it for good by spinning into the pit wall. Michael, meanwhile, was producing one of the greatest drives of all time as he made everyone look silly in the torrential conditions. Jacques finished an extremely creditable third, the last driver not to be lapped by Schumacher but putting to rest the idea that he could not race in the wet. I had forty-three points; Jacques twenty-six. Time to get out of there and forget. Canada was next and I knew Jacques would put everything into trying to win his home race on the track named after his legendary father.

Circuit Gilles Villeneuve may appear straightforward, but it's a really difficult track. A look at the statistics shows that the best drivers tend to win in Montréal. Lewis Hamilton took his fifth Canadian victory in 2016 and Michael won more races there than at any other circuit. A good lap is all about the braking and turning in. That, to me, is the most difficult skill of all in a racing car, the one that truly defines quality. When you look at speed traces, it's possible to see the guys who are really quick do something different, and I am sure that has to do with years of karting experience. In a kart, thanks to only having brakes on the rear, you have to have extreme sensitivity to the rear on turn-in to slow corners. Getting on the power is not so difficult, but braking in Canada is tricky because it's from such high speed and often in shadow. The change of light makes seeing the edge of the track difficult, added to which the surface is bumpy, making the car unsettled and nervous at that crucial moment. Added to which, at that time, we had a three-pedal system, unlike today, when the clutch is hand-operated. This meant your right foot would be hard on the accelerator through the long flat-out sections and then really pressed onto the brake pedal with loads of pressure for a long time. There was no respite, and consequently my right foot was on fire at the end of my first Canadian Grand Prix in 1993. It was agony. Canada has its special quirks that have to be learned. It's probably one of the most deceptively simple tracks of them all. I'm very proud to have won in Canada for that reason. Also, for this one, I had a really good coach yelling from the touchline.

Once again Williams filled the front row, with me edging out a quietly disappointed Jacques by a couple of hundredths of a second. It was a toss-up between one and two stops and I waited to see what Jacques opted for and then did the opposite. The last thing I wanted was to be on the same bit of track at the same time as Jacques, as we had been in Melbourne. Although Adrian Newey was interested in the performance of both cars he had chosen to work quite closely with me for this race, overseeing my engineer, Tim Preston. Adrian would be instrumental in me winning the race. On reflection, his interest may have had something to do with what he knew and I was very soon to learn.

Jacques opted for one stop, so I went for two. I led but could not see Jacques once I had made my first stop, and I had to rely on the pits giving me target lap times. Adrian had decided to do this job and was on the radio all the time saying, 'Damon, you need a bit more pace.' When I replied that I was flat out, he came back on and said, 'Just a bit more!' 'Bloody hell, Adrian!' I was thinking. But I really hammered home the laps, one after the other, absolutely on the limit. Jacques had made his single stop and, of course, I had to come in one more time, but when I finally rejoined after more fuel and tyres, I was miles ahead.

For the final laps I was cruising: conserving everything but keeping an eye on Jacques, who was guaranteed not to give up. He set his fastest lap two from the end and we crossed the line four seconds apart. There's no question Jacques gave me a good run for my money because he so badly wanted to win this race. It was an important victory for me because Jacques was definitely getting up to speed. Hill fifty-three points, Villeneuve thirty-two at the halfway point. After the race and after a few beers, Adrian had his Cheshire Cat grin on and I gave him a hard time for giving me a hard time. But thanks to

him, I was heading the right way again and there were smiles
all round.

The French Grand Prix of 1996 will forever be celebrated in
our house for an argument that ended with Georgie chucking
a flowerpot at me in Frank's plush motorhome office, whereas
it should really be celebrated for me winning another Grand
Prix. Unfortunately, she had tried to give me advice when I
was in no mood to take it, so soon after Michael Schumacher
had taken my pole position!

Given all the good work that had been done to get me out
of the previous year's slough of despond, Georgie thought she
would remind me about Mary Spillane's advice. But she had
started to do this in the garage when all the cameras were on
us and I had just got out of the car. Golden rule about racing
drivers; never go near them just as they get out of the car!
Her good intentions annoyed me, which in turn annoyed her,
and things quickly escalated into a thermonuclear conflict.
We wisely retreated to the relative privacy of Frank's office. It
didn't help matters that a woman had turned up at the gates
claiming she had my child, which didn't impress Georgie
much. Clive James had been doing a documentary on my year,
and they nearly caught a divorce for good measure. When
Georgie left the motorhome, I desperately tried to clean up the
flowerpot mess before anyone noticed. But Frank was right
outside and gave her a wry smile. He must have heard everything. He always liked a good punch-up between his drivers,
too.

Now I could imagine what it had been like for my parents.
As if worrying about death and injury wasn't enough, wives
have ambitious women to cope with, too, quite apart from the
normal stresses caused by competition. I could have done
without the argument, but maybe it had helped me win the
race, just like when Georgie had chucked the alarm clock at
me all those years ago?

This was not the only argument that was overheard from

outside Frank's office. The situation was reversed at the next race, the British Grand Prix, when Georgie overheard a disagreement between Jacques Villeneuve's lawyer and Frank. To add fuel to our concerns, Georgie had also been told by Ron Dennis that I should look for another drive and that he thought what Frank was doing was 'wrong'. Regardless of what was going on behind the scenes, I won easily in France and added another four points to my championship lead after Jacques had finished second. People were not only asking how I could possibly lose the title, but also saying I wasn't really proving anything. Anyone could drive the FW18 and win. It can look as if it's too easy when everything is good, but I had done all the nose-to-the-grindstone stuff, too. Nigel was accused of having it easy in 1992, and people quickly forget about all the bad years you've had before. The way I saw it, I deserved an easy time, and if I won the British Grand Prix I would be three clear wins ahead, assuming Jacques finished second at Silverstone; even better if he didn't. But I had been around long enough to know that, for some reason, the middle bit of an F1 season throws in a curveball or two. I beat Jacques to pole, but then the wheels started to come off, almost literally!

I made a bad start and dropped to fifth, then the car didn't feel right and I was struggling to make headway. Going into the massively quick Copse corner, the car just let go and I finished in the gravel, very fortunate not to have made it to the barrier. It was a left-front wheel bearing failure that left Jacques to win my home race in the same way I had denied him in Montreal. The gap was now fifteen points, healthy enough, but there was still a long way to go.

I had started the season knowing there would be blips, which is why I had wanted to make the early races count. Added to which, Jacques was bound to get better and better. In contrast to previous years, the mood within Williams was harmonious, despite the cryptic messages from Ron, and the team was being scrupulously fair to both of us, keen to maximise every advantage they had. I don't remember a single moment when there was any tetchiness between Jacques and me. I had the genuine feeling that Patrick and Frank both wanted me to make this one happen – but not that they didn't want Jacques to win; they knew that he would be there next year. This year I felt completely supported and knew they now had faith and confidence in me, which all felt great. It was a well-managed season from my point of view, as if the sun had suddenly come out. So what could possibly go wrong?

I always liked the Hockenheim track in the form we used back in 1996. It had three very long, curving straights punctuated by chicanes in the forest before finally returning us into the stadium section. It was very like coming into Clearways at Brands in that respect – except that there were 120,000 spectators. The straights were taken at well over 200mph, meaning we had to hit the brakes hard at 150 metres. This created 4g of deceleration, which had the effect of dangling us on the straps of the seat harness before we slithered through the chicane and could get on the power once again. Because we ran a wafer-thin rear wing to minimise drag and maximise straight-line speed, the car would accelerate like a rocket. I loved it. There were hardly any spectators out back, just tall fir trees strobing past. At the end of the first lap the spectators would let off fireworks and sometimes the grass would catch fire. You had to hope a rocket didn't land in the cockpit. The corners in the stadium were banked: really nice to drive and helping make the entire circuit a very interesting combination. Alas, that is all gone now, since spectators got bored waiting for us to reappear.

It was a little upsetting, then, to arrive at the Williams motorhome to read in the latest edition of *Autosport* (which someone had thoughtfully left lying around) that I was getting kicked out at the end of the year. And I thought everything had been going so well! My initial thought was that this was a journalist attempting to whip up a story because there was not much else going on. I met Andrew Benson, the author of the piece, and tore a strip off him. I felt it was incredibly unpatriotic to try and pull the rug from under me, a fellow Brit, just as I was heading towards a World Championship, but of course a journalist is obliged to chase any story that comes his way, and he turned out to be right on the money.

For years, I would think that this had come about because Frank had been so disillusioned by my downturn in form at the end of 1995 that he felt the need to replace me. I could have understood that. I had taken defeat badly and it must have seemed to Frank and Patrick that it wasn't good to have such a vulnerable driver. But now I was on fire. Why trade me in? Ron had clearly found out something about the situation and, seeing how well I was going in 1996, must have felt Frank was not playing straight and that I ought to know about it, which is why he said what he did to Georgie. Whatever his motivation was, it was not the news I needed. It wasn't Andrew Benson's fault, either. He was just the messenger who got shot.

As things turned out, it might not have had anything to do with my form; it might actually have been more to do with engines. BMW would link up with Williams in 2000, albeit with Ralf Schumacher instead of Frentzen. Frank knew that Renault were pulling out at the end of 1997, which meant he needed to find a replacement quickly. But if it was about power, it was probably just as much about money. Rothmans were also pulling out after 1997 and would be replaced as sponsors by Winfield Cigarettes, a British American Tobacco brand. BAT would go on to fund British American Racing, the new team set up by Craig and Jacques in 1999. The chips were piling up for German drivers, thanks to Michael's back-to-back championships awakening the huge industrial heartland of Germany to the marketing potential of F1. For 1997, Frentzen would also bring a large deal from Sonnax, an automotive product company.

But all this is with the benefit of hindsight. For the moment

I just had to sit tight and make the best of what I had. Fortunately, what I had was the best car in the world, and right now I had a race to deal with, plus an on-form Gerhard Berger, who really wanted to win this one. He led most of the way but I was right with him when, with four laps to go, the Benetton-Renault, sadly for Gerhard, blew up. Of course, at the post-race press conference, I was asked if this had been a lucky win. I said I felt really sorry for Gerhard – but understood exactly how he felt, having been in the same position previously at this very circuit. Once that had been dealt with, questions turned to my future with Williams. What could I say? What did I know? Nothing, was the answer to both.

My mood was confused – to say the least. The problem was that I had left negotiations to Michael Breen so that I could focus on driving. I knew I was on a very good deal in 1996; I had nothing to complain about. If Frank had said to me, 'Damon, for '97 we're going to give you the same deal and a bonus if you win the championship,' I would have been happy with that. However, the press obviously wanted to know about my future, so I had to be careful not to explode a bomb in the middle of my championship. Was I going the way of Nigel Mansell at the end of his championship year with Williams? That seemed to fit the storyline, because Williams had a record of falling out with almost every World Champion they had helped create. The typical and most obvious line was that my management must have asked for too much money: Damon is getting greedy, kind of thing, but the truth was I never had a discussion with Frank about money at all in 1996.

The Hungaroring was next: a circuit where I had won twice before. The chance of a third win would be scuppered when I made a poor start from the front row and had to spend the rest of an exciting race clawing my way into second place, closing right up on Jacques at the finish. After the race, I took Clive James with us on the police escort from the track to the airport. It's a crazy ride, with motorcycle outriders taking massive risks. On one occasion, Ayrton gave the police outriders all the cash he had as a tip when he arrived safely at the airport. Clive was clinging to the seat for all he was worth. It made good TV, as did the flight – by private jet – to Varna on the Black Sea coast to promote Rothmans cigarettes, which was a surreal experience with Clive and Peter Boutwood arguing about Dickens and the merits of various authors. However, it was not as surreal as the press conference the next day when I was asked if I knew that Frentzen was taking my seat, all of which Clive caught on film.

The gap between Jacques and me was seventeen points, but the situation got worse when I had a poor race at Spa, finishing fifth, three places behind Jacques – which is when I knew that I was a dead man walking as far as the team was concerned. To end my suffering, Frank called me at home in Ireland and said he was sorry, but he had to do what was right for the team, which left me in an invidious position. Williams had given me the biggest opportunity that any driver could wish for at a time when my career was on the verge of being over. I had mixed feelings about Williams because I'd been through a lot with them, but this latest development was very unceremonious and humiliating. I'd learned everything I needed with them and they had provided me with the chance to become a World Champion. Williams was a kind of F1 home for me, and Frank and Patrick had been father figures, but now I was to be kicked out of the nest to fend for myself. I'd had a good run, though, and I told myself that I needed to make the most of what was left of my contract and fight on until the bitter end.

I knew that walking into the paddock at Monza, the Circus Maximus of motor sport, would not be the heroic entrance I had hoped for. I anticipated an agitated press asking me what had gone wrong with negotiations. But this is F1. It's not just about the driving; it's about all the things you or someone else creates to put pressure on. If I was worth my salt, I should be able to cope with all of this by now. You don't get a soft landing anywhere in this game; you are in a circus and you're either being baited like a tiger in a cage or you're an acrobat doing amazing feats, a hundred feet up without a net. It's easy to enjoy it if you are watching in the crowd. But my whole career had been leading up to this point; it could either have a happy ending or a sad one, and it was all hanging in the balance and far from being decided by Monza. It would be really helpful to have a nice, clean victory to relieve some of the pressure.

I made a great start from pole, but Jean Alesi made an even better one from the third row and shot into the lead. I was pumped and utterly determined to deal with this. He was not going to take my race! I got a tow from the Benetton, dived down the inside as we went into the second Lesmo and slithered through into the lead. I don't think Alesi expected me to come through at that spot – it was the sort of thing that Ayrton would have tried to pull off – and I hammered on into the distance, banging in one fast lap after another. A few laps in, I checked myself, realising that I had this one in the bag provided I didn't take too many risks. That was my mistake. The irony was that I would have been better off taking risks.

As a rather poor method of stopping drivers from using the kerbs at the first chicane, stacks of tyres had been placed on the crowns. When I was pushing on, I had got a nice knack of turning in and making the car drift, then I would catch it and slide through. This was working perfectly every lap until I eased up a little at the start of the sixth lap. Instead of drifting around the first pile of tyres, the car gripped, turned in too soon and I clipped the tyres, taking off a front wheel. I walked back to the paddock to find the press were all over me. I remembered exactly what Mary had said: chin up, keep smiling, keep positive. She might have added 'and get the hell out of there!' The only consolation was that Jacques had an eventful race, damaging his car and finishing out of the points. He had started from the front row and been fourth at one point.

By putting myself out, I'd presented an open goal to Jacques – and he'd missed it. The relief was massive; as if someone had just stopped trying to strangle me. I could breathe again, for a while at least.

With two races left, I had a lead of thirteen points. Looking at the positives, I could come second to Jacques in both Grands Prix and still win the World Championship, but I also had to think about my choices for the future at this late stage in the negotiating season. The options were Arrows and the Stewart team, which was due to start in 1997. Jackie Stewart and his son Paul came to see me in Ireland, Jackie saying he knew it was a long shot but they would love to have me in the team, and it was difficult to say no. I have always felt close to Jackie because of my dad and it would have been terrific, but I knew I needed a team with a bit more experience. Arrows was different insofar as it was already established, and John Barnard, the brilliant designer who had turned things around at McLaren and Ferrari, was coming on board. Tom Walkinshaw, the owner of Arrows, had the wherewithal and he had just bought a new factory at Leafield in Oxfordshire. This was definitely worth considering.

Bernie must have thought I was going to win the championship at the penultimate round in Estoril, where we had done all our winter testing, because he had arranged for 'my biggest fan', Mick Jagger, to come to Portugal, along with Jerry Hall. Everyone was pumped up for the showdown and Estoril was touted as a nice place to come and see Damon win the championship. That meant that there was a good contingent of British fans-cum-holidaymakers present. I really liked the track and knew it like the back of my hand, but so did Jacques by now. According to the script, I was on pole, separated from Jacques by 0.009s.

It was amazingly close with not much to choose between us by this stage of the season. The grid, which is narrow at Estoril, was crammed with media and personalities, people tripping over things and the mechanics doing their best to keep everyone off the car. Mick Jagger and Jerry Hall turned up and wanted a picture with me and the car. I didn't really know them, but Mick put on the big smile and the paparazzi went berserk and I had to stop them trampling on the front wings. Everything was buzzing before we had so much as fired up an engine.

At first, it seemed I had this one under control. I opened a good lead while behind me, Jacques was pushing Michael like crazy, because he knew that he had to win this race. Then I got caught in traffic and began to receive messages about a problem with my clutch release bearing. The engineers were watching the rising temperature of this bearing and I had to make an adjustment in the cockpit. If the bearing failed, I would be out of the race. I backed off a little but, even so, I was surprised when Jacques came out ahead of me following his final pit stop. There wasn't much I could do to prevent him from taking the win he badly needed but, to do that, he would have to deal with Michael who was leading in the slowly improving Ferrari. With everything to play for, Jacques was true to his pre-season word and ran right round the outside of Michael at the final corner. I had a grandstand view of this amazing piece of driving, and I was impressed, even if Michael wasn't.

Before we went onto the podium, Michael had a word with Jacques about his 'dangerous' move around the outside. It was so like Ayrton having a word with me at Imola in 1993. I remember thinking, 'Good on you, Jacques!' I was pleased for him putting a move like that on Michael, of all people. Jacques had humiliated Michael: done him up like a kipper around the outside on one of the fastest corners on the circuit – just as he had predicted at the start of the year. The amazing thing is that, however great some drivers are, they can have one rule for them and another for everyone else. The next season, Michael would try to ram Jacques off the road at the final round of the championship in Jerez. He was penalised and had all his points taken away, but only because there was uproar, as there had been in 1994 – although then they didn't take his points away. I wasn't disappointed with third place because I had really feared my car wouldn't make it. At the end of the season John Sutton, the gearbox specialist at Williams, gave me the clutch release bearing on a plinth as a souvenir. John didn't know how that bearing made it to the end without melting.

There was an agonising three-week gap before the final round in Suzuka. Even though I had a handy nine-point advantage, I knew enough about motor racing to understand that it's not over until it's over. Some of the fans who had come to see me 'do the business' in Portugal were disappointed that they had travelled to the wrong race, but I promised myself I'd make it up to them. I had to stay at Estoril for some testing and, when that was finished, I went with my old flatmate, Mark Leveson, to a bar in Cascais and had one too many caipirinhas. I had a stinking hangover the next day as we flew into Kidlington in Oxfordshire and set off to see Tom Walkinshaw's factory and sign the contract. My head was pounding. I kept thinking, 'Just show me the bit of paper. I'll sign it and get the hell out of here.'

Tom had offered me a generous deal; the money was better than I'd been paid by Williams, but it still felt like severance pay. There could be no denying this was going to be a complete shot in the dark. There were several plus points, however. Tom was going to run with Bridgestone, which could turn out to be a big advantage once the Japanese tyre team understood the nuances of F1. Tom had bought the team from Jackie Oliver and he was sinking money into the project. This was the start of a ramp-up that included bringing John Barnard on board. They had been testing in Japan with a mule car, and the results were encouraging. I had already worked out that this was what I wanted to do, but given the state I was in I could have done without the factory tour. I signed the contract, flew home, went into the kitchen and said to Georgie,

'You'll never guess what I've just done.' She said, almost as a joke, 'What, signed for Arrows?'

Everyone else seemed equally amazed when the news came out, but the key thing was that Arrows had been the best deal among the few that were on the table. I knew they would be adequately funded because Bernie had said to me over the phone, 'Why don't you give Tom a ring?' Only Bernie would know about these things. The most important part of the contract was that it was a single-year deal. Tom was the only person prepared to give me that option. The plan was to follow Adrian to McLaren for 1998 and hope a seat might become free if either David Coulthard or Mika Häkkinen failed to agree terms with Ron. But before any of that, I still had to win the World Championship; for me and my family, for the fans, and for Britain.

I had one fan who had particularly impressed me; a young lad called William Taylor. Throughout winter testing at Silverstone, in all weathers, he had stood at Luffield corner and waved a huge Union flag. He'd also persuaded his family to take their summer holidays in Portugal in order to see me win! Feeling that he deserved something at least for his devotion, I arranged for him to fly out to Japan for the weekend. I thought he might very well bring me luck. This was when George and Olivia Harrison had some monks make offerings and chant for me somewhere in India. So the good vibes were everywhere. It would have been churlish not to want to win it for Williams, too, and for all my mechanics, who had worked loyally and tirelessly on the car all year. Either way, Team Willy, as we affectionately referred to ourselves, were going to win. So this was about me now: my hour had come. With a three-week break, I kept myself out of everyone's way. I stayed in Ireland and trained moderately, because I had overdone it for Estoril. At the start of the season I weighed 76kg and at the end I was 68kg. What I needed was a good meal and a rest.

24 » IT'S COMING HOME

For some reason, I get terrible jet lag going to Japan, so knowing what was in store I flew to Hong Kong a week before the race and arranged for Georgie to come out and join me for a stay in the Peninsular Hotel. They provided a service which involved sending an old, classic Rolls-Royce Silver Ghost to pick you up from the airport, but I didn't tell Georgie about it just yet. No more throwing alarm clocks and flowerpots this time, I thought.

Having spent a part of her childhood in Hong Kong, Georgie was keen to show me around all her old haunts, and we took a drive into the hills, where Georgie showed me her route to and from school. When we reached the top, there was a huge outcrop of rocks, which we climbed. To our absolute amazement we saw that someone had painted in large white letters the name 'Damon'. It was inexplicable why anyone would do that and it was extraordinary it should be here, but we looked upon it as a good omen.

Naturally, the tension began to build up when we reached Japan. This being the last race of the season there was an end-of-term atmosphere, and because the paddock was very small with each team working from Portakabins, we felt as if we were all in the same boat, despite being in competition. It didn't matter if you were the biggest or the smallest team; everyone had to work in the same cramped conditions.

The Japanese fans are very passionate about F1. Whereas in Europe people have photographs or bits of paper for you to sign, in Japan they have enormous tiles which are rock hard with sharp edges. Another novelty is staying in the nearby

Suzuka Circuit Hotel. The first time I went there, they got my name wrong and wrote 'Demon Hill' on my room key. Each year, when F1 descends on the hotel, the catering staff appear to be taken by surprise. They are completely unready and unable to work out where all these Europeans have come from. With a limited choice of eating places, the entire F1 paddock seems to use the same Italian restaurant every night, which adds to the F1 community feel.

Although the hotel is only a short walk from the track, the enthusiasm of the race fans makes going anywhere a nightmare as you'd set off alone and then hear the patter of feet building to a full-on assault. Within seconds, you are buried in these tiles and scrawled all over by the marker pens. On one occasion, I was actually lifted off my feet and carried away. I got them to all sing Beatles' songs: 'Love Me Do', that kind of thing. They loved it, and let me go.

Come qualifying, I thought, 'Well, I can go for pole, but I'm mindful of what happened to Nigel in 1987.' He had put himself in hospital because he crashed trying to take pole from Nelson Piquet. I thought, 'All I have to do is finish. If necessary, I can sit behind Jacques all day. Like Melbourne, only better.' After the events in Adelaide in 1994, I was a bit wary of being caught out by an 'accident'. I wasn't going to take Jacques out and I just wanted to have a good, clean race and not take unnecessary risks. Second to Jacques during qualifying was therefore not a problem. All good so far. If only I could sleep, though. Saturday night was relentlessly sleepless.

On the Sunday, there was more than the usual pre-race anticipation in the paddock. One of these two drivers would be Formula One Champion of the World in just over an hour. As I sat in my car on the grid, I thought, 'You've done everything you possibly could have done, Damon. Not left a stone unturned. You're not wishing you'd done this or done that. Well done: you are ready for whatever fate is going to serve up.' A calm descended on me and I knew that what would be, would be. The rest was out of my hands. Either way, I had enjoyed a bloody good run. I could look at myself in the mirror and think, 'At least you tried.' I didn't think of my father, or my mother, or my family. This place was where I went to work and did my thing, alone. I was at peace with myself and it was a lovely feeling sitting in the snug cockpit of that great car, ready to go racing and sort this thing out once and for all. I also knew this was a poignant moment: my last race with Williams, my last Grand Prix in the all-conquering FW18. One thing was certain: I would not have to spend another night anxiously waiting for this moment to arrive. It was here. Finally. Right now.

Compared to previous championship finales, this one was relatively simple. I led, Jacques made a bad start – and then his wheel fell off, literally. I don't know what happened exactly: maybe the same wheel bearing failure I had had at Silverstone? But my only rival was out. The team came on the radio and said, 'Damon, you're World Champion!' Now that's the kind of news you like to hear on the radio. While celebrations were beginning in the Williams office as Georgie opened champagne, I still had work to do because Michael was behind me somewhere and this Grand Prix remained up for grabs. That said, it was a very nice feeling driving that car in the knowledge that I was already officially the World Champion. After going through an enormous number of twists and turns, I had achieved what I had set out to achieve: to do my best and see where it took me. And it took me all the way to the top. No one could take that away from me. From my first race at Lydden Hill, my pitiful car racing debut at Brands, through the scrapheap of 1989, the hell of Imola and the capriciousness of business deals, politics and poundings from the press, I had prevailed to arrive at my appointed date with destiny. As all this was spinning through my head, Michael in his Ferrari closed as I slowly rolled over the line, spending nearly all of my luxurious advantage, and Murray Walker delivered his immortal line, '. . . and I'm going to have to stop talking because I've got a lump in my throat.' Job done. I'd won.

As I cruised around on the slow-down lap, I was even more aware that these were my last moments in the best car in the world and I tried to savour them. You have two minutes on your own before your private racing driver world that you've inhabited for the last hour and a half will be invaded by the other world and its frenzy. I'd gone through such intense experiences in that cockpit. It was where my whole consciousness had lived to the maximum; everything that I had wanted for my life had been invested in that cramped space, all the sweat and breath expended, and heartbeats thumped during all the laps. Every corner, every kerb, and every barrier. Every car in front, all the shunts and spray and fans waving, start lights intensely viewed through the tiny letter box of my visor: all of these were burned into my mind's eye forever. But soon it would be time to leave her for good. She'd looked after me, this one, my little FW18.

A lot goes on in a racing driver's world but you keep yourself a little detached when everything is kicking off all around. While everyone else is going nuts and trying to grab a quote or an interview, you remain slightly restrained – because you have to, as a racing driver. Racing drivers are quite often accused of being dull. But that's because they simply cannot afford to get overexcited. Michael may have been very good at prancing around on the podium, but he did it deliberately. It's not a normal racing-driver state to be hysterical and excited. You do that sort of thing for show, because you know it's what everyone wants. You have to go to the podium, go to the TV unilaterals and the press conferences, do all that and say the right things amid all the pushing and shoving, but you are actually waiting for the moment when you can go and reflect on things. At Suzuka, the normal rituals would have a very different significance because I had just won the championship, but for the moment, I was still one step back from letting it all in.

Karl-Heinz Zimmermann was a larger-than-life Austrian character who ran our hospitality unit. I had promised Karl-Heinz I would smoke one of his cigars if I won the championship, so if you see a photo of me smoking a cigar ever, that was the one and only time. Yuk! The schnapps got rid of the taste, though. And the beer chaser. One priority was to fight my way through the crowd of well-wishers and thank the boys who had prepared my car all season: Bob, Paul, Les, Matthew, and my engineer, Tim Preston. They had worked all hours; nothing had been too much trouble. Having been part of the test team in previous years, I had grafted with everyone else and felt like an integral part of this team. Now it was time to say thanks and, sadly, goodbye. Twelve months before it had been so bad that I hadn't known whether to laugh or cry. Now, I think, Frank and Patrick were happier with the outcome. We went to the same Italian restaurant as everyone else and Jacques sportingly joined me and congratulated me, keeping his huge smile going the whole time. He could have my supper now if he wished! I didn't care any more.

Another ritual at Suzuka – win or lose – is a visit to the karaoke cabins. My cabin was completely rammed with everyone jumping up and down and having a good time. Then they started singing 'It's coming home, it's coming home,' from *Three Lions*, but I had no idea what they were on about because I'd been in my own bubble all year. I quickly learned the lyrics though. At one point, Schumacher joined us but some mischievous person piped up with another song using the *Dads' Army* theme tune, after which he smirked and left the rowdy Brits to get on with their lager and singing. I hope we didn't offend him.

There was little time to recover from a hangover the following day, thanks to a bullet train ride to Tokyo and a lot of PR. A number of the regular British newspaper guys came on the train and we moved on to a smart hotel for a press conference. Georgie and I were given an absolutely huge suite, which had two floors, a boardroom – and a grand piano. I was exhausted and crashed into a deep sleep. No energy left for 'Let It Be' or even 'Chopsticks'.

The following morning, when Georgie went into the shower, I lay in bed alone – and as the emotion flooded in and the tension flowed out, more than a few tears found their way to the surface. I think that was the moment when I finally allowed myself to believe I'd done it. Because you know it's a mistake to believe it too soon, you always keep the cork in the bottle until it's truly over. But now I could believe. I'd put myself through quite a lot of stress one way or another over the last four years, but now all that was behind me, to be replaced by a sense of complete satisfaction.

On the return flight, they had all the papers for us to read and the crew had put *Georgie* and *Damon* on the cockpit window like people used to do on Ford Cortinas. There was another round of media work to be done as soon as we arrived back in the UK: wearing my overalls and standing by the car at Marble Arch; waving the Union Jack for the photographers. Then there was a press conference in Oxford Street with all sorts of people such as Jeffrey Archer turning up to offer congratulations. 'Hi, Jeffrey. Er, I don't remember meeting you before?' You get pulled around a little, which I had to accept was part of winning the championship and its accompanying celebrations.

One of the most memorable media events was being flown by Concorde to appear on the *Late Show with David Letterman* in New York. I bought a new suit made of a green velvet material, which made me looked like a leprechaun. But at the time I thought I had to put on a bit of a performance. You arrive by taxi, they throw you through the back door, into the green room – and straight into the show.

Letterman was a big motor sport fan and he asked me lots of questions about Senna, and was really intrigued by him almost to the point of being an anorak. We were chatting about my season and getting sacked, which got a laugh, and he 'bigged me up' about being the new F1 World Champion, which was good of him. Then he suddenly pulled out a huge picture of my dad in a book and said, 'Hey! What about this guy? Isn't that as good as it gets? He was World Champion, what is it – three times?' 'No. Two only,' I had to correct. 'Two, actually. And he won the Indy 500. First time.'

I wasn't ready for that. I felt like saying, 'Hi, Dad. Didn't expect to see you here.' I didn't mind – I understood why Letterman was doing it, but it was then that I realised that this would always be the case. Graham Hill was a massive star and I was just doing what he had done, but he had done it bigger, better and before me. There was no getting round that, even for a newly crowned World Champion. But better to be a 'chip off the old block' of Graham Hill than quite a few lesser alternatives.

The UK sports fans voted me BBC Sports Personality of the Year again, this time with Frankie Dettori and Steve Redgrave. I must have been nervous in front of the camera because Frankie turned to me and said in that squeaky voice, 'Smile, mate!' With him on one side and Redgrave towering over me on the other, we looked like the sketch from *That Was The Week That Was* with Cleese, Barker and Corbett, which is about as British a way to end a World Championship year as you could imagine.

25 » 1997: SLINGS AND ARROWS

F1 doesn't hang about. No sooner was I an ex-Williams driver, than I was instantly a rival to them. No long goodbyes, no lingering. Straight on to the next race, the next challenge, ever onwards to the Arrows of outrageous fortune! The ignominy of it! A World Champion being dropped from a great height into an almost 'no hope' car. Whatever happened to the old saying, 'To the victor; the spoils'? I'll admit my love for the business side of F1 was now at an all-time low. I may even have become a little jaded and cynical. I resigned myself to the fact that, if this was how it was going to be, then I would play by those rules and just take what I could while I could – and hope for the best. If all went to plan, it would only be for one year. But I didn't expect Arrows to be as bad as it was.

At the first race, the car was almost a non-runner. Frank Dernie, who had been with top teams like Williams and Benetton, had a limited budget to work with at first. But Frank was going to be replaced by John Barnard, ex-Ferrari, ex-McLaren design genius: the man who brought carbon fibre and semi-automatic transmissions to F1. When John came in, he said, 'Well, the first thing we've got to do is make the car safe,' which was disconcerting and reassuring at the same time.

John had not been at the forefront of F1 for some time but he was being drafted in by Tom, who was very pumped up and ready to make a good fist of his F1 team. I think Tom felt he had missed an opportunity with Benetton after being involved when Michael first arrived. Tom had put together the successful Jaguar Le Mans and World Sports Car programme with

Ross Brawn as designer and team leader. Ross stayed on with Flavio at Benetton and obviously remained with Michael throughout his career thereafter, but Tom was surplus to requirements at Benetton, it seemed. Perhaps F1 was unfinished business for him.

I didn't really know Tom that well. He was a barrel-chested, rugby-loving Scot who, among a myriad other projects, owned Gloucester Rugby Club. At the start of the year, he was on a big push to attract sponsors using the fact that he had the reigning F1 World Champion driving for him. The car would carry the highly prized number 1, which had a value to sponsors who often knew precious little about the sport. Tom would also impress these people by using his Agusta 109 helicopter to fly them into Leafield, rather like a James Bond villain showing off the operations centre of his world domination project. In every way, Tom was a very different fish from Patrick and Frank.

Arrows were going a different route by being the first in F1 to use Bridgestone tyres, whereas the remaining teams would continue with the tried-and-tested Goodyears. I had done a test at Suzuka in an old Ligier – basically a Benetton copy – to try out the Bridgestones. They were clearly going to be a key factor at some point or other, because the right tyres can be worth a gain of a second a lap or more. So it would just be a matter of getting the car to within about a second of the front runners and the tyres would do the rest. That is not as straightforward as it sounds though.

The engine was a Yamaha, which was a badged engine made by the Englishman John Judd. People like Ford used Yamaha cylinder heads or something like that, and there was also a connection with Renault. The motor industry is very incestuous, with brands competing and yet owning shares in their competitors. I wasn't sure if our Yamaha's parent company was into F1 as much as it should have been, but at least we had an engine.

The car was quite nice to drive, probably because it was

so slow. It didn't have any downforce but it was well balanced and felt really good on the Bridgestones; I was privately sceptical but in public cautiously optimistic. Ferretti, one of Tom's sponsors, manufactured luxury yachts. He invited me to meet them at his house. Tom, as was to be expected, was also very keen for me to download any knowledge I had from the engineering wizards at Williams. But there's only so much information a racing driver actually has; the important details are held by the engineering department, virtually under lock and key and unlikely to be divulged.

As we sat there in his sumptuous dining room drinking some very choice wines, Tom started to expound on his views about Formula One. 'Basically,' he explained to his guests, especially the man from Ferretti, 'if you want to win in F1, you've got to cheat . . .' I gulped. To some, perhaps, this was a valid philosophy. But the penny slowly dropped that, *ipso facto*, he was calling me a cheat. It was an uncomfortable moment, as you might imagine. I looked at Mr Ferretti to see if he was as amazed as I was, but he was too diplomatic to give anything away. Maybe Tom was joking? But it wasn't taken as a joke.

My father taught me not to cheat. I never do it, not even when playing golf on my own! What's the point? I could just write down seventy and call myself a scratch golfer and never hit a ball. In golf and, say, football, the rules are well known, change very little and are respected by the players because this gives their sport an integrity that is difficult to find in life. But when you have a very complicated set of technical regulations about machines that need hours to assemble and take apart, as in F1, there are bound to be opportunities for people to cheat and get away with it. The problem with Tom's attitude is that it deemed the crime to be getting caught, rather than breaking the rules. Our sport is riddled with examples of blatant cheating being either exposed and fudged over or else causing a crisis. It was later revealed, for example, that the so-called 2008 Singapore Crashgate scandal had involved

Nelson Piquet Jnr being asked to crash deliberately on a particular lap in order to help his team's race strategy. At the first race of 2007, Ferrari were found to be using a special floor stay. They went on to win the race using it but it was later found to be contravening the regulations. Nothing was done about the result because all the fuss was focused on finding the culprit in Ferrari who had divulged this secret device to their opponents. After what can only be described a forensic raid on McLaren's HQ and after all the dust had settled in the FIA court rooms, McLaren, ended up losing all their points for the season and were fined a nice round $100 million! Nothing more was said about the floor stay.

Similarly, there are opportunities to interpret the regulations however you want and argue your case afterwards. This is being clever and imaginative, not cheating. It is not always a clear-cut thing, unlike the speed limit, for instance, where either you are over, or you are not. F1 designers have to interpret the regulations and choose how far they are prepared to push the ambiguity, and they will often ask Charlie Whiting, the FIA's permanent technical delegate and Race Director, what he thinks a rule would permit. But what Tom was saying was hardly ambiguous. He meant that everyone in F1 was a cheat, so it was OK to cheat. The thought that everyone was consciously and deliberately entering a car they knew to be contravening the rules was both tragically disillusioning and thoroughly depressing. It was also, thankfully, complete rubbish. Some take the view that if you get caught once it is worth it, because you'll get away with it more often than not. I now realised that I was in a team whose owner thought it was acceptable to cheat. I had better watch myself very carefully, I thought. Fortunately, I trusted John Barnard who I saw as an ethical competitor, who had a fine reputation and wanted to win by being smarter than the other teams.

We may have had the number 1 on the car at the first race but it was certainly not a number-one car; we could hardly get it out of the garage. I did a couple of laps in the practice sessions but the engine kept cutting out. As the defending World Champion, it was ignominious and humiliating to find myself at the back of the grid at the beginning of the new season. As I keep saying, most of my career moves involved me starting badly and leaving lots of room for improvement. This was no exception, but I took the view that I had made my bed, so I had to lie in it. I would have to show what I could do with a no-hope car all over again. The journalists asked, 'Why are you doing it? Why would you suffer the humiliation of being at the back?' The answer I had learned from my father was that I am a professional racing driver and I am being paid to do it. His view was, if people felt embarrassed for him, that was their problem, not his. In truth, being that philosophical was a way of disguising the pain. Being demoted is something that happens to nearly every driver at some point; even Michael had to go to the back of the grid, although perhaps not quite as far back as me! Fernando Alonso has had to swallow a lot of humble pie since returning to McLaren in 2015. It's not quite like it was when you were coming up through the ranks and you can still dream of getting to the top. Once you've been there you imagine it to be your rightful place and not belonging to anyone else. When you reach the bottom, you have to start the climb towards the top again, but it is very painful to watch some other competitor running off with your old 'girlfriend' in the meantime.

After a slow start to the season, I got my first point with Arrows at Silverstone. The car was improving, with little changes and a bit more horsepower, but it was basically uncompetitive – and unreliable too. There was another classic pre-Silverstone hoo-ha in the press because Tom had decided to criticise me, saying I wasn't doing enough as a World Champion. I was obviously hurt by the jibe, but while I kept my mouth shut I kept thinking that if I had a decent car I would be seriously competitive. In any case, Tom and I posed for some photographs for the Fleet Street boys, trying to smooth it all over.

In Hungary, Bridgestone brought a fantastic tyre and Goodyear literally overcooked theirs. There was a lot at stake for Goodyear, but they played too bold a hand and their tyre was a little too 'racy'. My car was handling beautifully on this dinky little track where horsepower was not at a premium: you just needed a nimble car and a good driver, and I could hustle the Arrows car around that track better than most. As the sessions went by we were getting better and better and finally qualified third. It was good to see my name up on the timing monitor again at the sharp end of things. We were back in business and I was doing what Tom was paying me to do: seizing the day. Suddenly racing was fun again. I could feel my attention level doubling by the second as I started to realise that this could be a big opportunity for Arrows, a team that had never, ever won a single Grand Prix in their nineteen-season history.

People still mention the Hungary race to me. It was the classic David v. Goliath performance, especially memorable for one particularly sweet moment. I got a great start and slotted in behind Michael Schumacher. After a few laps I could see that his tyres were blistering and he had no traction. On lap 10 I got a better sprint down the pit straight and dived down the inside line into Turn 1. I had passed Michael and we hadn't crashed! Interesting, in view of the fact that he knew I had nothing to lose, but there was more. The car kept going and going, and with every lap that went by, I thought, 'This is ridiculous, beyond anyone's wildest dreams.' Of course, it couldn't continue. One lap from the end, the hydraulics, which operate the gear-change mechanism and throttle, failed. The engine was on tickover and stuck in fifth gear and I now had to get round the rest of the lap trying not to let the revs drop too low, otherwise the engine would stall.

Jacques Villeneuve was catching me and I thought, 'I'll try and make myself a bit wider and weave a bit on the straight.' I stayed in the middle of the track and did a bit of a weave. Jacques could have just gone past me at 40mph and still won, but must have been massively pumped up because he was fighting for the World Championship and he went for a big move on the grass. There's never a bad vibe between us but I was desperate and felt I had to do something, but it was all I could do to get the car over the line to take second place. It was good, but not nearly as good as it would have been if we'd won. Jackie Oliver, the founder of Arrows, was a bit emotional. It was the closest they would ever get to winning a Grand Prix.

The measure of any driver is whether you take the winning magic with you when you move from one team to another. I hadn't won, but I had come very, very close. Now it was time to press home my advantage with Ron Dennis regarding a contract for 1998.

For a few years we had rented a house in the South of France for the children's holidays. Ron's house was in Mougin and we had been invited round to play in the pool and so on because he was good friends with Ray Bellm, the guy who sponsored me on bikes with Mucron catarrh tablets. But Ron didn't mix business with pleasure, so nothing was said. Meanwhile, Adrian had completed the move from Williams to McLaren as planned and was now working on the 1998 car. Finding out he had not been included in decisions over which drivers Frank had signed was the last straw and partly explained why he had taken such a keen interest in helping me win the Championship in 1996. Plus McLaren had excellent facilities and resources for him to play with to make yet another world-smashing car. So, in my mind, it had to be McLaren for the next few seasons. With Mercedes engines, they would be a powerful force. If I could get in there, I would almost certainly be in contention for another World Championship, provided I could beat the Flying Finn, Mika Häkkinen.

My main support in McLaren came from Adrian, who had some faith in me and knew what I was capable of, but I needed to know whether Ron really wanted me. The problem was that Ron was very comfortable with having David as a McLaren driver: he fitted the bill in many respects. He was quick, younger than me and there was a suggestion that Mercedes liked him too. Mika was not leaving, so I found myself in competition for David's seat. It was obviously going to be a little bit of a push to get me in there. Also, I had seen the way David had had to play second fiddle to Mika a couple of times and I thought: 'I don't want to go to another team and be put in the B car again.'

Just in case the McLaren thing didn't work out, I had to keep some other irons in the fire too, which meant that it was a very hectic time between races. Over the summer, I would finish a Grand Prix, go back, swim in the pool and be with the family, but most of my time was spent on the phone in the office, much to the dismay of my long-suffering wife and children. Tabitha seemed to take particular offence at my phone time and decided to leave me a 'gift' on my desk! She was only just one year old, bless her.

With Michael Breen working hard in the background, the time came to make the call to Ron. He had convened a small board meeting with the key people at McLaren for a conference call. He kicked off with the message that there had been enough support for me driving for McLaren to prompt him to make me an offer, but I sensed there was a caveat. He said, in his inimitable Ron-ish way, 'OK, we would like to have you in the team, but we'll pay you on performances only.' And he offered me a million dollars per race win. That was it. No basic retainer. No talk of points for the team. If I won, I'd get paid.

McLaren are famously strong on marketing and I knew they worked their drivers really hard for their sponsors. I would be expected to be here, there and everywhere, having my photo used for all and sundry. And for that, he was prepared to pay me nothing. After a long pause I said, 'Hang on a minute. Obviously you're going to want me to do promotional work for your sponsors, and I'm carrying World Championship kudos. How are you going to value that?'

There wasn't a value, I was told, and he repeated his offer. I said, 'Listen, Ron, thanks very much, but no thanks.' And I put the phone down without saying goodbye. I was so incensed that I'd come all this way and he wasn't even going to acknowledge my record in any way whatsoever. If I had a weak point in these situations it was that I could be too easily hurt by the suggestion that I wasn't quite up to it. By this point in my career, I thought I had earned some respect for my abilities, but that was very naive of me. This was a negotiation, and I hated negotiations.

After slamming the phone down, I phoned Michael and I said, 'Oh shit, what have I done? Get him on the phone again.' Poor Michael had to phone back and say, 'You've got to understand Damon's very emotional about these things and he wants the best for himself.' But the door had closed. Once I had calmed down I reasoned that it would never have worked out as I couldn't drive for someone who wasn't sure they wanted me, although it would have been nice to have worked with Adrian again in a car that had a Mercedes engine. I wonder how many races I would have won? In 1998, Mika would win eight, David, one.

With McLaren out of the picture, Prost F1, Sauber and Jordan were the other options I was considering, together with Tom who was desperate to retain me. But with the best will in the world I couldn't see Arrows being competitive the following year with Yamaha engines and a Bridgestone deal that was no longer exclusive, McLaren and Benetton also having opted for the Japanese company's tyres. Sauber made me a ridiculous offer of £1 million a race, and I wouldn't have to win anything – which would probably be the case since I doubted the Swiss team had that potential. At the same time, Eddie Jordan was also offering a very good deal with a Honda-Mugen engine in which I had some faith, but having had experience of Eddie, I knew that for my own security I would have to get the sponsor, Benson & Hedges, to pay my retainer and have a separate contract with Eddie Jordan Racing for the drive. Alain Prost came to our villa in France and it must have been a bit awkward asking his last teammate to drive for him, but he did it with good grace, as always. He looked wistfully at my leisurely lifestyle, sunning by the pool and, laughing, he said, 'I remember how good it was to be a driver!' He would not have a good time with his eponymous F1 team. I rather clumsily said to a journalist that I wasn't going to drive for Prost F1 because it was 'too French', meaning I would be the only non-French person in a French team with French engines and a French teammate! But it rather upset them, understandably.

I looked at the Sauber deal one more time because it was a huge amount of money. We went to their factory in Switzerland and, as I sat in the meeting with Peter Sauber, I was so nervous that my shirt was soaked through with sweat. I had to make a decision and I wondered if I would regret saying no. I was coming up to my thirty-eighth birthday, and a two-year deal would be the last hurrah for me. In the end, I felt Sauber were deluded if they thought I could make them winners. At the end of the negotiation I had to say, 'I'll call you,' and we headed for the airport, landing at Kidlington to meet Tom one more time, who, to my great surprise, immediately matched Sauber's offer!

By then, I'd already mentally committed to Eddie. I needed something to keep me motivated. I'd been somewhat disillusioned by F1, being dumped at the back of the grid and then not getting the McLaren drive. Part of me thought, 'Sod it; I'll just sign for anyone and get paid a lot of money.' But I knew I needed to have a chance of winning to keep me motivated. Eddie Jordan Racing were the team with the most potential, and they were Irish. Having been made so welcome over there, I thought, this could be a good bit of craic, to use the vernacular. The situation was very similar to 1991, whereby Eddie had a deal with a large tobacco company, Gallaher, who were very keen to have me signed up to help promote Benson & Hedges. This desire gave me a bit of leverage over Eddie and I was determined to use it to the max. It wasn't really that difficult to choose Eddie Jordan Racing. They were going to be the most competitive available drive and I like Eddie; it's hard not to. And he really wanted me in his car; at least, at first he did . . .

So we had a meeting at Gallaher's plush offices at Brooklands in Surrey to finalise the big deal. Many millions of pounds were at stake and it was already quite late in the evening, so naturally the pressure was on to get it done before Michael and I decided to sleep on it or go back onto the driver market. EJ didn't like the fact that we had his title sponsor batting for us! He put on a good show by doing a perfect impression of the Tasmanian Devil cartoon character. EJ at full tilt is something to behold. He was insane. He was running backwards and forwards, shouting at people, jumping up and down, pointing his finger at Michael Breen. I can remember sweat coming off Michael's head as Eddie shouted at the top of his lungs and right in his face, 'Nobody's going to f**k me!' Michael never blinked. He grew up in Belfast so was not easily intimidated, I guess.

It was like being in a lunatic asylum. EJ's right-hand man, ex-*Autosport* editor and general Mr Fixer, Ian Phillips, reassured Nigel Northridge, the CEO of Gallahers, that this was all very normal, we'd get a deal sorted eventually and everything would be OK. I was watching this craziness, not understanding what it was all the fuss was about. All they had to do was give me what I wanted! At the end of it I had a two-year deal. This would take me to the end of my career because, having watched my father struggle on against all hope and reason, I had promised myself that I would not drive beyond the age of thirty-nine.

26 » THE LAST HURRAH

1998 started perfectly. Our last child, Rosie, was born in Dublin. The family was now complete but racing was just about to start again. Eddie Jordan was not about to forget the way in which I had circumvented him by securing my retainer directly though Gallahers. Normally it is the prerogative of the team to choose the driver and he had lost that power because of me. I viewed Eddie as a businessman who made his living though racing. He loved racing, but he knew the trick was to make money out of it – not easy at the best of times. I thought that if he could put on a respectable show in F1 and take home a good return, that would suit him just fine, but unlike Eddie, I didn't have many years ahead of me as a team owner. I had signed for his team because I thought they had winning potential, and I was still in F1 to win. So there was a little tension there, you could say, with EJ a little sore about not being in total control of his own team. Outwardly, of course, it was fantastically positive, with the PR machine going into full attack mode trying to attract smokers using a rival brand to switch to B&H while giving those who already smoked B&H something to feel proud about.

The 1998 Jordan F1 car was launched at the Royal Albert Hall, complete with Cirque du Soleil acrobats. But the other Eddie Jordan coup was to have Hill and Schumacher on the same team: Michael Schumacher's younger brother, Ralf. Trust Eddie to do something like that.

Money is a delicate subject to talk about. Only ten years earlier, I had been earning nothing, with a mortgage running at 17 per cent interest and a family to look after, and not long before that, I had been working as a labourer and dispatch rider. But in F1, the normal frame of reference is thrown out of the window, and I don't think EJ was calmed much by my decision to buy a jet and a house in Marbella. I was imagining a rosy post-driving career outlook that would see Michael finding me some cushy well-paid retirement jobs, but if that didn't materialise, well, at least I'd enjoy it while it lasted. Michael was dispatched to Wichita to spend quite a lot of money on this amazing flying machine, a Lear 31A. I got Peter Boutwood to design a colour scheme using the blue of the London Rowing Club and metalflake silver. Peter also produced a Damon Hill cap which, naturally enough, incorporated my helmet design. It sold like hot cakes and I still have people come up to me with the caps to sign. The Lear had pilots to fly it; I didn't want to learn to fly after what had happened to my father, but it was an exciting ride: a rocket ship, just incredible. I was definitely going for the luxury lifestyle, the rationale being that I had earned it! The plane enabled me to travel around Europe and get to all the testing and races easily, and also meant I could easily be based in Spain for the summer, the extra hot weather bringing the added bonus of acclimatising me for races run in blazing sunshine, but it proved to be the worst investment of my life, since I sold it in the middle of the dot-com bust. The house in Spain, however, became part of the family, the children spending long hot summers eating ice creams on the beach, jumping into the pool and running around naked most of the time.

The leading question for me with Jordan was: 'What do they have to change to become winners?' I had started to get to know them a little during the early season testing and I noticed that they liked to put in a quick time for the hell of it. At Williams, we never did that. We were always running with between forty and sixty kilos of fuel on board so as not to show our potential to the outside world. Jordan, on the other hand, constantly created false expectations, which is fine if you are trying to attract a sponsor, but has the knock-on effect of making the design team think they are doing a great job. As a result, their expectation was way beyond what it should have been after testing, only for it to be dashed come the race.

I had to readjust everyone's sights by saying they were continually kidding themselves. I tried to get that through to the engineering team led by Gary Anderson, who had been with Eddie's F1 team since the start. He had been used to dealing with a small group of engineers and doing most of it himself, but time had moved on and even at Williams, Patrick had realised where his strengths lay, and he knew exactly what Adrian's strengths were. You couldn't be an aerodynamicist, a car designer and a gearbox designer all by yourself. You needed to delegate. Eddie needed to change his team's philosophy in the design department and that may have put me slightly at odds with Gary, but as far as I was concerned I had worked with the best guys and I had seen from the inside what they did. Changes were instigated and Gary eventually made some room for a plucky, ambitious technical director in Mike Gascoigne, formerly with McLaren and Tyrrell.

There was also the question of the engine. Mugen-Honda were not making any progress and I felt I had to say something publicly. Ayrton Senna had got things done at Honda using the power of his personality to effect change, by publicly criticising McLaren's engine manufacturer. I thought, 'Well, you can keep talking behind closed doors, but they won't respond until the cat's out of the bag.' I told a journalist that we were never going to win with the engine as it stood. That gave Eddie an opportunity to accuse me of breach of contract because I was not supposed to be critical of the equipment, but the results started to come once I had made a noise.

The British Grand Prix at Silverstone was a carnival, with girls from the *Sun* newspaper drafted in to maximise the coverage; I was draped in Page Three girls, much to Georgie's annoyance. To be honest, I didn't put up much of a struggle to get away, but it did feel a bit wrong. Eddie, of course, loved it.

Ralf looked distinctly uncomfortable. I tried to get to know him a bit better, but he was very reserved. Franz Tost (later to become team principal at Toro Rosso) was Ralf's minder. Going out for a fun evening in Canada once, we tried to tempt Ralf to come with us. He almost agreed and then seemed to realise he couldn't because Franz was there to make sure he was in bed early. Ralf was very serious and in some ways almost repressed, as though by the fact that his brother was the great Michael Schumacher. There was never any friction between us but after Spa he felt he had good reason to be very upset with both Eddie and me, as would his big brother.

For some reason, the Jordan car had always gone well at Spa. This is a curious phenomenon in our sport; certain tracks suit certain marques. Whatever Jordan had been doing at Spa in the past, they were still doing it right in 1998 and I turned up to Spa in great form ready to take full advantage of it. Spa comes towards the end of August and I must have benefited from a long, hot summer relaxing down in Marbella doing a lot of water sports. Having spent so much of my career wrapped up in cotton wool, trying not to give anyone an excuse to drop me from the team by breaking a leg or doing something silly like that, I now felt I could now throw caution to the wind a bit more, and I loved blasting along on my super-fast 'Waverunner' that I had got from Yamaha. As a result, I was in a perfect relaxed state of mind before the race, and the water sport practice was to come in very handy.

As with the Arrows in Hungary, the Jordan was suddenly fantastic to drive and everything 'clicked' immediately I left the pits. We very rarely talk about 'form' in motor sport because it is so hard to quantify compared to the car's performance. I remember going round La Source hairpin and tapping the throttle to keep the rear moving slightly to balance the car. Jo Ramírez had been watching and commented in his laconic, smiling Mexican way that it was nice to watch because 'it was like Ayrton' in the way he used to blip the throttle while cornering. It meant a lot coming from him. But importantly it meant my form could actually be detected from outside the car. I was on form!

Everything was hooking up and it was immediately apparent there was a golden opportunity to do something special. That took me to the 'other level': the place beyond normal driving at the very end of the branch. When you're struggling in the middle of the field, you could go to the end of the branch and perhaps move from fourteenth to twelfth, but something tells you the risk is not worth it. When you get closer to the sharp end, it's as if you can see an apple just at your fingertips and you think, 'I want that apple!' So you reach out just a little bit more. This 'extra bit', that is otherwise dormant within you, comes alive. I could feel it again in Spa – and it was terrific. We were back in the game again. There was a tremendous buzz within the team after qualifying third, just ahead of Michael in the Ferrari and just behind the McLarens of Coulthard and Häkkinen. It was nice to be right up there with Ron's cars, if only to remind him that I was not done yet.

After qualifying at Williams, I used to spend an inordinate amount of time going through the race strategy and set-up changes to the car, often leaving the track late at night. These days, the rules do not permit changes to the car after qualifying, so that is one less job. But at Spa in 1998 we were utterly focused on winning and we buckled down to work. Mark Gallagher, the marketing director of Jordan, came into the office in the truck and said we had to meet sponsor guests at some event. It would have required travelling some distance and interrupting our race preparation. I flatly refused, even though this would create problems, given that EJ had probably guaranteed to bring me and Ralf over. Sure enough, EJ wasn't too happy, but I had to explain that this was what we needed to do if Jordan wanted to win. The pressure was increased when it became clear that many of the guests were actually from the Jordan factory and they worked on our cars! No matter; I coldly insisted, but said we would make their trip something to remember for the rest of their lives if we won tomorrow.

Come race day, it was typical Spa: rain tipping down all day. The exit of La Source, the tight hairpin first corner, has a bit of run-off that most people found they had to use, but there was a metal drainage grid running down on the edge of the track and a bump, which caused no concern in the dry, but in the wet felt like a patch of ice and needed respect.

As we all accelerated like maniacs out of La Source at the start of the first lap, Coulthard went over this bump with his right foot still planted firmly on the McLaren's throttle. The rear wheels spun on the metal and suddenly he was sideways and heading towards the wall, with the pack bearing down on him. I was right behind the McLaren and saw it all unfolding and I had just enough time to work out that when he hit the wall he was going to bounce back into the track. But should I aim behind or in front of him? It was like looking at a snooker break in slow motion; balls were going everywhere. It was also reminiscent of the huge shunt at the start of my dad's Indy 500 race in 1966 when he just managed to avoid the carnage. He described himself as being like an orange pip squeezed between thumb and finger, and I was about to find out exactly what he meant. I decided to wait for DC's car to finish rebounding across the track in front of me before continuing on my way, while absolute carnage was being unleashed behind me.

Unsurprisingly, the race was stopped, but I was still as pumped up as ever. Just as in Suzuka in 1994, I didn't get out of the car as I didn't want any distractions. I hadn't bargained on officials taking an hour to sort out the mess, during which time I was getting wet and cold, but I was determined to stay in the zone and not break my concentration. The temptation to get out was immense – if only to have a pee! – but I knew I had to sit tight. We took our original positions on the grid, with DC making the restart in the spare McLaren. Quite a few runners weren't that lucky.

I made a blinding start and shot straight into the lead, but once again there was an incident which brought out the safety car after Häkkinen had spun and been clouted by Johnny Herbert's Sauber. So here I was with my old foe, Michael, right behind me in his Ferrari. I was leading for the first time since Hungary the year before. At the very least, a podium finish was possible, provided the conditions didn't claim me. As the rain intensified on the eighth lap, Schumacher, the Reinmeister, passed me. Having started on intermediate tyres in the hope that the track would begin to dry, we now had to stop for full wets, at which point Michael was about sixteen seconds ahead of me, but I was twenty seconds ahead of Jean Alesi's Sauber.

On lap 25, the most amazing thing happened when Michael, coming up to lap Coulthard, failed to see the McLaren in the spray and wiped off the Ferrari's right-front wheel as he piled into the back of David's car. For reasons best known to himself DC had been tooling along on the racing line, and Michael thought he was getting into the slipstream of a faster car. Bang! The Ferrari was out of the race. Once the pair of them had limped back to the pits, Michael went storming up to the McLaren garage to have a word with DC. Michael was furious, and rightly so, his fear turning to anger. The upshot, however, was that I was now leading again.

Because Spa is so fast and protected by trees, the spray there is possibly the worst of any track. You simply have no idea how close you are to another car, or at what speed they are travelling. As I was building up speed towards the fast uphill return leg to the pits, I came across Jarno Trulli's Prost. We were both still drifting out of Stavelot corner and I knew there was a car in there somewhere, hidden by the spray. Not wanting to lift off the throttle, I pressed on and suddenly felt a gentle nudge. We had bounced off each other's tyres. Our relative speeds were very similar, which meant it was just a kiss and I was on my way. I'm not sure Trulli would thank me for using him as a buffer, but he finished in sixth place so I obviously hadn't knocked him off the track.

Ralf had just pitted for new tyres and was flying along when, as if we had not had enough drama for an entire season in one race, Giancarlo Fisichella hit the back of Shinji Nakano's Minardi, bringing out the safety car yet again. I dived in for a fresh set of wets, just in time to come out ahead of Ralf, but it had been close. As they tried to make an adjustment to my front wing, the mechanic couldn't remove the tool. 'Big Tim' Edwards, our chief mechanic, simply grabbed the poor guy, yanking him – complete with the previously jammed tool – clean off the car. Prior to that pit stop, the gap to Ralf had been a steady twenty seconds for most of the race, but now he could close right up and latch onto my tail. In my mind I thought I still had speed in reserve, but this incident had eradicated my lead. It was a crucial moment.

Jordan suddenly had both cars in the leading positions. From a possible podium we had leapt dramatically into a possible 1-2 for a team that had never even won a single F1 race before. The team might not have been familiar with such a situation, but I was. As we crawled along behind the safety car, I knew the restart could be an extra hazard Jordan could do without, if both drivers were allowed to race each other. Normally, there would be discussion about what we needed to do next, and I waited for some instruction to this effect but there was silence. Having spent several years dutifully coming second to the team leader at Williams, I thought, 'OK, now it's my turn now to say what I think should happen.' In the absence of any leadership, I came on the radio and said, 'I'm going to say something to you here and I think you'd better listen. If we both race, we could end up with nothing. So it's up to you, Eddie.'

You could construe this as gamesmanship, or you could say I was taking responsibility for the entire team's race weekend result. It made perfect sense, given that most of the opposition had eliminated themselves. We were sitting on an almost guaranteed 1-2, but if Ralf was going to race me, I would have to race him and we could both end up in the gravel. Was the risk worth it? I waited for news. Martin Brundle, who was commentating on the race, quite independently concurred with my assessment of the situation but added a key consideration that might have swung the deliberations going on in Eddie's already overloaded brain: Ralf was leaving the team at the end of the year and therefore had little incentive to obey any team orders. Eddie also had to consider that I was a key player in his main sponsor's plans. Reluctantly, I think, EJ ordered Ralf to stay behind me. No one likes to kill a race, but this was too important to throw away.

I received the news that Ralf would not race me. Did I believe it? Not entirely. I decided that when the safety car pulled in, I would leg it like a scalded cat. I was in the same position as Senna at Imola in 1994, complete with another Schumacher behind. There is no other mode to adopt, as it has to be flat out, and I made sure there would be no way Ralf would have any opportunity. In any case, we couldn't hang around because Alesi was closing in on both of us. I won't lie: the relief of crossing that line was massive, as was the joy. I had delivered again in some of the most difficult conditions imaginable and we had a Jordan 1-2 to boot. I thought to myself, 'That, Eddie, is what you are paying so much money for.'

We were put in a car to take us to the podium. Eddie did an Irish jig all the way from the paddock to join us but Ralf had a face like a wet weekend in – well, in Spa. He was really upset about the team order. Eddie looked at me and said in his best 'butter wouldn't melt in my mouth' voice, 'Is he miffed?' Tensions mounted later when Michael accosted Eddie and accused him of not letting his brother win. Meanwhile, when I stepped onto the podium, I thought, 'I'll give it the big Michael Schumacher jump up in the air!' But I was so cold and stiff that I only got about six inches off the ground, and when I landed, I jarred my back. In the midst of all this leaping about, my overalls had rucked up. Gallaher were not happy when they discovered that the Benson & Hedges logo was not clear in any of the podium photographs spread across the following morning's newspapers, but they got loads of coverage for what is often voted by fans as one of the most exciting F1 races of all time. It was a great feeling, and my refusal to be distracted by the hospitality plans had been vindicated. Everyone at Jordan would remember this weekend forever. We were soaked to the skin and freezing cold, but who cared? Everyone in the Jordan camp was an F1 winner and I had given them that breakthrough. It was, in some ways, more satisfying than winning the World Championship. I will always cherish the memories of that weekend.

After it was all over, I thought, 'That was hard. I don't know if I can do this much longer.' I had been sitting in that car for three hours, soaking wet, freezing cold, and the concentration needed was immense. The knock-on effect for the team, though, was huge: the whole team moved up a notch and the results started to come. The next day I sent a message to everyone at the Jordan factory: 'Make the most of this win. It's very, very special. The second win, the third and so on; these are very nice, of course they are. But they're not the first. There isn't the same feeling. Never will be. The next time you feel like this is when you win the championship. That's the next big one. So enjoy the first win. It's unique. You'll never experience its like again.'

The postscript to this is that a few years ago I was playing golf with EJ in Spain. I don't know if he was trying to wind me up, but he said his recollection was that I had said I would 'have Ralf in the wall' if he tried to pass me. I said, 'What? EJ, I never said anything of the sort!' But in EJ's mind there are all kinds of fantasies going on. I'm sure he heard what he wanted to hear, but can anyone seriously believe I would do such a thing to a Schumacher? On purpose, I mean.

I wasn't totally finished yet, though. At Suzuka, the final race, I pulled off what one journalist described as one of the best overtakes of the year when I came from way back to pass Frentzen into the chicane on the last lap. It was a massive lunge but I made it stick to gain the place. I'd lost my drive at Williams to Frentzen, so it had a sweet added significance. It was a fair move, though, and there were no ill feelings, which was just as well, because Heinz-Harald would join me at Jordan in 1999 after he and Ralf effectively swapped places, Ralf completing Frank's long and tortuous plan to secure Williams' future.

Although I hadn't advertised the fact, I had decided 1999 was to be my last season. Eddie knew my contract was up at the end of the year and so we would be back into the game-playing pretty soon. But you know it's nearly time to move on when you start getting plaudits. When I first got the Williams drive, I had been asked to go on Radio 4's *Desert Island Discs*, but it was way too soon for something like that. Then I received another BBC Sports Personality of the Year award and an OBE in 1996 – but now I was about to get completely stitched up.

I had been invited to a Down's Syndrome Association event at the Landmark Hotel, Marylebone. I was about to go into one of my amusing speeches when Murray Walker appeared from one corner to distract me and Michael Aspel materialised on the other side to surprise me as the subject of *This Is Your Life*. It was a totally surreal experience. They had my prep school headmaster, Mr Basil Flashman, who was charming and amusing and told a story of how, when asked by another boy, 'Hill, what does your father do?' I replied, 'He drives cars. He's a sort of chauffeur.' Barry Sheene flew all the way from Australia to tell his story of how I was too nice and should give the press more of a kicking. I reminded him that he had got me into enough trouble already! They showed the very amusing Pizza Hut commercial I had made with Murray when he went ballistic and I grabbed him by the throat. All my friends and colleagues were there. Schumacher couldn't make it, but Eddie was there, as were the Earl of March,

whom I had got to know when I raced a Manx Norton against
Barry Sheene at the newly created Goodwood revival the
previous September, and the 'Rat Pack': Donnelly, Herbert,
McCarthy and Blundell. They even had a clip showing me and
my sisters appearing on my father's *This is Your Life* in 1971,
all of which was excruciatingly embarrassing. Robert Sutton
cleared up the story about my punk years and Leo Sayer and
Mick Hucknall added a few nuggets, while Nigel Mansell
publicly thanked me for helping him become World Champion in 1992. Sir Jackie Stewart said I had honoured my father
and my family; even Mika and David were beamed in to say
nice things. It was all quite overwhelming. Frank also paid me
a very touching compliment by admitting that he had initially
had misgivings about me but now felt he had had no right to
have felt that way. He was particularly impressed by the way
I had recovered from the disaster of 1995 to come back, fitter
and stronger than ever, to win in 1996. I thought that was very
generous of him. To follow that, they brought on my entire
team of mechanics: Les Jones, Paul West, Matthew White, my
engineer Tim Preston, and even Adrian Newey. It is very odd
meeting everyone in an unnatural environment like that as
they shuffle on, say a few kind words and shuffle off again.
Then they brought on my whole family, complete with our
newest addition, Rosie. The last guest was George Harrison:
easily the most famous person in the room. Having been
recently diagnosed with throat cancer, George had bravely
made the trip from Henley-upon-Thames. He kept it simple
and said I was a nice lad and came from a nice family, which
my parents had a lot to do with; my driving was good and my
guitaring was 'coming along', which was stretching the truth
a bit, to be honest.

Once the party was over there was one more season to
get through before the mission was completed, but I have
to wonder if it would not have been better to have hung up
the helmet right there and then on the show. My final season
was going to be not only another year of pain but also an

inglorious one. Everything started off fairly well but then, for some reason, Heinz-Harald was suddenly a second quicker than me during testing. I thought, 'Bloody hell! Where did that come from?'

Frentzen was the funniest teammate I've ever had. He had the driest sense of humour and would say the most bizarre things. His dad had been an undertaker and growing up in that business had given Heinz-Harald a unique perspective on life. He told us a story about how his father found a good use for all Heinz-Harald's used karting tyres because they were the perfect size and shape for propping up the head of a corpse in the coffin. Frentzen is half German, half Spanish and I think that also had an effect on the way he thought. When talking, he would think really hard, make a strange clicking sound and then say something droll. In the engineer's room in the truck he often had us all in stitches. I thought, 'This is going to be great, having H-H as a teammate, but I had better watch myself because he can be phenomenally fast.' He had a reputation for being as fast as Michael Schumacher in their junior days but, even so, a full second was as hard to take as it was to understand.

In his infinite wisdom Max Mosley, President of the FIA, had brought in grooved tyres for 1998 to make the cars more exciting to watch, the theory being that they would slide around more. It was a bad idea from the start, and I hated them and so did everyone else. The change may have affected my performance more than Heinz-Harald's, although I didn't know for sure. It's also possible that thinking about my career coming to an end affected my commitment, because it is difficult to grind out the laps in testing if you know it won't make much difference and you are starting to think about life after racing. Bernie said that when a driver sees the 'red light' in his head, he should stop immediately. Something deserted me in 1999 and it was a frustrating mystery. I had wanted to go out on a high, but it was looking more as if I would go out on a raspberry.

At the first race of the season in Melbourne, I posed for the obligatory pre-season photographs for the FIA. The younger drivers were all full of excitement and there I was with a goatee beard and a few grey hairs, nearly twenty years their senior. I had always been an older driver, having arrived so late. Most of the drivers had usually been about ten years younger than me, if you discounted Senna, Prost and Mansell, but for these guys I could have been their father! Of course, I was as determined as ever, but I could not get used to the dreadful tyres, and with the thrill having gone, the motivation started to follow. This was going to be a long season.

A driver's mind is a fragile and dangerously deluded thing at times. If he is not quick, he looks for a reason everywhere but within himself. In any case, how does a driver measure himself? Inspiration is a completely subjective and illusory thing. I began to wonder where the lap time had gone. I became paranoid that perhaps Eddie was up to something. Eddie liked to keep drivers on contracts that were out of sync with each other. This was the only time I had managed to have a two-year contract and I was in the last year of it, and with Frentzen starting a two-year deal, it made sense to downgrade the driver who had to renegotiate. It meant Eddie could come to an agreement to pay him less, and it would discourage offers from elsewhere. But this was dangerous thinking, on top of which, my information was not coming from the horse's mouth; I had let Michael deal with all that stuff. By the time we reached the French Grand Prix at the end of June, I found I couldn't drive the car. I told Eddie I thought there was something wrong with it. That was when I began to think I'd had enough. I didn't want to wait till the end of the year; I wanted to go as soon as possible. After the British Grand Prix had a nice ring to it, as it was only one more race away. I could finish where I had started: at home, at Silverstone.

The race in France was horrific. It tipped down and I

couldn't see where I was going and that's when Bernie's red light came on in my mind. I had gone from being brilliant in the wet to being afraid and angry that we were expected to race in these conditions. It was time to stop, but thankfully, the car did that for me by developing an electrical problem. My performance could not have contrasted more starkly with Frentzen's, however, as he won the race. I told EJ that I wanted to do the British and then he could get another driver. We'd sort out the money somehow. What did Eddie do? He tried to replace me before Silverstone, although clearly B&H wanted me to do the race. This infuriated me, but it did leave Eddie caught on the horns of a dilemma again.

I have always felt that there was something very weird about my last season. I was puzzled by the way my form had completely disappeared. One minute, I was doing brilliantly in the Jordan and the next, the whole thing had started to collapse on me, but I didn't seem to have any fight left to deal with it any more. I was burned out. I wanted to have a big send-off, say sayonara and thanks for everything: everyone happy, last race at Silverstone, just like the old man. But it was not to be.

Michael and I spent a lot of time in Michael's London office on the phone to Eddie, trying to sort out the mess of my departure. Michael could hold him to the contract and for some reason Eddie caved in. But instead of having us part company amicably after Silverstone, he made me stay *after* the British Grand Prix too! I was trapped in a nightmare where I wanted to stop immediately but couldn't for fear of the financial consequences. By this stage, all that mattered was that I survived, could look after my family and that I did not inflict the same fate upon them that I had had to endure on losing my father. I was terrified of what might happen to me if I continued to race, but equally terrified of what might happen if tried to pull out, the legal consequences if I did not uphold my side of the deal being unthinkable.

As far as the fans were concerned, everything was still

hunky-dory with me and Jordan at Silverstone. I finished a creditable fifth just behind H-H Frentzen, so obviously I was getting the hang of things again, but it was the business side of things that caused so much grief now. I had so much stress, I was beginning to get panic attacks. Michael Schumacher had crashed and broken a leg during the British Grand Prix and was being treated in hospital in Northamptonshire, so I thought I would go and see him. During the journey, there were continual phone calls with Michael Breen about my contract with Jordan. Georgie was with me. At one point, I had to stop the car and say to her, 'I think I'm having a heart attack.' I couldn't breathe. Whatever was going on between Michael and Eddie, it was making my life hell. In retrospect, it might have been easier if I had phoned Eddie myself to sort it out, but by this point things were way too complicated.

After Silverstone, the next race at the Nürburgring was dreadful. We had been using a legitimate launch control device and to make it work, you had to go through a certain procedure that involved remembering to switch it off after the first lap of a race, otherwise the car would shut down. I was in the pack, but Frentzen was leading the race. Suddenly, my engine died at top speed just before reaching the end of the pit straight. I was trying to work out how to fix it as I decelerated with a dead car. Pedro Diniz was just behind me in his Arrows. We had been teammates two years before at Arrows. He was a gentle, intelligent fellow and I really liked him, but he was caught out by my sudden problem and went flying over the top of me and into a barrel roll. I thought, 'Oh f**k! I've killed him.' That was too much. I definitely didn't want to do this any more. If I was going to be incompetent and put people at risk, I wanted out as soon as possible. I was really down about the whole thing as I trudged back to the pits, the fact that my teammate was leading adding salt to the wound. Then, after a pit stop, exactly the same thing happened to Heinz-Harald! We had both been caught out by that stupid gizmo. It made me feel a little better, but not much. Johnny Herbert profited from our cock-up and won the race, which was one good thing.

But it wasn't only the cars that had technical issues. On the way home I had offered to take Peter and a few Jordan guests to the UK in my plane before heading back to Dublin. After we took off the pilots realised that the undercarriage light was displaying a fault. As we approached Farnborough, they warned us of their dilemma. Either the undercarriage was OK and the warning light was at fault, or there really was something wrong and the left undercarriage was in danger of collapsing under the load of landing. We were told to prepare ourselves for a dangerous situation and the fire engines were deployed. The pilots would have to make a low pass past the control tower so the air traffic controllers could have a look and see if we actually had the wheels down, but on the way through the clouds the pilots suddenly swerved. 'What the hell!' I thought, my heart even more in my mouth than before. It had been because of a hot air balloon! We never did find out what it was doing in a cloud near an international airfield. It was eventually registered as an official aviation 'near miss'. Too right! I could see the man in the basket's eyes popping out!

Eventually we got down in one piece, mightily relieved to be alive but with the next problem of how to get home. As luck would have it, a flying horse-box with one of the Aga Khan's horses on board was heading our way, so me and Dave Marron, who worked with Gallaher and Eddie, got in the windowless transporter and sat in the back on a bale of hay all the way home. They have a man in the back with a gun to shoot the poor thing if it gets too frightened. You can't have a race horse running around inside a plane when it's flying about!

Only a few months later, David Coulthard, his girlfriend and their dog walked out of the front of their plane miraculously unscathed after it crashed at Northolt. The two pilots were killed as the cabin folded under the fuselage. I'm guessing some of that Irish luck must have rubbed off on me.

Meanwhile, I was still concerned about being in breach of contract and feared I would end up with nothing, just as had happened to our family following my father's death. This thought alone was enough to send me into extreme anxiety. I was probably overreacting, but when you have no idea how to control a situation, it is easy to get things out of proportion. Everything I had gone through was motivated by the desire to restore and repair all the damage that was done to the Hills in 1975. If I thought getting into F1 was hard, getting out was turning out to be even harder, but we were nearly there. All I had to do was survive two more races and I'd be home for Christmas.

Malaysia was a new track: a fantastic, sweeping, fast circuit right on the equator. No one knew what to expect, except that it would be hot. And boy, was it hot! We all decided we would need extra preparation and defence against the heat and dehydration. If qualifying was anything to go by, we would be a dried-out bag of bones by lap 20. I actually qualified a respectable ninth, ahead of Frentzen, but no one was looking forward to the race. My method to mitigate the effects of the equatorial sun and humidity was to soak my overalls, turn the air conditioning up to full in the team office and just sit there for an hour to reduce my core temperature. Heinz-Harald went more radical: he had a doctor put him on a saline drip. When they had finished he looked green! You could almost see right through him. 'Heinz-Harald,' I said, 'you don't look at all well!' We went to the grid with him looking sick and me shivering. I was quite interested to see how this would work: how long would it be before I started to sweat? I got as far as Turn 1 before being shunted off. The press and TV caught up with me on the way back to the paddock and my teeth were still chattering, so I found it hard to give them much of a quote.

My last-ever F1 race, journey's end, would be at Suzuka,

the site of so many important dramas in my career: the circuit where the spirit of Senna had infused my being and I had driven the race of my life; the place where I had been crowned Champion. But it would now become the racetrack where the muse would desert me completely, overtaken by the instinct to survive to a ripe old age for the sake of myself and my wife and children. Halfway through the race, I couldn't take it any more. I'd been off once and was way out of the points with little hope of scoring anything. I came into the pits and parked the car. I didn't want to be doing 180mph any more – particularly on this track – hoping nothing went wrong. I'd done enough denying the fear; my motivation had completely gone. Some accused me of throwing in the towel, but as my father would have said, that's their problem. There was nothing left to gain by carrying on. I just wanted to walk away in one piece; too many of my friends and fellow drivers hadn't been so lucky. You could call it a kind of shell shock. I'd reached the maximum I could tolerate in this dangerous sport. The only other time in my career when I had come into the pits to retire a car was in my first-ever race at Brands Hatch in 1984. Then, they had sent me back out again and I became a World Champion! But this time I would never go out again. I was done for good.

I was so glad to get out of that car at Suzuka but I was overcome with a strong mix of emotions: sadness that it had ended like this, relief that I was unhurt and alive, and shame that I had let the team down. F1 had taken its toll on me. I'd been put through an emotional mangle; I'd pushed myself so many times to go through the limits. It had all been worth it, but this time I had found the absolute limit. So my racing days were over. All things considered, I hadn't done so badly. Now I could retire to reflect on my achievements, rest for a while on my laurels. I had money in the bank and four lovely children to take to school and spend time with. I'd be there for Georgie, too. Things were going to be different this time round. All I had to do was survive for a few more years and I would have outlived my father. But the spectre of the accident was not yet banished from my mind and I was about to enter a strange new life with no targets to meet, no races to win, no planes to catch and no hotels to check into. I had made no plans because I didn't want any. I had questions to answer. I needed time to understand what it had all meant and find out where I really wanted to go next. Shortly before he died, my father had with unwitting prescience said, 'Time is of the essence, and I'm very short of essence.' I was a very lucky man. I had won as much essence as I wanted. But I knew from bitter experience that it's not down to us, how much essence we have left.

27 » SEE YOURSELF

'It's easier to see the books upon the shelf . . .'
(George Harrison, *Thirty-Three & 1/3*)

Twenty years have flown by since Murray uttered his immortal words and carved my name into the hearts and minds of British motor racing fans. I have been thoroughly spoilt everywhere I go. I have outlived my father, who died over forty years ago, aged just forty-six. It seems impossible. All my children have grown up and have either left home or are off at college. It's just Georgie and me now. My mother passed her ninetieth birthday on 12 June. She is the same age as the Queen and I have earned enough in my career to be able to look after her, just as I had promised. She has lived to see her seven grandchildren growing up healthy and happy. The Rat Pack are looking a little fatter, balder and greyer than we were when we raced around England in the 1980s, but we still have as much to laugh about at Christmas. Perhaps more.

George Harrison died in 2001 on the same date as my father: 29 November. I wish I could have spent more time with him. He had a lot to teach all of us, not least that all things must pass. Barry Sheene died in 2003. He used to phone me up at ridiculous hours of the morning from Australia, just to say hello. I loved these guys. They had a knowledge about life: that it is a fleeting thing that will be gone before we know it. They were of the same tribe as my father and they left the world a better place for having been here. I am privileged and honoured to have been able to call them my friends. They came to me in my hour of need and gave me the best advice.

George's advice was, be as nice to everyone as you can, create good karma as much as you can, and that love is the only thing that matters. Barry's advice was more a little more controversial but basically not to worry about what anyone else thought of you and just be yourself. No one could accuse Barry of not being Barry.

I never got to know Michael Schumacher after racing and I guess it will never happen now, following his skiing accident in December 2013, though there is always hope. After my last race, *F1 Racing* magazine set me up to interview him in Suzuka. He was charming, friendly and with a broad smile. I will remember him like that and cherish the fact that he gave me some of the finest moments of my career. Amusingly, I was a driver steward in Monaco in 2010 and we had to penalise Michael for being a naughty boy. In fact, he had been typically clever and he knew the rules had an ambiguous loophole. But you can imagine: the irony of it. He thought it was quite funny, too. What has befallen him is beyond tragic.

I could not have asked for more than to have raced against the most successful racing driver of them all – and won! And to think of all the people who had told me that I was either too old, or too slow, or too late; or that I should get a proper job, or that I shouldn't waste my education on motor sport. When I think about that, I thank them for pressing my button: the button that makes me think, 'NO WAY!' That button is still there. I can't help it. It's deep, deep, deep inside me, but perhaps not so loud any more.

They said I should get someone to write this book for me, too. I couldn't have done it without Maurice Hamilton, but I had to do the actual writing myself. It wouldn't be my book if anyone else had done it. I wanted to get across to the reader, the fan, whoever you are, my story in my own way. If there is a point to any of this, it is that I have proved that it can be done – whatever that thing might be. It can be hard: very hard, to the point where you think it is impossible and you want to give up and cry. But then you get back up again and have another go, because that is how things happen; how they become reality, rather than just being stillborn dreams. And that is exactly how a guy who couldn't even drive in the beginning became an F1 World Champion. But like my old man said, 'If you try, you might fail. But if you never try, you'll never know.'

In 1999 we sold our house in Dublin and moved back to the UK just in time for the new millennium. We bought a massive project of a house on a stunningly beautiful hillside in Surrey. It had been owned by a man who had let it go, somewhat, and the garden was completely overgrown with wild rhododendrons. I discovered it hadn't been touched since 1975. It was as if time had stopped here the moment my father died and the house had been waiting for me all this time to bring it up the present. Semi-consciously, I was restoring the life that had been shattered in that dreadful accident. It became, *ipso facto*, Lyndhurst, the house I grew up in.

But if this was Lyndhurst, I could no longer be the young Damon. I would have to be my father, and that would mean something awful was about to happen to me. And if I was to prevent fate repeating itself, I would have to survive beyond forty-six years old. Did I do all this just to could get back to where we were in 1975? I'd done the racing and successfully survived that. The one thing I was definitely not going to do was start up a racing team like Dad. What I really wanted to do was to work out who I was and where I wanted to go next. But I had created quite a lot of complications that needed to be sorted out before I could finally break free from my former life.

There were the inevitable money issues; I had to look after my investments. A nice problem to have, you might think. Except, whom to trust? There were plenty of people who seemed to know what I should do with my money. I had told Michael in my last year in F1 that I would be stopping and that I would not be needing his management services any-more. But all my business had been done through his office; I had no experience and no idea about understanding where I stood financially. My career had moved so fast and so much had happened that there was no way I could have kept up with the thousands of necessary decisions. I was still very much dependent upon Michael's advice and yet I wanted to be independent and free to make my own choices. It worried the hell out of me. I had no idea how I could get to a position where I was in control of my wealth and my life. I was an adult and could make decisions, but I had relied on his protection for so long and I was baffled by the complexity of it all, on top of which, I was plagued with depression and anxiety. We put some money into P1, an idea he had come up with for an exclusive car-sharing club. I was also persuaded to invest in some BMW dealerships. To cut a long story short, I gradually realised that these ideas were not for me and I spent the next five or six years trying to get out of the complicated deals. It dragged me down and wasted a lot of energy, not to mention money!

During all this time, I had been trying to be a good dad: going to all the school sports days and plays, and doing the school runs. I let my hair grow and became a bit of a hippy. I went mountain biking around the beautiful Surrey hills and took the dogs for long walks in all weathers. Basically, I dropped out and just watched the wheels of life turning, as they always do, round and around, seemingly forever, repeating the same old stories.

I read a lot of books on philosophy and religion. I even became a vegetarian after reading Gandhi's autobiography, *The Story of My Experiments with Truth*. I hardly read the papers, seeing it as the confusing froth of life, but listened a lot to Radio 4, especially programmes such as *In Our Time*; anything that helped make some sense of the crazy mess we call 'civilisation'. I read obituaries, learning about incredible people who were never famous, but who led far more extraordinary lives than racing drivers do. I also enrolled on an Open University course and studied Literature, incredibly getting a first, albeit after almost six years. The reason it took so long was that I was phoned by Sir Jackie Stewart in the middle of the course to see if I wanted to succeed him as President of the British Racing Drivers' Club and help save the British Grand Prix! How could I refuse? Literature would have to wait.

I know I've done it all back to front but somehow it makes more sense when you've tried it yourself and failed. I should have listened a bit more when I was at school, but I had attention deficit disorder back then. What I've learned is that we can't do things on our own and there is this fantastic resource called the 'works of man' that can help us understand – if we can only get through it all in one lifetime.

I even started a band and fulfilled another ambition that I felt I'd missed out on during my career: playing music. I threw a massive party at the end of 2000 for my fortieth birthday and to celebrate my World Championship with friends who had not been able to celebrate with me in 1996 because I had been living in Ireland. Our band played all the hits and everyone was in fancy dress. The party's theme was, 'A film, or a character from a film', based on *The Italian Job*. It took place in a massive marquee in the garden. We held everyone in an antechamber and I showed a short film that made it look as if I had been driving a mini in the movie. Then I say, 'Hold on, fellas. I got a great idea . . .' and the curtain comes down to reveal a massive nightclub complete with flying Mini Coopers over the bar with their headlights blazing. To get the band onto the stage, we had the back end of a van protruding onto it and we 'blew the bloody doors off' and came though that!

It happened at the same time as a fuel tanker dispute and no one was sure if they would be able to get home. But they all came: everyone from George, Olivia and Dhani (who came as the Three Amigos) to Jeff Beck and Barry Sheene (who came as themselves). Martin Brundle was Bruce Willis in *Die Hard* and Jeremy Clarkson came as Crocodile Dundee or Indiana Jones, we weren't sure which. Ringo and Barbara came, since they lived close by, as did Roger Taylor. Leo Sayer was a dead ringer for Charlie Chaplin in *The Great Dictator* in an SS uniform, and Nick Mason came as some Kung Fu character. Georgie and I went as Sid and Nancy. By the end we had Jools Holland, Mick Hucknall, Gary Brooker, George Harrison, Leo Sayer, Nick Mason and Jeremy Clarkson holding an inflatable crocodile all on stage together with our band, the Conrods. By general consensus it was the best party anyone had ever been to, and it was worth every penny.

I had made a lot of sacrifices to get to where I was. Now I wanted to make up for lost time and just play around. In many ways it was ideal, but the change from having a full-on exciting job with a very rigid schedule to having to make up my own mind about what I really wanted to do was also quite bewildering. I went cold turkey, in effect, from the routine and the adrenaline. But I knew I had to kick this habit: the need for speed.

And I had had a bellyful of F1. I was jaded and disillusioned by the whole thing; I never even wanted to see a race on the television. When Michael started to clean up and win absolutely everything, I'm afraid I took the view that there was something wrong with our sport, and by extension, our world. It seemed to me that he was getting an unfair advantage for some reason or other. Oddly, when races were on I quite often found myself in the garden with a chainsaw clearing away decades of undergrowth. I obviously still needed the power tool and the adrenaline! But there could hardly have been a better metaphor for my state of mind. I really needed to clear away this confusing jungle of crap inside my head that had accumulated over the years, going way back to my dad's accident and even before.

It was during this time that I started to have a crisis in my life and sought help from a therapist. I learned an awful lot about how our minds work and how we map relationships onto other relationships. How, in effect, we don't clearly see what is happening around us until we can see life as following patterns that repeat, and repeat through generations. Larkin's line, 'They fuck you up, your mum and dad' is perhaps taking it too far, but there is some truth in there. Well, I was a dad and I had four lovely children who had every right to get the best start in life. I didn't want them to experience what I was going through as well.

Depression is what it says on the tin: a big downer, like the ground has fallen away from under you and then the earth has fallen in. Sometimes you can hardly get up. You look at the world and it makes you more depressed, and then you see extremes of beauty. It's the contrast that screws you up; you can't take the massive swings. You want to know that when you say 'yes' to something, you will still like it when you get it, instead of finding out this was an awful decision and you are hating every minute of it. You lose trust in yourself. All this has an effect on those around you, so you feel worse.

In truth, it was hardly surprising that I developed full-blown depression. It had been lurking below the surface virtually all my life. When I started to ask questions about my parents' relationship, the picture began to become clearer. Of course, the big problem was that I couldn't ask my father anything, so I had to talk to his friends and people who had known him. Slowly the picture becomes clearer and the pennies start to drop. You realise that this is their crap you are dealing with, not yours.

But the added grief of my father's accident didn't help at all. It created scar tissue around the problems, so I had to go through proper grieving for the loss of my father, too. When all this started to unravel, I became acutely aware of how scared I was of dying unexpectedly, just as he had. Once, I had to take a trip to the south of France, which meant flying, and I couldn't face it. I found myself curled up in a ball in the fetal position on the floor of the bedroom before I could summon up courage to fly. It wasn't that I was scared for myself; it was the fear of inflicting on my family the same godawful experience that I had gone through in November 1975. After a while, though, you start to realise that you are not your father – or your mother, for that matter. You are you. I am me, Damon Hill, Parts I and II, and this is 'now', not 1975.

I have to say a big thank you to Louise Webb, who steered me in the right direction. She had lost her whole family save for two sisters, and her then boyfriend, in her father's helicopter accident. Not surprisingly, she had to sort out one or two issues of her own relating to that episode. She eventually became a therapist herself, and it was Louise who gave me the number of another therapist to call, should I need to talk. And I did need to talk. A lot. That poor man. He has listened to no end of rubbish for years, but he never made me feel as if I was not a valuable human being. Eventually, all the rubbish is dumped in his room and he clears it away after you leave. That's how it works. But it took a few years, as I said at the beginning of this book.

Eventually, I had a moment: a split second of absolute clarity, when my mind experienced what I can only call 'unification with the cosmos'. I was on a beach in Kos on a family holiday, feeling utterly useless. I had taken Oliver for breakfast and then we went for a walk up the beach to a secluded spot. He sat with his feet in the calm blue sea looking like the Buddha and I sat behind him on a deckchair, head in hands, just looking out towards the far horizon, feeling frustrated, confused and angry with myself. All of a sudden, my mind just disappeared, by which I mean my consciousness of my 'self' disappeared. My mind became connected to everything all at once. There was no 'in' or 'out'; there was just 'oneness'. It only lasted for a few seconds, but it was really an infinite time. At that moment, I realised that the universe could not be complete without me in it. I was meant to be; this is all meant to be.

I have not been idle in the meantime. It was in 2006, when 'uncle Jackie' called to see if I wanted to become President of the BRDC. So that was six years of my life spent sorting out other people's problems – but we got a deal with the irrepressible Mr Ecclestone, who had us running around like chickens in a coop being visited by a fox when he decided to do a deal for the British Grand Prix to go a rival circuit, Donington Park. What a fiasco! We got it back eventually after a lot of nonsense. But it was all good fun.

Then one day in 2006 my son Josh rather sheepishly said, 'Dad? I want to be a racing driver.' Oh my God! No! That's what I thought. But what I said was, 'Oh. OK! Great!' Evidently he had been inspired by a passenger ride with me driving a two-seater GP Masters Car around Silverstone. I should blame myself, but I thought he'd passed the window of interest. This entailed going through the not entirely unpleasant, but not all that lovely either, experience of taking him karting so he could catch up with all the other baby karters who had been doing it since they were four. I had never said no to Josh being a racing driver but, conversely, I had never taken him somewhere to arouse his interest. He had been to a few Grands Prix when he was younger, but I had never deliberately led him towards motor sport. Who would want their child to become a racing driver?

Weekends were spent next to hot dog stands and push-starting smoky karts. He made me enter one or two races, which was very hairy since I had a huge target on my back, but I pulled off one or two famous moves they will be talking about at Club100 for a few years to come. Josh was growing into quite a competitor. It's amazing to see the little flashes at first, then the more solid performances. Then he would do something totally mind-blowing like storming through the pack from the back on slicks in the wet and in semi-darkness! It seemed always to be freezing, wet and dark at kart meetings.

He progressed all the way to European F3 before telling his parents in 2013 that he no longer had the ambition to be a racing driver. No matter. He had proven his credentials and won quite a few races. Right up to the time he finished he was looking good, and he had taken the London Rowing Club helmet across the line in first place to make it three generations of winning Hills. We were very proud of him and delighted that he had found out which direction he wanted his life to go in. He now drums in a band called the Severs. We last saw them play in the Isle of Wight rock festival this summer; they were great and went down a storm.

My other children have thrived, too. Rosie is eighteen and a very talented artist-cum-designer, just like her mother, who does amazing life drawings. Tabitha has received a 2:1 in Law from Bristol University. She is only twenty-one. We are so proud of them all. But not last or by any means least is Oliver, who is now twenty-seven.

In 2007 we joined a group of concerned parents of children with learning disabilities in our area and decided to form HALOW: a charity named by using the initials of all our children. The goal was to fill the gap between higher education and full-time employment where, typically, there is no support. The tag line is, 'Nurturing Independence'. We put on learning and fun experiences for the young people. It has a heavy social activity emphasis, but we also provide supported living. Fundraising is a never-ending task but we have what is called the HALOW250 / Two Boats Cycle Ride, which entails 120 riders cycling eighty miles from Putney to Portsmouth, getting on a ferry to St Malo, cycling 120 miles to Caen, returning on another ferry to Portsmouth, then riding a leisurely fifty miles to Guildford for a drink and a hamburger. I've done about three of the five rides, and it's tough!

We also do the Damon Hill Karting Challenge, which is simply a fun kart race of 2.5 hours in teams of four at Daytona in Sandown Park. Being involved in the start of HALOW has been amazingly challenging and rewarding. Oliver is now in supported living and is leading his own life: just as he should; just as we all want for ourselves. HALOW supports nearly 170 young people with learning disabilities in and around the Guildford area and has been a big success.

In 2012, I was offered a job with Sky F1, the new F1 sport channel. Martin Brundle, whose son Alex also races, gave me the call. He has been doing F1 commentary for over twenty-five years now. In order to get a bit closer to the motor sport world again, for the sake of Josh's career, I thought it would be a good idea. Then Josh stopped! This is my fifth year with the Sky F1 gang. I've loved working with true talents like David Croft, Ted Kravitz and the incomparable Simon Lazenby. We have a lot of fun and it's been very educational to see the sport from this side of the fence. Sky F1 has raised the bar and does a fantastic job. As ex-F1 driver expert analysts, Johnny Herbert, Anthony Davidson, Paul di Resta, Martin and I watch the poor souls of today struggling through all the trials and tests of their character and talents. They have no idea what awaits them. Joni Mitchell was right when she wrote, 'You don't know what you've got till it's gone.' But life after racing is very good. I thank my lucky stars.

This book has been quite an experience for me; I have had to go back one more time to places and through experiences that I really wanted to let lie. But in doing so I have become even clearer than before about who I am and what I have actually achieved in my life. I'm only fifty-five and, God willing, there will be more things I can do with the time left, but twenty years on from becoming an F1 World Champion seemed like the perfect opportunity to celebrate having got to the top of the F1 world. In any case, an explanation and an apology were way overdue to all my fans and supporters who cheered me on when I was racing. The apology is for leaving you all high and dry when I stopped; I never really said thanks properly. I hope this book has explained why I had to wait a while and makes up for the delay by being a better and fuller picture than I could have produced before. But as I started by saying, if you have ten years to chop down a tree, then spend nine years sharpening the axe. The question I'll leave you to ponder is: what was the tree?

Acknowledgements

For over thirty years, Georgie has had to tolerate and endure the fallout from my crazy projects. I thought this book was going to be the last straw. But typically, she could see how important it was for me to get all this stuff down and out there. So thank you Georgie, yet again. I needed your support and I got all of that and more.

My mother was obviously crucial in helping me try to piece together the parts of our family history that had not been so well documented. Her book *The Other Side of the Hill* was extremely useful, as were my father's two books, *Life at the Limit* and *Graham*. I'd like to thank both parents for taking the trouble to leave some clues for the Hill family to go on.

While I'm at it, I should thank all those who wrote articles and took copious amounts of photographs in an era when it wasn't so easy to upload them to the internet. The problem was I had too much material to go through, not lack of evidence! So thanks to all the writers and photographers.

I should thank all my children, too, because I have had to use up a lot of home time to lock myself away and get this monumental work completed. But unlike this book, they didn't need putting to bed any more. So thanks, Oliver, Josh, Tabitha and Rosie for being so understanding. I hope this book makes up for it.

To Sir Jackie Stewart, many thanks for agreeing to write my Foreword. It is by far the best school report I have ever had! As always, you have shown that you understand that winning is not enough; it's also how you play the game.

To Clive James, thanks for writing *Damon's Bravest Day*,

and for being there when I got the sack from Williams to film how I dealt with the yin and yang of F1. To have a great writer like yourself even utter my name is the highest praise.

Going through one's whole life is a pretty daunting task even for the person concerned, but to have to endure someone else's agonies requires immense patience and understanding. As one of F1's most experienced and respected journalists, and witness to the whole of my F1 career, Maurice Hamilton was the perfect man for the job. This is our second book together. Or is it the third? Anyway, this one would never have happened if Maurice hadn't set me up with David Luxton who brought me back to Pan Macmillan with whom I did my very first book, *My Grand Prix Year*, in 1993. So either I never escaped, or I've returned home! But an enormous thanks is due to both of you for helping me get this from hot air to dry print.

Robin Harvie deserves massive thanks for driving me like a slave to do better and carve some sense out of my ramblings. To all at Pan Macmillan for choosing to get behind my story, another big thank you.

I have had to ask a few friends for their recollections of what happened. Niki Lauda reminded me of events at Imola and Eddie Jordan and Ian Philips reminded me of events at Jordan. So a big thanks for your time guys. Please don't sue! Sir Patrick Head, Ron Dennis and Craig Pollock also took the time to explain some more details from their recollection, so many thanks for taking the calls.

I have to say special thanks to Peter Boutwood, who was my closest confidant and most loyal friend throughout my time in F1, before and after, and helped me piece together some of the complicated historical events. He was there. He remembers what really happened. Thanks, my friend.

To some more Irishmen, Dave Marron and Mark Gallagher, I thank them for their recollections that helped put together events at Gallaher's offices and Spa 1998.

Additionally, to Konrad Bartelski, who brought his father's

book on my father's crash to my attention. Thank you to you and your amazing father for taking so much trouble and care. The same also goes to Terry Lovell, whose book *Bernie's Game* explained some of the complicated events at the time of my father's team being set up.

Also, I have to thank Nigel Roebuck, who put me in touch with Quentin Spurring, who worked with Dad at Embassy Racing and gave me some interesting insights into operations.

To those who helped me achieve success on the track 'back in the day', John Bright, Ray Boulter, the whole Manadient Team, Glen Walters, Murray Taylor, Kevin Corin, and of course all the teams I drove for in all the races I did in F1, thanks guys and girls for tolerating me and even giving me a chance to do my thing.

Erwin Golner deserves special thanks, too, for showing such faith in me and getting me fighting fit for 1996. I'm still training, Erwin!

Mary Spillane's advice, 'Save it for the book!', was crucial to my success in 1996 and so thanks for letting me tell your story that literally changed my mind and my life.

To Murray Walker, a massive thanks for delivering the line of the year 1996. You will for ever be a legend.

Last but not least, to everyone I have forgotten to mention, I'm so sorry my scatterbrain has let me down, but if you feel you really should have been thanked, you have now. This publication was on a tight deadline. Next life, I will take a longer run-up!

Index